Frommer's

S0-AHR-840

PORTABLE
New Orleans

8th Edition

by Mary Herczog

Here's what critics say about Frommer's:

"Amazingly easy to use. Very portable, very complete."

—*Booklist*

"Detailed, accurate, and easy-to-read information for all price ranges."

—*Glamour Magazine*

WILEY

Wiley Publishing, Inc.

Published by:

WILEY PUBLISHING, INC.

111 River St.
Hoboken, NJ 07030-5744

ISBN: 978-0-470-19405-8

Editor: Cate Latting
Production Editor: Eric T. Schroeder
Photo Editor: Richard Fox
Cartographer: Guy Ruggiero
Production by Wiley Indianapolis Composition Services
Front cover photo: Performance of the Preservation Hall Jazz Band

For information on our other products and services or to obtain technical
support, please contact our Customer Care Department within the U.S. at
800/762-2974, outside the U.S. at 317/572-3993 or fax 317/572-4002.

Wiley also publishes its books in a variety of electronic formats. Some content that appears in print may not be available in electronic formats.

Manufactured in the United States of America

5   4   3   2   1

Contents

List of Maps   v

Introduction   1

1   Planning Your Trip to New Orleans   4

  1   Visitor Information 4
  2   Money 4
  3   When to Go 5
      New Orleans Calendar of Events 6
  4   Planning a Visit for Mardi Gras or Jazz Fest 13
  5   Getting There 21
  6   Specialized Travel Resources 22

2   Getting to Know New Orleans   24

  1   Orientation 26
      The Neighborhoods in Brief 27
  2   Getting Around 32
      Fast Facts: New Orleans 35

3   Where to Stay   38

  1   The French Quarter 42
  2   The Faubourg Marigny 57
  3   Mid-City/Esplanade 59
  4   Central Business District 62
      Spending the Night in Chains 65
  5   Uptown/The Garden District 72

4   Where to Dine   79

  1   The French Quarter 82
  2   The Faubourg Marigny 100
  3   Mid-City/Esplanade 102

4 Central Business District 106

5 Uptown/The Garden District 112

6 Coffee, Tea & Sweets 121

5   Sights to See & Places to Be   125

1 The French Quarter 128

2 Outside the French Quarter 138

3 Parks & Gardens 146

4 New Orleans Cemeteries 149

5 Organized Tours 152

6 Especially for Kids 155

7 Gambling 156

8 The Top Nearby Plantations 156

9 A Side Trip to Cajun County 158

6   Shopping   165

1 Major Hunting Grounds 165

2 Shopping A to Z 166

7   New Orleans After Dark   178

1 Jazz & Blues Clubs 179

2 Cajun & Zydeco Joints 185

3 Rhythm, Rock & the Rest of the Music Scene 186

4 The Bar Scene 190

5 Gay Nightlife 195

Index   198

General Index 198

Accommodations Index 201

Restaurant Index 202

List of Maps

The City at a Glance   29

Where to Stay in New
   Orleans   40

Where to Stay in the French
   Quarter   43

Where to Stay & Dine in
   Mid-City   61

Where to Stay & Dine
   Uptown   73

Where to Dine in New
   Orleans   80

Where to Dine in the French
   Quarter   83

New Orleans Attrac-
   tions   126

French Quarter Attrac-
   tions   129

Mid-City Attractions &
   Nightlife   139

Cajun Country   159

New Orleans Nightlife   180

French Quarter Night-
   life   183

ACKNOWLEDGMENTS

Thank you to the city of New Orleans and its greatest asset, its people. Thank you to Frommer's and Cate Latting, for their continued support of the city, and me, through difficult times. Thank you to the Metropolitan Convention and Visitor's Bureau for help with arrangements. Thanks to the Fat Pack (Chuck, Wesly, Diana, Robin, Dave, Nettie, John, and Fiona) for valuable pork-based research. This year's Stunt Stomachs (Caroline, Jean, and Debi) did their parts with gusto. I love the North Rendon All Stars and I love our house, even the parts that have to be fixed all the time. Nothing can fix Steve Hochman because he is perfect.

ABOUT THE AUTHOR

Mary Herczog remains a proud New Orleans homeowner. In addition to this book, she writes *Frommer's Las Vegas, California For Dummies,* and other Frommer's titles. She has also written about Bali for *Frommer's Dream Vacations* and *Frommer's Southeast Asia.* She is the author of the young adult novel *Figures of Echo,* the basis for the recent Lifetime movie *Custody.*

AN INVITATION TO THE READER

In researching this book, we discovered many wonderful places—hotels, restaurants, shops, and more. We're sure you'll find others. Please tell us about them, so we can share the information with your fellow travelers in upcoming editions. If you were disappointed with a recommendation, we'd love to know that, too. Please write to:

Frommer's Portable New Orleans, 8th Edition
Wiley Publishing, Inc. • 111 River St. • Hoboken, NJ 07030-5744

AN ADDITIONAL NOTE

Please be advised that travel information is subject to change at any time—and this is especially true of prices. We therefore suggest that you write or call ahead for confirmation when making your travel plans. The authors, editors, and publisher cannot be held responsible for the experiences of readers while traveling. Your safety is important to us, however, so we encourage you to stay alert and be aware of your surroundings. Keep a close eye on cameras, purses, and wallets, all favorite targets of thieves and pickpockets.

FROMMER'S STAR RATINGS, ICONS & ABBREVIATIONS

Every hotel, restaurant, and attraction listing in this guide has been ranked for quality, value, service, amenities, and special features using a **star-rating system.** In country, state, and regional guides, we also rate towns and regions to help you narrow down your choices and budget your time accordingly. Hotels and restaurants are rated on a scale of zero (recommended) to three stars (exceptional). Attractions, shopping, nightlife, towns, and regions are rated according to the following scale: zero stars (recommended), one star (highly recommended), two stars (very highly recommended), and three stars (must-see).

In addition to the star-rating system, we also use **seven feature icons** that point you to the great deals, in-the-know advice, and unique experiences that separate travelers from tourists. Throughout the book, look for:

Finds	Special finds—those places only insiders know about
Fun Fact	Fun facts—details that make travelers more informed and their trips more fun
Kids	Best bets for kids and advice for the whole family
Moments	Special moments—those experiences that memories are made of
Overrated	Places or experiences not worth your time or money
Tips	Insider tips—great ways to save time and money
Value	Great values—where to get the best deals

The following **abbreviations** are used for credit cards:

AE	American Express	DISC	Discover	V	Visa
DC	Diners Club	MC	MasterCard		

FROMMERS.COM

Now that you have this guidebook, to help you plan a great trip, visit our website at **www.frommers.com** for additional travel information on more than 3,600 destinations. We update features regularly, to give you instant access to the most current trip-planning information available. At Frommers.com, you'll find scoops on the best airfares, lodging rates, and car rental bargains. You can even book your travel online through our reliable travel booking partners. Other popular features include:

- Online updates of our most popular guidebooks
- Vacation sweepstakes and contest giveaways
- Newsletters highlighting the hottest travel trends
- Online travel message boards with featured travel discussions

Introduction

One of the pleasures of New Orleans was that the city changed very slowly, if at all. This was a city that objected strenuously when a certain decades-old restaurant dared to switch from hand-chipped ice to machine made. This was a city where 10 years could go by between visits, but your favorite bookstore would still be in business when you came back, and your favorite bookseller would still be behind the counter, possibly with a volume he had been holding for you until the day you finally returned. Still, change is the one constant in life, and yet we never think about it applying to an entire city, an entire culture, an entire way of life.

On August 29, 2005, New Orleans changed forever. In the wake of Hurricane Katrina, which was not quite as strong as the direct hit originally predicted, at least three of the levees designed to keep the below-sea-level city safe from the waters of Lake Pontchartrain either broke or were breached, with the result that 80% of one of the most charming and historic cities in America was under water. The water remained for weeks—months in certain places—and by the time it was done, the landscape of New Orleans was forever altered.

Throughout that time there were impossible images. Faces massed in the Superdome and the Convention Center, stranded for days without sufficient food or water. People stuck on rooftops, baking in the hot sun, waiting for rescue. Lacy wrought-iron balconies, stately oaks, and street signs with unbearably ironic names like Flood, all hovering inches above water. People wading through a fetid stew, carrying a few meager possessions. As the floodwaters were pumped out, more shocks followed. There was the ravaged Lower 9th Ward, where house after house was reduced to a rubbish heap of piles of random lumber, unrecognizable as anything, much less someone's home, while other houses were pushed into one another, once lined up in an orderly row, now smashed at various angles into each other, sometimes, incredibly, sitting on top of one another. Vacant lots materialized as homes had literally been blown away. Sometimes, concrete pilings were left behind, making the lot look like a cemetery, which it was, in a sense. Sometimes just the front steps were left, leading to nowhere, a metaphor that doesn't bear explication. Across town, in Lakeview, homes appeared fine outside, but inside, furniture lay out of place in careless heaps, like the contents of a snow globe shaken by a giant, the consequence of floating in 10 feet or more of water for weeks on end. Everything, from stuffed toys to pianos to pictures on the wall, was covered in thick fuzzy mold—family homes, rotten to the core. And adding to the brokenness of it all was the color: Verdant, tropical New Orleans was brown, gray, and dusty. The vegetation itself had drowned. The official death toll will likely never be known, because many remain missing, and such death counts do not cover those who died after the storm, during evacuation and exile, from stress or illness, or even suicide and despair.

It takes a long time to come back from something like this. But New Orleans was given two gifts. The first was that the narrow band of land that did not flood at all included the most historic and best-loved areas: the French Quarter and the part of Uptown that included the Garden District. New Orleans is considerably more than those much-photographed neighborhoods, make no mistake, but what the average visitors imagine when they think of New Orleans remains much as it ever did. One can walk through those areas and not know that anything of the magnitude of the disaster ever came close.

The second is the spirit of the people of New Orleans. Within weeks of the catastrophe, intrepid remaining citizens threw a jazz funeral, complete with an exalting, rejuvenating second line for the disaster, for its victims, and for its citizens. Then they got their hands down in the muck and began to clean. Restaurants and clubs reopened even when it meant grilling on the sidewalk and keeping the beer cold with a generator. Plans were made for Mardi Gras and pleas were made for the return of Jazz Fest, because this is a city that loves its parties, and what's a party for except to celebrate life and survival? And sure enough, Mardi Gras parades rolled, and many contained floats openly mocking the terrible thing that had happened just 6 months before, a thumbing of the nose at events that may have left the city broken but not bowed. An only slightly truncated Jazz Fest went on during its usual weekends, featuring headliners such as Bruce Springsteen, and attracted as large a crowd as usual. Mardi Gras 2007, though still not quite as crowded as pre-Katrina days, was otherwise unremarkable, which is as it should be—the past is done and celebrants were embracing the present. Jazz Fest 2007 was as crowded, musically, and attendance-wise, as ever. The refurbished Superdome reopened on September 25, 2006, with a bang-up party including performances by U2 and Green Day, and the usually hapless Saints responded with a winning season that saw them one victory away from their first Super Bowl appearance ever. To help aid the recovery of the vital music and cultural scene, the prestigious Thelonious Monk School of Jazz is relocating from Los Angeles to the campus of Loyola University. The movie business continues to be loyal—every time you turn around, it seems you stumble on some movie or TV crew. Even Donald Trump is getting in on the act, with a planned massive development in the heart of the CBD.

But over all, recovery is slow going. All manner of important things are, maddeningly, no closer to being resolved than in the early days after the storm, while the fate of many citizens and establishments remains in question. Crime is notably on the rise, and is a serious problem, though it is largely confined to the poor and still badly damaged areas of town. It is mostly drug related, and the tourist areas of town remain no more dangerous than in any other big city. There are increased patrols in the most visible parts of town, but visitors should exercise caution and typical big-city common sense when entering questionable neighborhoods after dark.

All of this likely prompts a question of your own, probably: Should you go?

Oh, yes.

Go, because everything in life is fragile and precarious, and we can take nothing for granted, and some day it really will all be gone. Go, because it's not gone, not at all. Go, because the things you wanted—the beautiful architecture, the majestic oaks, the river wind, the quality of light that makes even the most mundane just a little bit magic—all remain. Go, because there are people there, and as long as they are, there will be music and food, and it will be some of the best of your life. Go, because perhaps you've wanted to help in any way you can, and now the best way you can is to help a historic city regain its economic feet. Go, because every brick in the French Quarter has a story to tell, and so does the damaged ground of the 9th Ward, and you should bear witness. Go, because there is much to celebrate, and this is still the best place there is to do so.

"I want to be in that number," goes the song. I do indeed. I hope you do, too.

1

Planning Your Trip to New Orleans

No matter what your idea of the ideal New Orleans trip is, this chapter will give you the information to make informed plans and help point you toward some additional resources.

1 Visitor Information

Even a seasoned traveler should consider writing or calling ahead to the **New Orleans Metropolitan Convention and Visitors Bureau,** 2020 St. Charles Ave., New Orleans, LA 70130 (© **800/672-6124** or 504/566-5011; www.neworleanscvb.com). The staff is extremely friendly and helpful, and you can easily get any information you can't find in this book from them.

2 Money

Not surprisingly, prices are flopping every which way these days as local businesses try to get themselves righted again. Even once things stabilize, expect prices for accommodations to skyrocket during major events and festivals (see "Planning a Visit for Mardi Gras or Jazz Fest," later in this chapter). New Orleans generally is quite popular in the fall during the convention season. The heat and humidity of the summer months (July–Aug) keep tourism in the city to its yearly low, so if the weather doesn't bother you, you can find some incredible hotel bargains, though even at other times these days, if a hotel is feeling a paucity of tourists, you can get some good deals.

Almost all New Orleans **ATMs** are linked to a national network that most likely includes your bank at home. **Cirrus** (© **800/424-7787;** www.mastercard.com) and **PLUS** (© **800/843-7587;** www.visa.com) are the two most popular networks.

Some centrally located ATMs in New Orleans are at the **First National Bank of Commerce,** 240 Royal St.; **Hibernia National Bank,** 701 Poydras St.; and **Whitney National Bank,** 228 St.

Charles Ave. There are now ATMs all over the French Quarter, a big change from some years ago when there was just one.

3 When to Go

With the possible exception of July and August (unless you happen to thrive on heat and humidity), just about any time is the right time to go to New Orleans, particularly now. Mardi Gras is, of course, the time of year when it's hardest to get a hotel room, but it can also be difficult during the various music festivals throughout the year, especially the Jazz & Heritage Festival.

It's important to know what's going on when; the city's landscape can change dramatically depending not just on what festival or convention is happening, but also on what is happening with recovery efforts, and prices can also reflect that. The best time of year to go, in our opinion, is December, before and during Christmas. The town is gussied up with decorations, there are all kinds of seasonal special events, and the weather is nice—but for some reason, tourists become scarce. Hotels, eager to lure any business, lower their rates dramatically, and most restaurants are so empty that you can walk in just about anywhere without a reservation. Take advantage of it.

THE WEATHER

The average temperature in New Orleans is an inviting 70°F (21°C), but it can drop or rise considerably in a single day. (We've experienced 40°F/4°C and rain one day, 80°F/27°C and humidity the next.) Conditions depend primarily on two things: whether it rains and whether there is direct sunlight or cloud cover. Rain can provide slight and temporary relief on a hot day; for the most part, it hits in sudden (and sometimes dramatically heavy) showers, which disappear as quickly as they arrived. Anytime the sun shines unimpeded, it gets much warmer. The region's high humidity can make even mild warms and colds feel intense. Still, the city's semi-tropical climate is part of its appeal—a slight bit of moistness makes the air come sensually alive.

New Orleans should be pleasant at almost any time of year except July and August, which can be exceptionally hot and muggy. If you do come during those months, you'll quickly learn to follow the natives' example, staying out of the noonday sun and ducking from one air-conditioned building to another. Winter is very mild by American standards but is punctuated by an occasional cold snap, when the mercury can drop below the freezing point.

In the dead of summer, T-shirts and shorts are absolutely acceptable everywhere except the finest restaurants. In the spring and fall, something a little warmer is in order; in the winter, you should plan to carry a lightweight coat or jacket, though umbrellas and cheap rain jackets are available everywhere for those tourists who inevitably get caught in a sudden, unexpected downpour. Also note that many restaurants are overzealous with air-conditioning, so bring those light wraps along on warm nights just in case.

New Orleans Average Temperatures & Rainfall

	Jan	Feb	Mar	Apr	May	June	July	Aug	Sept	Oct	Nov	Dec
High (°F)	63	64	72	79	84	90	91	90	88	79	70	64
Low (°F)	43	45	52	59	64	72	73	72	70	59	50	45
High (°C)	17	18	22	26	29	32	33	32	31	26	21	18
Low (°C)	6	7	11	15	18	22	23	22	21	15	10	7
Days of Rainfall	10	9	9	7	8	10	15	13	10	5	7	10

NEW ORLEANS CALENDAR OF EVENTS

For an exhaustive list of events beyond those listed here, check http://events. frommers.com, where you'll find a searchable, up-to-the-minute roster of what's happening in cities all over the world. For general information, contact the **New Orleans Metropolitan Convention and Visitors Bureau**, 2020 St. Charles Ave., New Orleans, LA 70130 (© **800/672-6124** or 504/566-5011; www.neworleanscvb.com).

January

Allstate Sugar Bowl Classic. First held in 1934, this is New Orleans's oldest yearly sporting occasion. 2007 marked Allstate's first sponsorship of this college football championship, in the triumphantly refurbished, if still emotionally tarnished, Superdome. The football game is the main event, but there are a series of other fan- and visitor-related activities. Fans tend to be really loud, really boisterous, and everywhere during the festivities. For information, contact Allstate Sugar Bowl, 1500 Sugar Bowl Dr., New Orleans, LA 70112 (© **504/828-2440;** www.allstatesugar bowl.org). January 1, 2008.

February

Lundi Gras. This is an old tradition that has been revived in the last decade or so. It's free, it's outdoors (celebrations are at Spanish Plaza), and it features music (including a jazz competition) and the arrival of Rex at 6pm, marking the beginning of Mardi Gras, plus an appearance by the King of Zulu. For more information, contact New Orleans Riverwalk Marketplace, 1 Poydras St., New

Orleans, LA 70130 (© **504/522-1555**). See also p. 14. Monday before Mardi Gras. February 4, 2008.

Mardi Gras. The culmination of the 2-month-long Carnival season, Mardi Gras is the big annual blowout, a citywide party that takes place on Fat Tuesday (the last day before Lent on the Christian calendar). The entire city stops working (sometimes days in advance!) and starts partying in the early morning, and the streets are taken over by some overwhelming parades—which, these days, go through the Central Business District instead of the French Quarter. Day before Ash Wednesday. February 5, 2008.

March

St. Patrick's Day Parades. There are two: One takes place in the French Quarter beginning at Molly's at the Market (1107 Decatur St.) on March 14, and the other goes through the Irish Channel neighborhood following a route that begins at Jackson Avenue and Magazine Street, goes over to St. Charles Avenue, turns uptown to Louisiana Avenue, and returns to Jackson Avenue. The parades have the flavor of Mardi Gras, but instead of beads, watchers are pelted with cabbages, carrots, and other veggies. For information on the French Quarter parade, call Molly's at the Market (© **504/525-5169**). The Irish Channel parade takes place in early March. Because there's no organization to contact about this one, you can try the New Orleans Metropolitan Convention and Visitors Bureau (p. 4) for more information.

St. Joseph's Day Parade. This is another city-centric festivity that gets little play outside of the area. St. Joseph is the patron saint of families and working men. His veneration was brought to New Orleans by Italian and Sicilian immigrants. On his saint's day, in addition to the parade, which takes place the weekend around March 19, you may want to visit the altars devoted to St. Joseph, moving and elaborate works of art featuring food, candles, statues, and much more, all of which takes days to construct. You can find them all over the city, at various churches (where you might get fed after services), private homes (where you will likely also get fed) and at the American Italian Museum and Library, 537 S. Peters St. For more information, call © **504/522-7294.** March 17 to March 19.

Super Sunday. This is the annual Mardi Gras Indians showdown, which takes place on the Sunday nearest St. Joseph's Day. This is an incredible but sadly underappreciated event in New Orleans, when the Indians are all in one place; the feathers fly and the chants are ongoing. These days more than ever, it's hard to say who will show. Unfortunately, there are neither contact numbers nor firm times or locations for this event (though it's roughly in the Bayou St. John area and Uptown, around the intersection of LaSalle and Washington), and for that matter, recently the two neighborhoods have been doing their respective things on Sundays 2 weeks apart. For more information, you can try checking with www.nola.com or the Metropolitan Tourism board, or just show up in town and drive into that area and ask around, or just watch for feathers and listen for drums. Usually in mid- to late March.

Tennessee Williams New Orleans Literary Festival. The 22nd anniversary of the festival takes place in 2008. A 5-day series celebrating New Orleans's rich literary heritage, this festival includes theatrical performances, readings, discussion panels, master classes, musical events, and literary walking tours dedicated to the playwright. By the way, the focus is not confined to Tennessee Williams. Events take place at venues throughout the city. For info, call © **504/581-1144** or go to www.tennesseewilliams.net. March 26 to March 30, 2008.

Spring Fiesta. The fiesta, which begins with the crowning of the Spring Fiesta queen, is more than half a century old and takes place throughout the city—from the Garden District to the French Quarter to Uptown and beyond. Historical and architectural tours of many of the city's private homes, courtyards, and plantation homes are offered in conjunction with the 5-day event. For the schedule, call the Spring Fiesta Association (© **504/581-1367**). Last 2 weekends in March or early April.

April

The French Quarter Festival. For hard-core jazz fans, this is rapidly becoming an alternative to Jazz Fest, where actual jazz is becoming less and less prominent. It kicks off with a parade down Bourbon Street. Among other things, you can join people dancing in the streets, learn the history of jazz, visit historic homes, and take a ride on a riverboat. Many local restaurants set up booths in Jackson Square, so the eating is exceptionally good. Events are held all over the French Quarter. For information, call or write French Quarter Festivals, 400 N. Peters St., New Orleans, LA 70130 (© **504/522-5730;** www.fqfi.org). Usually mid-April.

New Orleans Jazz & Heritage Festival (Jazz Fest). A 10-day event that draws musicians, music fans, cooks, and craftspeople to celebrate music and life, Jazz Fest rivals Mardi Gras in popularity.

Lodgings in the city tend to sell out up to a year ahead, so book early. Events take place at the Fair Grounds Race Track and various venues throughout the city. For information, call or write New Orleans Jazz & Heritage Festival, 1205 N. Rampart St., New Orleans, LA 70116 (© **504/522-4786;** www.nojazzfest.com). Usually held the last weekend in April and first weekend in May.

May

Greek Festival. Located at the Holy Trinity Cathedral's Hellenic Cultural Center, this 3-day festival features Greek folk dancing, specialty foods, crafts, and music. For more information, call or write Holy Trinity Cathedral, 1200 Robert E. Lee Blvd., New Orleans, LA 70122 (© **504/282-0259;** www.greekfestnola. com). Last weekend of May.

New Orleans Wine & Food Experience. During this time, antiques shops and art galleries throughout the French Quarter hold wine and food tastings, winemakers and local chefs conduct seminars, and a variety of vintner dinners and grand tastings are held for your gourmandistic pleasure. More than 150 wines and 40 restaurants are featured every day. For information and this year's schedule, call or write Mary Reynolds, P.O. Box 70514, New Orleans, LA 70172 (© **504/529-9463;** www.nowfe.com). Five days toward the end May.

June

The Great French Market Tomato Festival. A celebration of tomato diversity, this daylong event features cooking and tastings in the historic French Market. For more information, call or write the French Market, P.O. Box 51749, New Orleans, LA 70151 (© **504/522-2621;** www.frenchmarket.org). First Sunday in June.

International Arts Festival. This 3-day gathering of calypso, reggae, and soca (a blend of soul and calypso) musicians is held in City Park and includes a heady helping of ethnic foods and arts and crafts. For more information, call or write Ernest Kelly, P.O. Box 6156, New Orleans, LA 70174 (© **504/367-1313**). Second week of June.

July

Go Fourth on the River. The annual Fourth of July celebration begins in the morning at the riverfront and continues into the night, culminating in a spectacular fireworks display. For more information, go to www.go4thontheriver.com or contact the New Orleans Metropolitan Convention and Visitors Bureau at © **800/ 672-6124.** July 4th.

Essence Music Festival. The return to the Superdome of this 3-day event, sponsored by the venerable magazine, is a significant one for the city. Nighttime entertainment brings the top names in African-American entertainment. (The 2007 lineup included Beyonce, Ludacris, the O'Jays, the Isley Brothers, Lionel Richie, and many others.) Known as a "party with a purpose," the daytime offers seminars with motivational speakers, crafts and trade fairs, and other activities, not to mention huge crowds. www.essence.com. Early July.

Tales of the Cocktail. The first mixed drink was invented right here in New Orleans, where they still love to drink (you may have noticed!), and eat, and talk about both those activities. With cocktail tours of local bars, tie-ins with local restaurants, panels featuring local restaurant owners, chefs, drinks specialists, authors, and plenty of clever, quirky events, it's quickly becoming one of the year's top events. For information, go to www.talesofthecocktail.com. Mid-July.

August

Satchmo Summerfest. Hometown boy made very good is now celebrated with his own festival, held around his real birthday (he claimed to be born on July 4th, but records prove otherwise). It includes the usual local food and music in Satchmo's honor, with the emphasis on jazz entertainment and education, including activities for kids to ensure that Satchmo lives on for generations to come. For location updates and information, call or write French Quarter Festivals, 400 N. Peters St., New Orleans, LA 70130 (© **504/522-5730;** www.frenchquarterfestivals.org). August 2 to August 5, 2008.

September

Southern Decadence. This is the pinnacle of gay New Orleans, where more than 100,000 gay men come to town to flaunt it, whether they got it or not. The multiday party hits its frenzied peak on the Sunday before Labor Day as participants flock to follow a secret parade route, making sure to stop into many bars along the way. People travel from far and wide to be a part of the festivities. There is only an informal organization associated with the festival, and it's hard to get anyone on the phone. For information, try the website **www.southerndecadence.com** or contact *Ambush Magazine* (© **504/522-8047;** fax 504/522-0907). Labor Day weekend.

The Rayne Frog Festival. Cajuns can always find an excuse to hold a party, and in this case they've turned to the lowly frog as an excuse for a *fais-do-do* (dance) and a waltz contest. Frog races and frog-jumping contests fill the entertainment bill—and if you arrive without your amphibian, there's a Rent-a-Frog service. A lively frog-eating contest winds things up. For dates and full details, contact Lafayette Parish Convention and Visitors Commission, P.O. Box 52066, Lafayette, LA 70505 (© **800/346-1958** in the U.S., 800/543-5340 in Canada, or 337/232-3808; www.lafayettetravel.com). Labor Day weekend.

October

Art for Arts' Sake. The arts season begins with gallery openings throughout the city. Julia, Magazine, and Royal streets are where the action is. For more information, contact the Contemporary Arts Center, 900 Camp St., New Orleans, LA 70130 (© **504/523-1216;** www.cacno.org). Throughout the month.

Gumbo Festival. This festival showcases one of the region's signature dishes and celebrates Cajun culture to boot. It's 3 days of gumbo-related events (including the presentation of the royal court of King and Miss Creole Gumbo), plus many hours of Cajun music. The festival is held in Bridge City, on the outskirts of New Orleans. For more information, contact the Gumbo Festival, P.O. Box 9069, Bridge City, LA 70096 (© **504/436-4712**). Second weekend in October. October 10 to October 12, 2008.

Festivals Acadiens. This is a series of happenings that celebrate Cajun music, food, crafts, and culture in and near Lafayette, Louisiana. (Most of the events are in Lafayette.) For more information, contact the **Lafayette Parish Convention and Visitors Commission,** P.O. Box 52066, Lafayette, LA 70505 (© **800/346-1958** in the U.S., 800/543-5340 in Canada, or 337/232-3737; www.lafayettetravel.com). October 10 to October 12, 2008.

New Orleans Film Festival. Canal Place Cinemas and other theaters throughout the city screen award-winning local and international films and host writers, actors, and directors over the course of a week. Admission prices range from $6.25 for NOFF members to $7.25 for general admission. For dates, contact the New Orleans Film and Video Society, 843 Carondelet, No. 1, New Orleans, LA 70130 (© **504/309-6633;** www.neworleans filmfest.com). Mid-month.

Halloween. Rivaling Mardi Gras in terms of costumes, Halloween is certainly celebrated more grandly here than it is in any other American city. After all, New Orleans has a way with ghosts. Events include Boo-at-the-Zoo (end of Oct) for children, costume parties (including a Monster Bash at the Ernest N. Morial Convention

Center), haunted houses, formal and informal costume extravaganzas, and much more. Apart from Southern Decadence, it's the biggest magnet for gay and lesbian visitors. You can catch the ghoulish action all over the city—many museums get in on the fun with specially designed tours—but the French Quarter, as always, is the center of the Halloween-night universe. October 31.

Voodoo Music Experience. This 2-day music festival, set in City Park, was the first major event to return to the city, 2 months after Hurricane Katrina, buoying the spirits of the first wave of people working on reconstruction, with a lineup that featured Nine Inch Nails. In 2007 the lineup included Rage Against the Machine, Ben Harper, Wilco, Dr. John, Common, The Smashing Pumpkins, and The Black Crowes, among many others. An increasingly big draw, there are seven stages, with top regional and international acts (www.voodoomusicfest.com). Last weekend in October.

November

Swamp Festival. Sponsored by the Audubon Institute, the Swamp Festival features long days of live Swamp Music performances (lots of good zydeco here), as well as hands-on contact with Louisiana swamp animals. Admission to the festival is free with zoo admission. For information, call or write the Audubon Institute, 6500 Magazine St., New Orleans, LA 70118 (© **504/861-2537**; www.auduboninstitute.org). First weekend in November.

Words & Music: A Literary Fest in New Orleans. This highly ambitious literary and music conference (originated in large part by the folks behind Faulkner House Books) offers 5 days' worth of round-table discussions with eminent authors (with varying connections to the city), original drama, poetry readings, and master classes, plus great music and food. For authors seeking guidance and inspiration and for book lovers in general, call © **504/586-1609** or visit their website at www.wordsandmusic. org for exact dates.

December

Christmas New Orleans–Style. New Orleans loves to celebrate, so it should be no surprise that they do Christmas really well. The town is decorated to a fare-thee-well, there is an evening of candlelit caroling in Jackson Square, bonfires line the levees along the River Road on Christmas Eve (to guide Papa Noël, his sled drawn by alligators, on his gift-delivering way), restaurants offer specially created multicourse Réveillon dinners, and hotels throughout the city offer "Papa Noël" rates.

Why? Because despite all the fun and the generally nice (read: not hot and humid) weather, tourism goes *waaay* down at this time of year, and hotels are eager to lure you all in with cheaper rates. This is one of the top times to come to town—you can have the city virtually to yourself. For information, contact French Quarter Festivals, 400 N. Peters St., Suite 205, New Orleans, LA 70130 (✆ **504/522-5730;** www.frenchquarterfestivals.org). All month.

Celebration in the Oaks. Lights and lighted figures designed to illustrate holiday themes bedeck sections of City Park. This display of winter wonderment is open for driving and walking tours. Driving tours are $12 per family car or van, and walking tours are $5 per person. For information, contact Celebration in the Oaks, 1 Palm Dr., New Orleans, LA 70124 (✆ **544/482-4888;** www. neworleanscitypark.com). Late November to early January.

New Year's Eve. The countdown takes place in Jackson Square and is a big street party. In the Southern equivalent of New York's Times Square, revelers watch a lighted ball drop from the top of Jackson Brewery. December 31.

4 Planning a Visit for Mardi Gras or Jazz Fest

MARDI GRAS

There was a great deal of speculation about whether New Orleans should cancel Mardi Gras in 2006, whether it was appropriate to hold the traditional massive celebration at such a somber time. The opposition failed to take into account several things: Because it is a holiday separate from any observation of it, one can no more "cancel" Mardi Gras than one can cancel Christmas. Secondly, Mardi Gras celebrations—that is, parades and parties—are all privately funded and operated, so it's not really a city decision. And finally, for a town that tends to throw a party just because it's a day with a "Y" in it, the response to any suggestions that official celebrations should be postponed for a year was "Fine. Then we will load up little red wagons with a bunch of beads, and walk down the streets and do it ourselves."

It didn't come to that after all. Six months virtually to the day after Katrina, Zulu and Rex paraded as usual, along with the other krewes who march earlier. Some parades were a little shorter, but the beads and other throws were even more plentiful. The crowds may not have been as thick as usual (though conversely, Sun night may have set a record for attendance), but that wasn't unexpected. More to the point, the spirit was immeasurably high, as New Orleanians and lovers of same alike turned out in their most glittery or satirical costumes, screaming for beads, engaging in their traditions, and generally exalting in a moment that not that long before seemed like it would never come again. They had survived, and they were filled with hope that their city would, too. That there was not this same focus on Katrina during Mardi Gras 2007 was as good a sign as the continuity of the previous year; it meant the city and its loyal residents were moving into the future that brought along the best, not the worst, of the past.

Forget sensational media reports that tend to focus on the salacious action. There is a lot more to Carnival than that, and it remains one of the most exciting times to visit. You can spend several days admiring and reveling in the traditions and never even venture into the frat-party atmosphere of Bourbon Street.

THE SEASON   The date of Fat Tuesday is different each year, but Carnival season always starts on **Twelfth Night,** January 6, as much as 2 months before Mardi Gras. On that night, the Phunny Phorty Phellows kick off the season with a streetcar ride from Carrollton Avenue to Canal Street and back.

Two or 3 weeks before Mardi Gras, parades begin chugging through the streets with increasing frequency. There are plenty of parodies, such as the parade of the **Mystick Krewe of Barkus.** Barkus is, as you might guess, a krewe for pets that parades through the Quarter (some of the dogs get quite gussied up) and is a total hoot.

If you want to experience Mardi Gras but don't want to face the full force of craziness, consider coming for the weekend 10 days before Fat Tuesday (the season officially begins the Fri of this weekend). You can count on 10 to 15 parades during the weekend by lesser-known krewes such as Cleopatra, Pontchartrain, Sparta, and Camelot. The crowds are more manageable during this time.

The following weekend there are another 15 parades—the biggies. Everything's bigger: The parades are bigger; the crowds are bigger; the city has succumbed to Carnival fever. After a day of screaming for beads, you'll probably find yourself heading somewhere to get a drink or three. The French Quarter will be the center of late-night revelry; all of the larger bars will be packed. The last parade each day (on both weekends) usually ends around 9:30pm or later.

LUNDI GRAS   In the 19th century, Rex's **King of Carnival** arrived downtown from the Mississippi River on this night, the Monday before Fat Tuesday. Over the years, the day gradually lost its special significance, becoming just another day of parades. In the 1980s, however, Rex revived Lundi Gras, the old tradition of arriving on the Mississippi.

These days, festivities at the riverfront begin in the afternoon with lots of drink and live music leading up to the king's arrival at around 6pm. Down the levee a few hundred feet, at Wolfenberg Park, Zulu has its own Lundi Gras celebration with the king arriving at around 5pm. In 1999, for the first time, King Zulu met up with Rex in an impressive ceremony. That night, the **Krewe of Orpheus** holds their parade. It's one of the biggest and most popular parades, thanks to the generosity of the krewe's throws. It holds fast to old Mardi Gras traditions, including floats designed by master float creator Henri Schindler. For Mardi Gras 2000, venerable Proteus returned to parading, right before Orpheus.

Because Lent begins the following night at midnight, Monday is the final dusk-to-dawn night of Mardi Gras. A good portion of the city forgoes sleep so as not to waste the occasion—which only adds to the craziness.

MARDI GRAS The day begins early, starting with the two biggest parades, **Zulu** and **Rex,** which run back to back. Zulu starts near the Central Business District (CBD) at 8:30am; Rex starts Uptown at 10am. Generally, the best place to watch parades on St. Charles Avenue is between Napoleon and Jackson avenues, where the crowds are somewhat smaller and consist mostly of local families and college students.

It will be early afternoon when Rex spills into the CBD. Nearby at about this time, you can find some of the most elusive New Orleans figures, the **Mardi Gras Indians.** The "tribes" of New Orleans are small communities of African Americans and black Creoles (some of whom have Native American ancestors), mostly from the inner city. Their elaborate (and that's an understatement) beaded and feathered costumes, rivaling Bob Mackie Vegas headdresses in outrageousness and size, are entirely made by hand.

After the parades, the action picks up in the Quarter. En route, you'll see that Mardi Gras is still very much a family tradition, with whole families dressing up in similar costumes. Marvel at how an entire city has shut down so that every citizen can join in the celebrations. Some people don't bother hitting the streets; instead, they hang out on their balconies watching the action below or have barbecues in their courtyards. If you are lucky and seem like the right sort, you might well get invited in.

In the Quarter, the frat-party action is largely confined to Bourbon Street. The more interesting activity is in the lower Quarter and the Frenchmen section of the Faubourg Marigny (just east of the Quarter), where the artists and gay community really know how to celebrate. The costumes are elaborate works of art. Although the people may be (okay, probably *will* be) drunk, they are boisterous and enthusiastic, not (for the most part) obnoxious.

PLANNING A VISIT DURING MARDI GRAS

LODGING You can't just drop in on Mardi Gras. If you do, you may find yourself sleeping in Jackson Square or on a sidewalk somewhere. Accommodations in the city and the nearby suburbs are booked solid, *so make your plans well ahead and book a room as early as possible.* Many people plan a year or more in advance. Prices are usually much higher during Mardi Gras, and most hotels and guesthouses impose minimum-stay requirements.

CLOTHING As with anything in New Orleans, you must join in if you want to have the best time. Simply being a spectator is not enough. And that means a **costume** and **mask.** Once you are masked and dressed up, you are automatically part of it all. (Tellingly, the Bourbon St. participants usually do not wear costumes.) As far as costumes go, you need not do anything fancy. If you've come unprepared, several shops in town specialize in Mardi Gras costumes and masks. Or just don an old suit and a cheap Halloween mask.

DINING If you want to eat at a restaurant during Mardi Gras, make reservations as early as possible. And pay very close attention to **parade routes,** because if there is one between you and your restaurant, you may not be able to cross the street, and you can kiss your dinner goodbye. This might work to your advantage; often restaurants have a high no-show rate during Mardi Gras for this reason, and so a well-timed drop-in may work.

PARKING Even though the huge crowds everywhere add to the general merriment, they also grind traffic to a halt all over town. So our admonition against renting a car is even stronger during Mardi Gras. *Don't drive.* Instead, relax and take a cab or walk. Remember, the fun is everywhere, so you don't really have to go anywhere. Parking along any parade route is not allowed 2 hours before and 2 hours after the parade. In addition, although you'll see people leaving their cars on the "neutral ground" (the median strip), it's illegal to park there, and chances are good that you'll be towed. Traffic in New Orleans is never worse than *in the hour after a parade.*

Tips **For More Information . . .**

You'll enjoy Mardi Gras more if you've done a little home-work before your trip. Contact the **New Orleans Metropolitan Convention and Visitors Bureau,** 2020 St. Charles Ave., New Orleans, LA 70130 (© 800/672-6124 or 504/566-5011), and ask for current Mardi Gras info.

You'll also want to get your hands on the latest edition of *Arthur Hardy's Mardi Gras Guide.* This will tell you which krewes are parading where and when, among much other useful information. Your best bet is to contact the magazine directly (© **504/838-6111;** www.mardigrasneworleans.com/arthur). This valuable guide is sold all over town and is full of history, tips, and maps of the parade routes.

SAFETY Many, many cops are out, making the walk from uptown to downtown safer than at other times of year, but, not surprisingly, the streets of New Orleans are a haven for pickpockets during Mardi Gras. Take precautions.

CAJUN MARDI GRAS

Mardi Gras in New Orleans sounds like too much for you, no matter how low-key you keep it? Consider driving out to Cajun country, where Mardi Gras traditions are just as strong but considerably more, errr, wholesome. **Lafayette,** the capital of French Acadiana, celebrates Carnival in a different manner, one that reflects the Cajun heritage and spirit. Three full days of activities lead up to Cajun Mardi Gras, making it second in size only to New Orleans's celebration. There's one *big* difference, though: The Cajuns open their final pageant and ball to the general public. Don your formal wear and join right in!

MASKED MEN AND A BIG GUMBO In the Cajun countryside that surrounds Lafayette, there's yet another form of Mardi Gras celebration, one tied to the rural lifestyle. Cajuns firmly believe in sharing, so you're welcome to come along. The celebration goes like this: Bands of masked men dressed in raggedy patchwork costumes (unlike the New Orleans costumes, which are heavy on glitter and shine) and peaked hats known as *capichons* set off on Mardi Gras morning on horseback, led by their *capitaine.* They ride from farm to farm, asking at each, *"Voulez-vous reçevoir le Mardi Gras?"*

("Will you receive the Mardi Gras?") and dismounting as the invariable *"Oui"* comes in reply. Each farmyard then becomes a miniature festival as the revelers *faire le macaque* ("make monkeyshines") with song and dance, much drinking of beer, and other antics loosely labeled "entertainment." As payment for their show, they demand, and get, "a fat little chicken to make a big gumbo" (or sometimes a bag of rice or other ingredients).

When each band has visited its allotted farmyards, they all head back to town where there is dancing in the streets, rowdy card games, storytelling, and the like until the wee hours, and you can be sure that all those fat little chickens go into the *"gumbo gros"* pot to make a very big gumbo indeed.

You can write or call ahead for particulars on both the urban and rural Mardi Gras celebrations. For the latter, the towns of **Eunice** and **Mamou** stage some of the most enjoyable celebrations. Contact the **Lafayette Convention & Visitors Commission,** P.O. Box 52066, Lafayette, LA 70505 (© **800/346-1958** in the U.S., 800/543-5340 in Canada, or 337/232-3737; www.lafayettetravel.com), for more information.

THE NEW ORLEANS JAZZ & HERITAGE FESTIVAL

People call it "Jazz Fest," but the full name is the New Orleans Jazz & Heritage Festival, and the heritage is about as broad as it can get. Stand in the right place and, depending on which way the wind's blowing, you can catch as many as 10 musical styles from several continents, smell the tantalizing aromas of different food offerings, and meet a United Nations–like spectrum of fellow fest goers all at once.

In the days immediately following Katrina, one of the things lovers of the city wondered about was the fate of Fest. It seems like a trivial thing to focus on, but it wasn't. The music festival is one of the city's two largest tourist draws (Mardi Gras being the other), and much of the local economy (particularly hotels and restaurants) relies on it. But it goes deeper than that; over more than 35 years, Jazz Fest has come to encompass everything the city has to offer, in terms of music, food, and culture. That, and it's a hell of a party. When its return was announced (thanks in part to Shell Oil, the festival's first corporate underwriters, a necessary step under the circumstances), it was seen as a sign that the city really would survive, after all. Jazz Fest 2006 was a moment of resurrection for the city, as crowded as any year, with virtually the same amount of music and food, and highlighted by an emotional and resonant set by Bruce

Springsteen and his Seeger Sessions band. The traditional songs about hard times and hope, coupled with Springsteen's own ire about the state of a city he loved, in front of tens of thousands who had endured much in the previous months, was a confluence of artist, material, time, and place like no other.

And yet, you don't need a star to have musical and emotional epiphanies at Fest. While such headliners as Van Morrison, Dave Matthews, Bob Dylan, Sting, and Paul Simon have drawn record-setting crowds in recent years, serious Jazz Fest aficionados savor the lesser-known acts. They range from Mardi Gras Indians to old-time bluesmen who have never played outside the Delta, from Dixieland to avant-garde, from African artists making rare U.S. appearances to the top names in Cajun, zydeco, and, of course, jazz.

EVERY DAY IS A GOOD DAY   Hotel and restaurant reservations, not to mention choice plane flights, fill up months (if not a year) in advance, but the schedule is not announced until a couple of months before the event. That may mean scheduling your visit around your own availability, not an appearance by a particular band. Just about every day at Jazz Fest is a good day, however, so this is not a hardship—at least, until you learn about an extraordinary group that is playing on a day you won't be in town. Or you could do like we do: Go for the whole 11 days so you won't miss a thing.

The second Saturday does attract some of the top acts, and each year it sets a record for single-day attendance. But we feel the fun tends to diminish with that many people. Still, the tickets are cheap enough (provided you buy them in advance; prices at the gate have become rather costly) that going early in the day and leaving before the crowds get too big is a viable option. The Thursday before the second weekend is traditionally targeted to locals, with more local bands and generally smaller crowds because fewer tourists are around than on the weekends. It's a great time to hit the best food booths and to check out the shopping in the crafts areas.

Contact the **New Orleans Jazz & Heritage Festival,** 1205 N. Rampart St., New Orleans, LA 70116 (© **504/522-4786;** www. nojazzfest.com), to get the schedule for each weekend and information about other Jazz Fest–related shows around town.

JAZZ FEST POINTERS

A typical Jazz Fest day has you arriving sometime after the gates open at 11am and staying until you are pooped or until they close at around 7pm (incredibly the whole thing runs as efficiently as a Swiss train). After you leave the Fair Grounds for the day, get some dinner and then hit the clubs. Every club in the city has Jazz Fest–related bookings (of special note is the **Ponderosa Stomp,** a 3-day event featuring "unsung heroes" of the blues, rockabilly, Swamp Pop, and New Orleans R&B). Bouncing from one club to another can keep you out until dawn. Then you get up and start all over again. This is part of the reason we think Jazz Fest is so fun.

There are also many nonmusical aspects of Jazz Fest to distract you, particularly the crafts. Local craftspeople and imported artisans fill a sizable section of the Fair Grounds with demonstrations and displays of their products during the festival. You might get to see Louisiana Native American basket making; Cajun accordion, fiddle, and triangle making; decoy carving; boat building; and Mardi Gras Indian beading and costume making.

And then there's the food. The heck with the music—when we dream of Jazz Fest, we are often thinking more about those 50-plus food booths filled with some of the best goodies we've ever tasted. The food ranges from local standbys—red beans and rice, jambalaya, étouffée, and gumbo—to more interesting choices such as oyster sacks, the hugely popular sausage bread, *cochon de lait* (a mouthwatering roast pig sandwich), alligator sausage po' boys, and quail and pheasant gumbo. There's plenty of cold beer, too, although you'll probably have to wait in some mighty long lines to get to it.

Try to purchase tickets as early as February if possible. They're available by mail through **Ticketmaster** (© **800/488-5252** or 504/522-5555; www.ticketmaster.com). To order tickets, get information about transportation shuttles to and from the Fair Grounds, or to find out what you are allowed to bring in to Jazz Fest, contact **New Orleans Jazz & Heritage Festival** (© **504/522-4786;** www. nojazzfest.com). Admission for adults is $20 to $30 in advance (depending on when you buy the tickets) and $45 at the gate; $5 for children. Evening events and concerts (order tickets in advance for these events as well) may be attended at an additional cost—usually between $20 and $30, depending on the concert.

JAZZ FEST PARKING & TRANSPORTATION   Parking at the Fair Grounds is next to impossible. The few available spaces cost $10 a day, but it's rare to get a space there. We strongly recommend that you take public transportation or one of the available shuttles.

The **Regional Transit Authority (RTA)** operates bus routes from various pickup points to the Fair Grounds. For schedules contact © **504/827-7802** (www.norta.com). Taxis, though probably scarce, will also take you to the Fair Grounds at a special event rate of $3 per person (or the meter reading if it's higher). We recommend **United Cabs** (✆ **504/524-9606**).

PACKAGE DEALS   If you want to go to Jazz Fest but would rather have someone else do all the planning, consider contacting **Festival Tours International,** 15237 Sunset Blvd., Suite 17, Pacific Palisades, CA 90272 (✆ **310/454-4080;** www.gumbopages.com/festivaltours), which caters to music lovers who don't wish to wear name tags or do other hokey tour activities. Packages include accommodations, tickets, and also a visit to Cajun country for unique personal encounters with some of the finest local musicians.

If you're flying to New Orleans specifically for the festival, visit **www.nojazzfest.com** to get a Jazz Fest promotional code from a list of airlines that offer special fares during the event.

5 Getting There

BY PLANE

Among the airlines serving the city's **Louis Armstrong New Orleans International Airport (MSY)** are **American** (✆ **800/433-7300;** www.aa.com), **Continental** (✆ **800/525-0280** or 504/581-2965; www.continental.com), **Delta** (✆ **800/221-1212;** www.delta.com), **JetBlue** (✆ 800/538-2583; www.jetblue.com), **Northwest** (✆ **800/225-2525;** www.nwa.com), **Southwest** (✆ **800/435-9792;** www.southwest.com), **US Airways** (✆ **800/428-4322;** www.usairways.com), and **United** (✆ **800/241-6522;** www.ual.com).

The airport is 15 miles west of the city, in Kenner. You'll find information booths scattered around the airport and in the baggage claim area.

BY CAR

You can drive to New Orleans via **I-10, I-55, U.S. 90, U.S. 61,** or across the Lake Pontchartrain Causeway on **La. 25.** From any direction, you'll see the city's distinctive and swampy outlying regions; if you can, try to drive in while you can enjoy the scenery in daylight. For the best roadside views, take U.S. 61 or La. 25, but only if you have time to spare. The larger roads are considerably faster.

It's a good idea to call before you leave home to ask for directions to your hotel. Most hotels have parking facilities (for a hefty daily fee); if they don't, they'll give you the names and addresses of nearby parking lots.

Driving in New Orleans can be a hassle, and parking is a nightmare. It's a great city for walking, and cabs are plentiful and not too expensive, so you really don't need a car unless you're planning several day trips.

Nevertheless, most major national car-rental companies are represented at the airport including **Alamo** (© 800/327-9633; www.alamo.com), **Avis** (© 800/331-1212; www.avis.com), **Budget Rent A Car** (© 800/527-0700; www.budget.com), **Dollar Rent A Car** (© 800/800-4000; www.dollar.com), **Hertz** (© 800/654-3131; www.hertz.com), and **National** (© 800/227-7368; www.nationalcar.com).

BY TRAIN

As with the interstates and highways into New Orleans, the passenger rail lines cut through some beautiful scenery. **Amtrak** (© 800/USA-RAIL or 504/528-1610; www.amtrak.com) trains serve the city's **Union Passenger Terminal,** 1001 Loyola Ave.

The New Orleans train station is in the Central Business District. Plenty of taxis wait outside the main entrance to the passenger terminal. Hotels in the French Quarter and the Central Business District are just a short ride away.

6 Specialized Travel Resources

TRAVELERS WITH DISABILITIES

Be aware that although New Orleans facilities are mostly accessible (especially in the Quarter), with proprietors being most accommodating (making narrow doors wider to fit wheelchairs and such), you are still dealing with older structures created before thoughts of ease for those with disabilities. Before you book a hotel, **ask questions** based on your needs. If you have mobility issues, you'll probably do best to stay in one of the city's newer hotels, which tend to be more spacious and accommodating.

For information about specialized transportation systems, call **LIFT** (© 504/827-7433). Organizations that offer a vast range of resources and assistance to travelers with disabilities include **MossRehab** (© 800/CALL-MOSS; www.mossresourcenet.org); the **American Foundation for the Blind (AFB)** (© 800/232-5463; www.afb.org); and **SATH** (Society for Accessible Travel & Hospitality) (© 212/447-7284; www.sath.org). **AirAmbulance Card.com** is now partnered with SATH and allows you to preselect top-notch hospitals in case of an emergency.

GAY & LESBIAN TRAVELERS

New Orleans is a very gay-friendly town with a high-profile homosexual population that contributes much to the color and flavor of the city. You'll find an abundance of establishments serving gay and lesbian interests, from bars to restaurants to community services to certain businesses.

Ambush Magazine, 828-A Bourbon St., New Orleans, LA 70116 (© **504/522-8047;** www.ambushmag.com), is a weekly entertainment and news publication for the Gulf South's gay, lesbian, bisexual, and transgender communities. One useful website is **www.gayneworleans.com**, which provides information on lodging, dining, arts, and nightlife as well as links to other information on New Orleans gay life.

The International Gay and Lesbian Travel Association (IGLTA) (© **800/448-8550** or 954/776-2626; www.iglta.org) is the trade association for the gay and lesbian travel industry, and offers an online directory of gay- and lesbian-friendly travel businesses and tour operators.

SENIOR TRAVEL

Don't be shy about asking for discounts, but always carry some kind of identification, such as a driver's license, that shows your date of birth, especially if you've kept your youthful glow.

Mention the fact that you're a senior when you make your travel reservations. Many hotels offer discounts for seniors. Seniors who show their Medicare card can ride New Orleans streetcars and buses for 40¢.

Members of **AARP,** 601 E St. NW, Washington, DC 20049 (© **888/687-2277;** www.aarp.org), get discounts on hotels, airfares, and car rentals.

2

Getting to Know New Orleans

At the time of this writing, New Orleans has in many ways shrunk to its 1878 borders. It was always a manageable size (only about 7 miles long), and if you didn't count the unusual directions and the nearly impossible-to-pronounce street names, it was a very user-friendly city, with most of what the average tourist would want to see concentrated in a few areas. As it happens, those areas were the least damaged by Hurricane Katrina and the flooding aftermath. Aerial maps of the flooded sections show a thin sliver of dry running alongside the river, with other little pockets here and there, nearly all corresponding to the best-known districts. While the city still debates about rebuilding plans, those neighborhoods are the heart of revitalization for the city, a city that currently looks like a small funky town.

The greatest damage occurred from the post-Katrina flooding; the storm itself was just enough off-center so that the city in many parts experienced less damage than might be expected. The average tourist could confine him- or herself to certain areas (truth be told, the only areas the average tourist went to in the first place) and barely know a disaster ever occurred, much less one of this magnitude. However, we encourage you to take the time to tour some of the devastated areas—it's the only way to even begin to comprehend the extent of what happened and what will be needed in the future. Further, while neighborhoods such as the Lower 9th Ward and the Treme were not part of the regular tourist routes, the city owes much of its heart and soul to the inhabitants and history of these regions. While the survival of the French Quarter and Garden District should be celebrated, the future of these lesser-known neighborhoods must not be neglected if New Orleans is to flourish fully again.

The major breaches in the levee system happened at the 17th Street Canal (at the rough border between Orleans and Jefferson Parish), the London Street Canal (between City Park and Elysian Fields Ave.), and the Inner Harbor Navigation Canal, known locally as the Industrial Street Canal, the border between the 9th and the Lower 9th wards. The waters of Lake Pontchartrain rushed in until the more or less bowl-shaped city became a level extension of the lake itself. Because of the varying levels of higher ground, the depth of flooding sometimes varied from block to block, with the result that one stretch might have been subjected to no more than a foot or so in the street, while just a few blocks away, the water was as deep as 6 feet. The closer one gets to the lake, the more serious the flooding, particularly north (or lakeside) of St. Claude Avenue and Claiborne Avenue in the 9th and Lower 9th wards (the now-iconic photo of the swamped Circle Foods store was taken at the corner of Claiborne and St. Bernard aves., looking under the 10 freeway), and north (lakeside) of the 610 in Lakeview and Gentilly in that neighborhood. Disconcertingly, buildings perched on patches of high ground may have avoided serious damage while neighborhoods such as the Broadmoor section of Mid-City, far from a lakeshore, suffered deep flooding. For a detailed look at the flood levels, see the map, **"Post-Katrina Flood Levels,"** on the inside back cover of this book.

Though much may have changed by the time you read this, in terms of bulldozing and rebuilding, driving through some of the flooded areas can be deceptive. If an area took on only a few feet of water, the buildings may not show many signs of damage, just the telltale brown water line revealing the level at which the floodwaters sat (it likely initially flooded even higher, but there was a drop in the water level after the storm surge passed), or cryptic florescent spray-painted symbols, indicating a search was done of the premises and what was found within—the graffiti of disaster. By mid-2007, most of the flood lines and spray-painted marks had been either painted over or had faded away, but some are still visible. Mid-City, with its 4 to 6 feet of water on average, has some parts that still seem ghostly and abandoned, but overall it is making a steady comeback. Even badly flooded residential Lakeview can appear normal—unless, that is, you were to enter one of the houses that sat for weeks under as much as 12 feet of water. Within these family homes, furniture was tossed about like the toys of a disgruntled giant child, and every exposed inch was sometimes covered in mold. Most of these houses are now gutted. As reconstruction continues, throughout the city you are still likely to see piles of trash in front of many buildings, as ruined interiors are ripped out, down to the studs, in an attempt to salvage a structure.

And all of that pales compared to the utter devastation of the Lower 9th Ward, where houses were pushed into each other, as if kicked about, or in many cases, reduced to indistinguishable piles of lumber and rubble. Those piles sat for a disgracefully long time, but by summer 2007, most of them had been bulldozed, reducing this once-complex neighborhood to a series of vacant lots. Here and there is the occasional brand-new house, as an intrepid owner takes a stand in isolation.

So what should you see? Whatever you like. New Orleans is a very convenient and hospitable city—that is, if you don't count the unconventional directions, tangled roads, and the nearly unpronounceable street names. This chapter contains some of the ins and outs of New Orleans navigation and gives you some local sources to contact for specialized information.

1 Orientation

ARRIVING

From the airport, you can get to your hotel on the **Airport Shuttle** (© **504/522-3500**). For $13 per person (one-way), the van will take you directly to your hotel. There are Airport Shuttle information desks (staffed 24 hr.) in the airport.

Note: If you plan to take the Airport Shuttle *to* the airport when you depart, you must call a day in advance and let them know what time your flight is leaving. They will then tell you what time they will pick you up.

A **taxi** from the airport to most hotels will cost about $28 for one to two people; if there are three or more passengers, the fare is $12 per person plus a $1 gas surcharge.

From the airport, you can reach the **Central Business District** by **bus** for $1.50 (exact change required). Buses run from 6am to 6:30pm. From 6 to 9am and 3 to 6pm, they leave the airport every 12 to 15 minutes and go to the downtown side of Tulane Avenue between Elks Place and South Saratoga Street; at other times, they leave every 23 minutes. For more information, call the **Regional Transit Authority** (© **504/248-3900;** www.norta.com).

VISITOR INFORMATION

The **New Orleans Metropolitan Convention and Visitors Bureau,** 2020 St. Charles Ave., New Orleans, LA 70130 (© **800/672-6124** or 504/566-5011; www.neworleanscvb.com), not only has a wide array of well-designed and well-written brochures that cover everything from the usual sightseeing questions to cultural history, but the incredibly friendly and helpful staff can answer almost any random question you may have. If you're having trouble making decisions, they can give you good advice; if you have a special interest, they'll help you plan your visit around it—this is definitely one of the most helpful tourist centers in any major city.

Once you've arrived in the city, you also might want to stop by the **Visitor Information Center,** 529 St. Ann St. (© **504/568-5661**), in the French Quarter. The center is open Tuesday to Saturday from 9am to 5pm and has walking- and driving-tour maps and booklets on restaurants, accommodations, sightseeing, special tours, and pretty much anything else you might want to know about. The staff is friendly and knowledgeable about both the city and the state.

CITY LAYOUT

"Where y'at?" goes the traditional local greeting. "Where" is easy enough when you are in the French Quarter, the site of the original settlement. A 13-block-long grid between Canal Street and Esplanade Avenue, running from the Mississippi River to North Rampart Street, it's the closest the city comes to a geographic center.

After that, all bets are off. Because of the bend in the river, the streets are laid out at angles and curves that render north, south, east, and west useless. It's time to readjust your thinking: In New Orleans the compass points are *lakeside, riverside, uptown,* and *downtown.* You'll catch on quickly if you keep in mind that North Rampart Street is the *lakeside* boundary of the Quarter and that St. Charles Avenue extends from the French Quarter, *downtown,* to Tulane University, *uptown.*

Canal Street forms the boundary between new and old New Orleans. Street names change when they cross Canal (Bourbon St., for example, becomes Carondelet St.), and addresses begin at 100 on either side of Canal. In the Quarter, street numbers begin at 400 at the river because 4 blocks of numbered buildings were lost to the river before the levee was built.

THE NEIGHBORHOODS IN BRIEF

The French Quarter Made up of about 90 square blocks, this section is also known as the *Vieux Carré* ("Old Square") and is enclosed by Canal Street, North Rampart Street, the Mississippi River, and Esplanade Avenue. The Quarter is full of clubs, bars, stores, residences, and museums; its major public area is Jackson Square, bounded by Chartres, Decatur, St. Peter, and St. Ann streets. The most historic and best-preserved area in the city, a survivor of two major fires in the 1700s in addition to Katrina, it's likely to be the focal point of your stay.

Faubourg Marigny This area is east of the French Quarter (on the other side of Esplanade Ave.). Over the past decade, the Marigny has emerged as one of the city's vital centers of activity, and it was fortunate that it did not experience flooding from Katrina. Here, you can still find the outlines of a small Creole suburb, and many old-time residents remain. Younger urban dwellers have moved into the area in significant numbers recently. Today some of the best bars and nightspots in New Orleans are along Frenchmen Street, the Marigny's main drag. Along with the adjacent sections of the French Quarter, the Marigny is also a social center for the city's gay and lesbian communities.

Bywater This riverside neighborhood is past the Faubourg Marigny and is bounded on the east by an industrial canal. It is tempting to misspeak and call it "Backwater" because at first glance it seems like a wasteland of light industry and run-down homes. In fact, Bywater has plenty of nice, modest residential sections. Furthermore, it's home to the city's artists-in-hiding, and many local designers have shops among the urban decay. This is in keeping with the history of the area, which early on was home to artisans as well as communities of immigrants and free people of color. The lower Bywater adjacent to the Marigny suffered relatively little damage and looks pretty good until one travels past St. Claude toward the lake, where there was severe flooding thanks to the breach in the Industrial Canal.

Mid-City/Esplanade Ridge Stretching north from the French Quarter to City Park, Esplanade Ridge hugs either side of Esplanade Avenue. This area encompasses a few distinct neighborhoods, all of which have certain things in common. In the 19th century, Esplanade was the grand avenue of New Orleans's Creole society— the St. Charles Avenue of downriver. Many sections of the avenue and houses along it have seen better days, but there is still evidence of those times, especially in the ancient oak trees forming a canopy above the road. If you drive or stroll toward City Park along Esplanade, you can measure the progress of the avenue's development in the styles of its houses. Because of this relatively high ground, most of the buildings along Esplanade escaped damaging flooding.

The oldest section of Esplanade Ridge, **Faubourg Treme,** is located directly across Rampart Street from the French Quarter. Like the Quarter, it was a dense 19th-century Creole community.

The City at a Glance

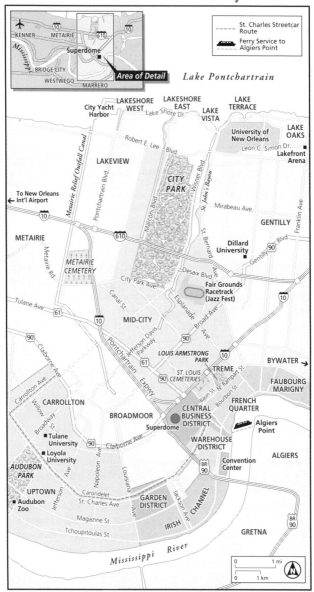

St. Charles Streetcar Route

Ferry Service to Algiers Point

Lake Pontchartrain

Area of Detail

KENNER METAIRIE Superdome BRIDGE CITY WESTWEGO MARRERO

LAKESHORE WEST LAKESHORE EAST LAKE VISTA LAKE TERRACE LAKE OAKS

City Yacht Harbor *Lake Shore Dr.*

University of New Orleans Leon C. Simon Dr. Lakefront Arena

Robert E. Lee Blvd.

LAKEVIEW

CITY PARK

Metairie Relief Outfall Canal Pontchartrain Blvd. Marconi Blvd. Wisner Blvd. *St. John's Bayou* Mirabeau Ave. Franklin Ave.

To New Orleans Int'l Airport

GENTILLY

METAIRIE Metairie Rd.

METAIRIE CEMETERY

Dillard University *Gentilly Blvd.*

City Park Ave. Desaix Blvd. St. Bernard Ave.

Canal St. Esplanade Ave. Broad Ave.

Fair Grounds Racetrack (Jazz Fest)

Tulane Ave.

MID-CITY

Pontchartrain Expwy Jefferson Davis Parkway

LOUIS ARMSTRONG PARK

BYWATER

ST. LOUIS CEMETERIES TREME Basin St. N. Rampart St.

FAUBOURG MARIGNY

Carrollton Ave. Willow St. Broadway

CARROLLTON

BROADMOOR

CENTRAL BUSINESS DISTRICT Superdome

FRENCH QUARTER Bourbon St.

Algiers Point

Tulane University Loyola University

Claiborne Ave.

Napoleon Ave. Louisiana Ave.

WAREHOUSE DISTRICT

Convention Center

ALGIERS

AUDUBON PARK

UPTOWN Audubon Zoo

Jefferson Ave. Carondelet St. Charles Ave.

GARDEN DISTRICT

Jackson Ave.

IRISH CHANNEL

Magazine St. Tchoupitoulas St.

GRETNA

Mississippi River

0   1 mi
0   1 km

Unlike the Quarter, Treme (pronounced Treh-*may*) has remained almost untouched by preservationists (apart from some plucky folks who have beautifully restored a number of turn-of-the-20th-century and older houses) and so has continued to be an organic residential community. Prior to Katrina, it was one of the most vibrant African-American neighborhoods in New Orleans, home to more than a few of the city's best brass bands. Despite major community efforts to reclaim the neighborhood, Treme is usually plagued by severe crime, and it is not advisable to walk through at night. Hurricane and flood damage has set back this historic neighborhood, and there is fear that reconstruction may lead to the sort of gentrification that could force out families who have lived here for generations.

Central Business District Historically, **Canal Street** has been New Orleans's main street, and in the 19th century it also divided the French and American sections of the city. (By the way, there's no canal—the one that was planned for the spot never came to be.)

The **Central Business District (CBD)** is roughly bounded by Canal Street and the elevated Pontchartrain Expressway (Business Rte. U.S. 90) between Loyola Avenue and the Mississippi River. Some of the most elegant luxury hotels are in this area. Most of the district was known as Faubourg St. Mary when Americans began settling here after the Louisiana Purchase. Lafayette Square was the center of life here during the 19th century.

Within the CBD is the **Warehouse District.** More than 20 years ago, this area was full of abandoned warehouses and almost nothing else. With the efforts of some dedicated individuals and institutions, however, it's steadily evolving into a residential neighborhood with some commercial activity. Furthermore, this area also serves as the city's art gallery district, with many of the premier galleries concentrated along **Julia Street.**

Uptown/The Garden District Bounded by St. Charles Avenue (lakeside) and Magazine Street (riverside) between Jackson and Louisiana avenues, the Garden District remains one of the most picturesque areas in the city. Originally the site of a plantation, the area was subdivided and developed as a residential neighborhood for wealthy Americans. Throughout the middle of the 19th century, developers built the Victorian, Italianate, and Greek Revival homes that still line the streets. Most of the homes had elaborate lawns and gardens, but few of those still exist. The Garden District is located uptown (as opposed to the CBD, which is downtown); the neighborhood west of the Garden District is often called Uptown.

Because it did not flood, much of Uptown looks as it always did, although some trees toppled and others look like they were pruned by drunks.

The Irish Channel The area bounded by Magazine Street and the Mississippi River, Louisiana Avenue, and the Central Business District got its name during the 1800s when more than 100,000 Irish immigrated to New Orleans. As was true elsewhere in the country, the Irish of New Orleans were often considered "expendable" labor, and many were killed while employed at dangerous construction work and other manual labor.

These days, the Channel is significantly less Irish, but it retains its lively spirit and distinctive neighborhood flavor. Much of the area is run-down, but just as much is filled with quiet residential neighborhoods. To get a glimpse of the Irish Channel, go to the antiques-shop district on Magazine Street and stroll between Felicity Street and Jackson Avenue.

Algiers Point Directly across the Mississippi River from the Central Business District and the French Quarter and connected by the Canal Street Ferry, Algiers Point is the old town center of Algiers. It is another of the city's original Creole suburbs but probably the one that has changed the least over the decades. Today you can't see many signs of the area's once-booming railroad and dry-docking industries, but you can see some of the best-preserved small gingerbread and Creole cottages in New Orleans. The neighborhood has recently begun to attract attention as a historic landmark, and it makes for one of the city's most pleasant strolls.

SAFETY

New Orleans's crime rate is an area of difficulty. Over the years, it climbed so high the city became the murder capital of the country. Concentrated efforts paid off, and the city became pretty safe again. But even before Katrina, crime was starting to rise, and now after the storm, there are even more problems, thanks to a decreased police force and a low-income population under great stress and frustration. Most of the serious crime is drug-related, and confined to areas where tourists do not go, but once again, we urge you to be very cautious about where you go at night.

The **French Quarter** is fairly safe, especially during the daytime, thanks to the number of people present at any given time, but some areas are better than others. (Rampart and the north part of Esplanade have had bad reputations.) On Bourbon Street be careful when socializing with strangers and in particular be alert to distractions by potential pickpocket teams. Dauphine and Burgundy are in quiet, lovely old parts of the Quarter, but as you near Esplanade, watch out for purse snatchers. At night stay in well-lighted areas with plenty of both street and pedestrian traffic and take cabs down Esplanade and into the **Faubourg Marigny.**

Conventional wisdom holds that one should not go much above Bourbon toward Rampart alone after dark, so it's best to stay in a group (or near one) if you can; and if you feel uncomfortable, consider taking a cab, even if it seems silly, for the (very) short ride. In the **Garden District,** as you get past Magazine toward the river, the neighborhoods can be rough, so exercise caution (more cabs, probably).

2 Getting Around

You really don't need to rent a car during your stay in New Orleans. Not only is the town just made for walking, but most places you want to go are easily accessible on foot or by some form of the largely excellent public transportation system. At night, when you need them most, cabs are easy to come by. Meanwhile, driving and parking in the French Quarter bring grief. The streets are narrow and crowded, and many go one way only. Street parking is minimal (and likely to attract thieves), and parking lots are fiendishly expensive.

BY PUBLIC TRANSPORTATION

DISCOUNT PASSES If you won't have a car in New Orleans, we strongly encourage you to invest in a **VisiTour** pass, which entitles you to an unlimited number of rides on all streetcar and bus lines. It costs $5 for 1 day, $12 for 3 days. Many visitors think this was the best tip they got about their New Orleans stay and the finest bargain in town. Passes are available from VisiTour vendors—to find the nearest one, ask at your hotel or guesthouse or contact the **Regional Transit Authority (RTA)** (© **504/248-3900;** www. norta.com). You can contact the RTA for information about any part of the city's public transportation system.

BUSES   New Orleans has an excellent public bus system, so chances are there's a bus that runs exactly where you want to go. Local fares at press time are $1.25 (you must have exact change in bills or coins), transfers are an extra 25¢, and express buses are $1.25 (or you can use a VisiTour unlimited pass; see above). You can get complete route information by contacting the RTA (© **504/248-3900;**

www.norta.com) or by picking up one of the excellent city maps available at the Visitor Information Center, 529 St. Ann St., in the French Quarter.

STREETCARS   Besides being a National Historic Landmark, the **St. Charles Avenue streetcar** is also a convenient and fun way to get from downtown to Uptown and back. Unfortunately, the overhead system was badly damaged by Katrina, and the route is only coming back in stages. The first section to return travels only from Canal to Lee Circle, with the next stretch to Napoleon to be up and running by the end of 2007. The entire line should be completed by mid-2008. In the meantime, the iconic green cars survived fine and have been transferred to the newer Canal and riverfront lines (see below). There is presently a bus that serves the St. Charles route. When restored to full service, the streetcars will run 24 hours a day at frequent intervals, and the fare is $1.25 each way (you must have exact change in bills or coins). Streetcars can get crowded at rush hour and when school is out for the day. Board at Canal and Carondelet streets (directly across Canal from Bourbon St. in the French Quarter) or anywhere along St. Charles Avenue, sit back, and look for landmarks or just enjoy the scenery.

The streetcar line extends beyond the point where St. Charles Avenue bends into Carrollton Avenue. The end of the line is at Palmer Park and Playground at Claiborne Avenue. It will cost you another $1.25 for the ride back to Canal Street. It costs 10¢ to transfer from the streetcar to a bus.

The **riverfront streetcar** runs for 2 miles, from the Old Mint across Canal Street to Riverview, with stops along the way. It's a great step saver as you explore the riverfront. The fare is $1.50, and there's wheelchair ramp access (but not on the St. Charles line).

The **Canal Street streetcar** line started running just in time for Jazz Fest 2006. Naturally, all of the spiffy new air-conditioned bright red cars flooded; hence the use of the historic green cars on this line. Be sure to check the destination sign, because one branch, Cemeteries, only goes there (to several of the older cemeteries, in fact), while the other, labeled either City Park or Beauregard Circle, is the one you want if you are taking it to Mid-City, City Park/the New Orleans Museum of Art, or Jazz Fest. Be prepared for jammed cars during Jazz Fest, because the line runs to within a few blocks of the Fair Grounds. If your destination is strictly Canal Street/Carrollton, any of the cars will take you there. One-way fares are $1.25.

BY CAR

If you must have a car, try one of the car-rental agencies listed on p. 22.

New Orleans drivers are often reckless, so drive defensively. The meter maids are an efficient bunch, even now, so take no chances with parking meters and carry quarters. It's probably best to use your car only for longer jaunts away from congested areas. Most hotels provide guest parking, often for a hefty daily fee; smaller hotels or guesthouses (particularly in the French Quarter) may not have parking facilities but will be able to direct you to a nearby public garage. The narrow streets and frequent congestion make driving in the French Quarter more difficult than elsewhere in the city. Streets are one-way, and on weekdays during daylight hours, Royal and Bourbon streets between the 300 and 700 blocks are closed to vehicles. The blocks of Chartres Street in front of St. Louis Cathedral are closed at all times. Driving is also trying in the Central Business District, where congestion and limited parking make life difficult for motorists. Do yourself a favor: Park the car and use public transportation in both areas.

Once you get into more residential areas like the Garden District and off main drags like St. Charles Avenue, finding where you are going becomes quite a challenge. Street signs are often not legible until after you cross an intersection, if they are present at all. At night they aren't even lit, so deciphering where you are can be next to impossible. If you must drive, we suggest counting the number of streets you have to cross to tell you when to make any turns rather than relying on street signs.

BY TAXI

Taxis aren't quite as plentiful as they have been in New Orleans, but they can still be hailed easily on the street in the French Quarter and in some parts of the Central Business District, and they are usually lined up at taxi stands at larger hotels. Otherwise, telephone and expect a cab to appear in about 15 minutes. The rate is $2.50 when you enter the taxi and $1.60 per mile thereafter. During special events (like Mardi Gras and Jazz Fest), the rate is $4 per person (or the meter rate if it's greater) no matter where you go in the city. It is a $10 fee for transfers between hotels no matter how short the ride.

The city's most reliable company is **United Cabs** (© **504/524-9606;** www.unitedcabs.com).

Most taxis can be hired for a special rate for up to five passengers. It's a hassle-free and economical way for a small group to tour far-flung areas of the city (the lakefront, for example). Within the city you pay an hourly rate; out-of-town trips cost double the amount on the meter.

ON FOOT

We can't stress this enough: Walking is by far the best way to see New Orleans. Sure, sometimes it's too hot or humid—or raining too hard—to make walking attractive, but there is always a cab or bus nearby. Remember to drink lots of water if it's hot and pay close attention to your surroundings. If you enter an area that seems unsafe, retreat.

BY BIKE

One of the best ways to see the city is by bike. The terrain is flat, the breeze feels good, and you can cover a whole lot of ground on two wheels. A bike store near the French Quarter rents bikes by the hour, day, or longer. **Bicycle Michaels,** 622 Frenchmen St. (© **504/945-9505;** www.bicyclemichaels.com), rents mountain and hybrid bikes; during Jazz Fest it has a fleet of 100 bikes at the ready.

FAST FACTS: New Orleans

American Express The local office (© **800/508-0274**) is at 201 St. Charles Ave. in the Central Business District. It's open weekdays from 9am to 5pm.

Babysitters It's best to ask at your hotel about babysitting services. If your hotel doesn't offer help finding child care, try calling **Accent on Children's Arrangements** (© **504/524-1227**) or **Dependable Kid Care** (© **504/486-4001**).

Emergencies For fire, ambulance, and police, dial © **911**. This is a free call from pay phones.

Hospitals Because so many residents, including medical personnel, were displaced by the hurricane, and their offices or hospitals remain closed, medical care in New Orleans is far more limited than it should be. If you have an ongoing problem or condition that may require very specific medical care, please take the time to find out what the current situation is before planning your trip. Should you become ill, call or go to the emergency room at **Ochsner Medical Center,** 1514 Jefferson Hwy. (© **504/842-3460**), or the **Tulane University Medical Center,** 1415 Tulane Ave. (© **504/588-5800**).

Liquor Laws The legal drinking age in Louisiana is 21, but don't be surprised if people much younger take a seat next to you at the bar. Alcoholic beverages are available round-the-clock, 7 days a week. You're allowed to drink on the street but not from a glass or bottle. Bars will often provide a plastic "go cup" that you can transfer your drink to as you leave (and some have walk-up windows for quick and easy refills).

One warning: Although the police may look the other way if they see a pedestrian who's had a few too many (as long as he or she is peaceful and is not bothering anyone), they have no tolerance at all for those who are intoxicated behind the wheel.

Newspapers & Magazines To find out what's going on around town, you might want to pick up a copy of the daily *Times-Picayune* (www.nola.com) or *Offbeat* (www.offbeat.com), a monthly guide (probably the most extensive one available) to the city's evening entertainment, art galleries, and special events. It can be found in most hotels, though it's often hard to locate toward the end of the month. The *Gambit Weekly* (www.bestofneworleans.com) is the city's free alternative paper and has a good mix of news and entertainment information. It comes out every Sunday. The paper conducts an annual **"Best of New Orleans"** readers' poll; check their website for the results.

Pharmacies There is a Walgreens located on the corner of Iberville and Royal (© 504/525-2180), but the closest 24-hour pharmacy to the Quarter is Walgreens at 1801 St. Charles (© **504/561-8458**). There is also a 24-hour **Rite Aid** at 3401 St. Charles Ave., at Louisiana Avenue (© **504/896-4575**), which is more convenient if you're staying Uptown or in the Garden District.

Police Dial © **911** for emergencies. This is a free call from pay phones.

Post Office The main post office is at 701 Loyola Ave. In the Quarter, there is one at 1022 Iberville. If you have something large or fragile to send home and don't feel like hunting around for packing materials, go to **Royal Mail Service,** 828 Royal St., near St. Ann Street (© **504/522-8523**) in the Quarter.

Radio WWOZ (90.7 FM) is *the* New Orleans radio station. They say they are the best in the world, and we aren't inclined to disagree. New Orleans jazz, R&B, brass bands, Mardi Gras Indians, gospel, Cajun, zydeco—it's all here. It's such a vital part of the city's soundtrack that during the days the station was off the air, another public radio station took to broadcasting old OZ tapes on the Internet, to help keep it alive. Its studio in Armstrong Park was damaged, so its temporarily located near the French Market. Tune in, feel the beat, and support it. The city's NPR station is **WWNO** (89.9 FM). Also, Tulane's station, **WTUL** (91.5 FM), plays very interesting, eclectic, art-rock, college-radio music.

Taxes The sales tax in New Orleans is 9%. An additional 4% tax is added to hotel bills for a total of 13%. There is also a nightly tax of 50¢ to $2 based on the number of rooms a hotel has.

Time Zone New Orleans observes Central Standard Time, the same as Chicago. Between the second Sunday in March and the first Sunday in November, daylight saving time is in effect. During this period, clocks are set 1 hour ahead of standard time. Call © **504/828-4000** for the correct local time.

Transit Information Local bus routes and schedules can be obtained from the **RTA Ride Line** (© **504/827-7802;** www.norta.org). **Union Passenger Terminal,** 1001 Loyola Ave., provides bus information (© **504/524-7571**) and train information (© **504/528-1610;** www.amtrak.com) and is the place where trains and buses deliver and pick up their passengers who are traveling away from or into New Orleans.

Weather For an update, call © **504/828-4000.**

3

Where to Stay

If you're doing your New Orleans trip right, you shouldn't be doing much sleeping. But you do have to put your change of clothes somewhere. Fortunately, New Orleans is bursting with hotels of every variety (though increasingly of the brand-name chain sort), so you should be able to find something that fits your preferences. The path of Hurricane Katrina and the resulting flooding meant that the main areas of the city with the largest concentration of hotels were largely unscathed or at least sustained repairable damage. Hotels that had minor leaks and the like, which could be treated or repaired, easily reopened almost immediately. By mid-2006, more than 30,000 hotel rooms in downtown were back in business.

And how do those New Orleans hotels look? Pretty much the same as always, and in some cases, even better, as some properties took advantage of the downtime to upgrade. Further, many hotels have dropped their prices in an attempt to lure back tourists. On the other hand, persistent staff shortages may mean less than swift and flawless service, though every establishment is doing its best to fill in gaps. Still, keep this in mind if housekeeping is lax or room service slow (if not nonexistent). As always, during crowded times (Mardi Gras, for example), however, just finding anything might have to be good enough. After all, serious New Orleans visitors often book a year in advance for popular times.

Given a choice, we tend to favor slightly faded, ever-so-faintly decayed, just-this-side-of-elegant locales; a new, sterile chain or even a luxury hotel doesn't seem right for New Orleans, where atmosphere is everything. Slightly tattered lace curtains, faded antiques, mossy courtyards with banana trees and fountains, a musty, Miss Havisham air—to us, it's all part of the fun. We prefer to stay in a Tennessee Williams play if not an Anne Rice novel (though in summertime, we'll take air-conditioning, thank you very much).

Understandably, this may not appeal to you. It may, in fact, describe your own home, and who wants one's own home on vacation? Nevertheless, here are a few tips. Don't stay on Bourbon Street unless you absolutely have to or don't mind getting no sleep. The open-air frat party that is this thoroughfare does mean a free show below your window, but it is hardly conducive to . . . well, just about anything other than participation in the same. On the other hand, making a night of it on your balcony, people-watching—and people-egging-on—is an activity with its own merits, one enjoyed by a number of happy tourists. If you must stay on Bourbon Street, try to get a room away from the street.

A first-time visitor might also strongly consider not staying in the Quarter at all. Most of your sightseeing will take place there, but you may want to get away from it all after dinner or simply see a neighborhood whose raison d'être isn't to entertain first-time visitors. Try the beautiful Garden District instead. It's an easy streetcar (or rather, bus, until sometime in 2008, depending on your location Uptown) ride away from the Quarter, and it's close to a number of wonderful clubs and restaurants. Finally, while staying in the Garden District and the Quarter means you can avoid seeing any Katrina damage, staying in the increasingly interesting Mid-City might bring you in proximity, depending on which place you choose.

All of the guesthouses in this chapter have their merits. If you want more information, we recommend **PIANO,** the Professional Innkeepers Association of New Orleans. Their website (www.bbnola. com) will provide you with quick descriptions and photos of and quick links to a variety of B&Bs, inns, and more. All members must be licensed by the city and inspected by a state official.

Though tourism is not what it was pre-Katrina, as a general rule, just to be on the safe side, always book ahead in spring and fall. And if your trip will coincide with Mardi Gras or Jazz Fest, book *way* ahead (and we can't stress this enough—*please* look at the calendar of events in chapter 1, "Planning Your Trip to New Orleans," to make sure)—up to a year in advance if you want to ensure a room. Sugar Bowl week and other festival times when visitors flood New Orleans also require planning for accommodations, and there's always the chance that a big convention or sports event will be in town, making it difficult to find a room. (Though we have to admit that's often when the maligned anonymous chain hotels do come in handy because they may not be the first choice of regular visitors. If a convention didn't take one over with block booking, there is often an extra room for a decent rate floating around.) You might conceivably run across a cancellation and get a last-minute booking, but the chances are remote at best. You should also be aware that rates

Where to Stay in New Orleans

Astor Crown Plaza Hotel: The Alexa **36**	The Frenchman **41**
Ashton's Bed & Breakfast **38**	The Grand Victorian Bed & Breakfast **6**
B&W Courtyards Bed & Breakfast **42**	Hampton Inn Garden District **5**
Chimes B&B **4**	Harrah's **17**
The Columns **3**	Hilton New Orleans Riverside Hotel **16**
Cotton Exchange **34**	Hilton St. Charles **23**
Courtyard by Marriott **14**	Holiday Inn Express **35**
Dauphine Orleans Hotel **39**	Homewood Suites **31**
The Depot at Madame Julia's **12**	Hotel InterContinental **28**
Drury Inn & Suites **29**	The House on Bayou Road **37**
The Fairmont New Orleans **33**	International House **26**

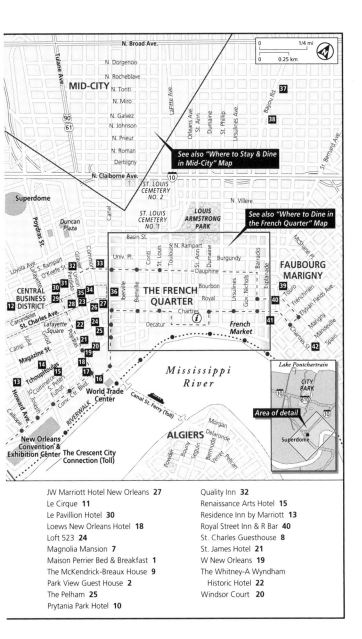

JW Marriott Hotel New Orleans **27**
Le Cirque **11**
Le Pavillion Hotel **30**
Loews New Orleans Hotel **18**
Loft 523 **24**
Magnolia Mansion **7**
Maison Perrier Bed & Breakfast **1**
The McKendrick-Breaux House **9**
Park View Guest House **2**
The Pelham **25**
Prytania Park Hotel **10**

Quality Inn **32**
Renaissance Arts Hotel **15**
Residence Inn by Marriott **13**
Royal Street Inn & R Bar **40**
St. Charles Guesthouse **8**
St. James Hotel **21**
W New Orleans **19**
The Whitney-A Wyndham
  Historic Hotel **22**
Windsor Court **20**

41

frequently jump more than a notch or two for Mardi Gras and other festival times (sometimes they even double), and in most cases, there's a 4- or 5-night minimum requirement during those periods.

If you want to miss the crowds and the lodgings squeeze that mark the big festivals, consider coming in the month immediately following Mardi Gras or, if you can stand the heat and humidity, in the summer, when the streets are not nearly as thronged. December, before the Sugar Bowl and New Year's activities, is a good time, too, but perhaps a bit chilly and rainy. In both cases, hotel prices fall dramatically and great deals can be had just about everywhere. (And these prices might not be accounted for in the rack rate quoted in this guide, so you might have a pleasant surprise!)

There are no recommendable inexpensive *hotels* in the French Quarter. If you're on a budget and must stay there, consider a guesthouse. On the whole, however, you'll have a better selection of inexpensive lodgings outside the Quarter. There are also a couple of hostels in New Orleans; check the website **www.hostels.com** for more information.

The rates we've given in this chapter are for double rooms and do not include the city's 11% hotel tax. You may see some wide ranges of room rates below, which hotels were not eager to break down more specifically for us. Realize that rates often shift according to demand. Unless our entry includes the caveat "higher rates for special events" (implying higher prices then) or "seasonal rates apply" (implying lower prices during same), the high end of the range is for popular times such as Mardi Gras and Jazz Fest, and the low end is for quieter periods such as the month of December. ***Note:*** Some of the hotels listed under "Expensive" have some surprisingly low numbers at said low end of their range. These could indicate certain times of year or even just whim. Therefore, it's worth searching those out and making a call; you might get very lucky!

1 The French Quarter
VERY EXPENSIVE

Hotel Maison de Ville ℛ   A member of the *Small Luxury Hotels of the World,* the Maison de Ville is not quite as sterling as it has been, despite taking advantage of some storm damage to do some sprucing up in the form of new bedding, new paint, and replaced ceilings. Overall, it remains so romantic and charming that complaints (that it's not exactly run-down but not quite on the ball with all things as it used to be) only seem intermittently important. A newish owner

Where to Stay in the French Quarter

Bienville House **12**

Bourbon Orleans-A Wyndham
Historic Hotel **18**

Bourgoyne Guest House **20**

Chateau LeMoyne-
French Quarter **4**

Chateau Sonesta Hotel
New Orleans **3**

Dauphine Orleans Hotel **5**

The Garlands Historic
Creole Cottages **21**

Hotel Maison de Ville **14**

Hotel Monteleone **9**

Hôtel Provincial **25**

Hotel St. Marie **16**

Hotel Villa Convento **24**

JW Marriott Hotel
New Orleans **10**

Lafitte Guest House **23**

Lamothe House **28**

Le Richelieu Hotel **27**

Maison Dupuy **17**

Maison Orleans **2**

Melrose Mansion **29**

New Orleans Guest House **22**

Omni Royal Orleans **13**

Place d'Armes Hotel **19**

Prince Conti Hotel **6**

Ramada Plaza Hotel-
The Inn on Bourbon **15**

Ritz-Carlton, New Orleans **1**

Royal Sonesta **7**

Soniat House **26**

St. Louis **8**

Westin New Orleans at
Canal Place **11**

might also change things, but we reluctantly think the prices may be too high to justify it (especially since some rooms have rather stinky air-conditioning). Still, this was the hotel where Tennessee Williams was a regular guest in room no. 9, which, along with atmosphere, has to count for something. Most of the rooms surround an utterly charming courtyard (complete with fountain and banana trees), where it's hard to believe you're in the thick of the Quarter. Rooms vary dramatically in size, however; some can be downright tiny, so ask when you reserve, as price is no indicator of size. Be careful you don't get a room overlooking the street—Bourbon is less than half a block away and makes its sorry presence known.

The far more spacious **Audubon Cottages** (larger than many apartments, some with their own private courtyards), located a few blocks away and including a small, inviting pool, can go for less than the cramped queen rooms in the main hotel (and are farther from the hubbub of Bourbon). All rooms are thoroughly lush, with nice touches such as feather beds; the service is helpful and courteous, and the continental breakfast disappointing. Overall, it's a romantic getaway—we just wish it weren't so expensive.

727 Toulouse St., New Orleans, LA 70130. © **800/634-1600** or 504/561-5858. Fax 504/528-9939. www.maisondeville.com. 16 units, 7 cottages. $179–$239 double and queen; $219–$259 king; $329–$399 suite; $239–$329 1-bedroom cottage; $599–$699 2-bedroom cottage; $770–$960 3-bedroom cottage. Rates include continental breakfast. DISC, MC, V. Valet parking $30. **Amenities:** Restaurant; outdoor pool; concierge; massage; laundry; dry cleaning; shoeshine. *In room:* A/C, flatscreen TV, Wi-Fi, dataport, minibar, hair dryer, iron, CD clock radio, robes.

Maison Orleans ★★★   This is for those who say, "I'd stay at the Ritz-Carlton if only it were even nicer and had even better service." *Voilà!* Originally conceived as a boutique hotel attached to the Ritz, it now operates as the Ritz's Club Level, but with, get this, 24-hour butler service. Yes, ring a special button, "ask for the sun" (they say themselves), and your own personal Jeeves will fetch it for you.

Largely untouched by Katrina, the rooms here are gorgeous little classics of NOLA style: wood floors, paneling, and furniture; superb moldings; fireplace facades; and bathrooms containing about the deepest hotel tubs we've seen, a separate shower (though rooms whose numbers end with 05s have smaller bathrooms, with tub/shower combinations), quality amenities, and thick bath sheets. You get both local aesthetics *and* modern comforts, though window size can vary. Beds are so ultralush, with feather beds, down comforters with soft covers, and a half canopy, that we had to be dragged out of ours in the morning. All of this doesn't come cheap. However, because there are also five food servings a day (enough so that you need not eat anywhere else, though that would be a mistake in New Orleans!), and drinks are free, a case can be made that there is a certain economy to staying here, depending on the extent to which you take advantage of these inclusions.

904 Iberville St., New Orleans, LA 70112. © **504/670-2900.** Fax 504/670-2910. 75 units. $304–$715 double and suite. Rates include continental breakfast plus daily snacks. AE, DC, DISC, MC, V. Valet parking $32. **Amenities:** 2 restaurants; health club; spa; full access to Ritz-Carlton shops; room service; babysitting; dry cleaning and laundry; 24-hr. butler service; special baths drawn by butler. *In room:* A/C, TV, Wi-Fi, CD and DVD players (and complimentary selections), iPod docking station, minibar (stocked according to personal preference), coffeemaker, hair dryer, iron, robes and slippers.

Melrose Mansion ✫ A standout even on a street full of mansions in a town full of pampering guesthouses, the Melrose Mansion has long combined luxury-resort living with the best guesthouse offerings. Unfortunately, it seems somewhat to be resting on its laurels, needing some paint touch-ups and the like here and there. Service is still attentive and accommodating, and the breakfasts, once handsome feasts, aren't elaborate, though they do include delicious pastries from Croissant D'or, and the staff does try to address dietary needs. It still remains a charming old mansion, with well-maintained grounds, but it may no longer be justifying its high cost. (For which, please note, it has a very strict cancellation policy).

The rooms vary from classic Victorian antiques to lighter country-style decor. Bathrooms can be small, but fancy linens help.

937 Esplanade Ave., New Orleans, LA 70116. ℂ **800/650-3323** or 504/944-2255. Fax 504/945-1794. www.melrosegroup.com. 20 units. $225–$275 double; $300–$450 suite. Rates include continental breakfast and cocktail hour. AE, DC, DISC, MC, V. Private parking $23. **Amenities:** Heated outdoor pool. *In room:* A/C, TV, Wi-Fi, minibar, hair dryer, iron.

Ramada Plaza Hotel—The Inn on Bourbon A too-pricey chain hotel, with modestly good-looking, vaguely Southern decor, plus cottage-cheese ceilings and fluorescent lights in the hallways. The justification for staying here is the location: the former site of the 1859 French Opera House—the first opera house built in the United States (it burned down in 1919). Party animals should note that this means the hotel is right in the middle of the liveliest action on Bourbon, and many rooms (not standards, though) have balconies overlooking the mayhem below. All rooms have king-size or double beds. The pool is fine but unheated. The **Bourbon Street Cafeteria** serves breakfast.

541 Bourbon St., New Orleans, LA 70130. ℂ **800/272-6232** or 504/524-7611. Fax 504/568-9427. www.innonbourbon.com. 186 units. $219–$299 double. AE, DC, DISC, MC, V. Valet parking $20. **Amenities:** Bar; outdoor pool; fitness room; concierge; jewelry shop; gift shop; laundry; dry cleaning; express checkout. *In room:* A/C, TV, minibar, coffeemaker, hair dryer.

Ritz-Carlton, New Orleans ✫✫✫ The Ritz was occupied during the hurricane and its aftermath and as such took a serious beating, requiring a major renovation that kept it closed until December 2006. Given the standards of the brand name, it was no surprise it returned as good as, if not better than, ever.

Sentimentalists that we are, we were deeply sad to see the venerable Maison Blanche department store go the way of Woolworth's,

D. H. Holmes, and other Canal Street shopping landmarks. But for the city's sake, we are pleased to have the Ritz-Carlton take its place, preserving the classic, glazed terra-cotta building and bringing a high-end luxury hotel to the Quarter. Service is sterling, and there may be some surprises along the way that will tickle you. Room color scheme varies according to the size (double rooms are light blue, queen purple, and so on), and rooms have lovely beds. King rooms are nicer than doubles, while rooms on the 12th, 14th, and 15th floors are the largest (some ridiculously large). Consider pony-ing up for the Club Level over at the Maison Orleans (see above). The spa is by far the nicest and largest in town, and though unde-niably expensive, it's gorgeous, and the treatments are utter perfec-tion. Look for fun site-specific events in the courtyard, such as crawfish boils and voodoo ceremonies.

921 Canal St., New Orleans, LA 70112. ⓒ 800/241-3333 or 504/524-1331. Fax 504/524-7675. www.ritzcarlton.com. 452 units. $169–$419 double; from $569 and way, way up for suites. AE, DC, DISC, MC, V. Valet parking $32. Pets welcome. **Amenities:** 2 restaurants; 2 bars; top-of-the-line spa (w/brand-new treatment rooms) and health club (w/resistance pool, Jacuzzi, and personal trainers); concierge; shops; room serv-ice; babysitting; laundry/dry cleaning; Wi-Fi in public areas. *In room:* A/C, TV, high-speed Internet ($9.95/day), minibar, coffeemaker, iron, safe, Nintendo, newspaper delivery, robes and slippers.

Royal Sonesta ⓡⓡ   The Royal Sonesta brags that it never closed, providing refuge during and after Katrina, bless its heart. (Anderson Cooper stayed here!) As one of the classiest hotels in the Quarter, the contrast between the boisterous hurly-burly of Bourbon Street and the Sonesta's marbled and chandeliered lobby couldn't be greater. Inside, all is quiet and gracious, and if your room faces the courtyard (complete with a large pool), you are in another world altogether. Big and bustling (a favorite of business travelers, so it always seems busy), this is considered the only acceptable, top-flight Bourbon Street hotel, though noise is still a problem in rooms that face Bourbon (or even the side streets). But because the Sonesta is so large, reaching nearly to Royal Street, unless you do have one of those rooms, you won't believe you are so close to such craziness. Rooms underwent a major renovation a couple of years ago, adding posher bedspreads and the like, but the designers miscalculated by including an enor-mous combo armoire/TV cabinet—leaving scant few inches between it and the end of the king-size beds. The bathrooms gleam with mar-ble and tile, but don't bring a cat inside if you want to swing it.

300 Bourbon St., New Orleans, LA 70130. ⓒ 800/766-3782 or 504/586-0300. Fax 504/586-0335. www.sonesta.com/royalneworleans. 500 units. $249–$389 double;

$479–$1,250 suite. AE, DC, DISC, MC, V. Parking $25 car, $30 oversize. **Amenities:** 2 restaurants; bar; pool; exercise room; concierge; business center; room service; massage. *In room:* A/C, TV, Wi-Fi, dataport, minibar, hair dryer, iron, safe.

Soniat House ⋆⋆   The recipient of endless tributes from various prestigious travel journals, the wonderful and romantic Soniat House lives up to the hype. Keeping a low profile behind a solid wood gate, it is classic Creole—the treasures are hidden off the street. Inside this nonsmoking property you will find a perfect little hideaway, an oasis of calm that seems impossible in the Quarter. The beyond-efficient staff will spoil you, and the sweet courtyards, candlelit at night, will soothe you. The entire establishment is very particular and detail-oriented, and the experience here is gracious and adult.

Rooms do vary, if not in quality then at least in distinction. All have antiques, but if you want, say, high ceilings and really grand furniture (room no. 23 has a 17th-c. bed), you are better off in the main house or the suite-filled annex across the street. The rooms in the old kitchen and other buildings are not quite as smashing by comparison. On the main property, bathrooms are small, though some rooms have their own private balconies, but across the street they gain size, not to mention Jacuzzi bathtubs, custom decor, and antique furnishings. Many rooms have nonworking fireplaces, and all are decorated in simple, elegant good taste, including original art on the walls. Our only real complaint is the extra charge ($13) for the admittedly delicious, but small, breakfast.

1133 Chartres St., New Orleans, LA 70116. **℃ 800/544-8808** or 504/522-0570. Fax 504/522-7208. www.soniathouse.com. 33 units. $265–$325 double; $395–$675 suite; $750 2-bedroom suite. AE, MC, V. Valet parking $25. No children under 12. **Amenities:** Access to nearby health club (for additional charge) and business center; concierge; same-day laundry; dry cleaning. *In room:* A/C, TV, Wi-Fi, hair dryer, safe, robes.

EXPENSIVE

Chateau LeMoyne—Holiday Inn French Quarter ⋆   The Chateau LeMoyne is in a good location, just around the corner from Bourbon Street but away from the noise and not far from Canal. It's a nice surprise to find a Holiday Inn housed in century-plus-old buildings, but the ambience stops at your room's threshold. Once inside, matters look pretty much like they do in every Holiday Inn. Famed architect James Gallier designed one of these 19th-century buildings, and you can still see bits of old brick, old ovens, and exposed cypress beams here and there, along with a graceful curving outdoor staircase. You wish they'd made more of their space, but even the spacious courtyard feels oddly sterile. Suites aren't much different from standard rooms, just with frillier furniture, though the enormous Executive Suite is probably worth budget busting for its four large (if dark) rooms that include a Jacuzzi and sauna.

301 Dauphine St., New Orleans, LA 70112. ℂ **800/447-2830** or 504/581-1303. Fax 504/525-8531. www.chateaulemoyneneworleans.com. 171 units. $89–$309 double; $159–$499 suite, depending on season. Extra person $15. AE, DC, DISC, MC, V. Valet parking $28. **Amenities:** Restaurant (breakfast only); bar; outdoor swimming pool; breakfast room service 7–11am. *In room:* A/C, TV, Wi-Fi, coffeemaker, hair dryer, iron, safe.

Chateau Sonesta Hotel New Orleans ⭐⭐ On the site of the former D. H. Holmes Canal Street department store (1849), the Chateau Sonesta Hotel maintains the structure's 1913 facade. Thanks to Canal Street flooding, the hotel had to renovate over 50% of its guest rooms (which are now quite spiffy and fresh), plus their famous Clock Bar. Many rooms feature balconies overlooking Bourbon or Dauphine Street, which you might want to avoid if you are a light sleeper or request if you want the party action that encourages. High ceilings and a fairly spacious layout, not to mention that proximity to Bourbon, make this a potentially well-priced (if slightly generic) choice, already popular among business groups for its meeting rooms and location.

800 Iberville St., New Orleans, LA 70112. ℂ **800/SONESTA** or 504/586-0800. Fax 504/586-1987. www.chateausonesta.com. 251 units. $99–$350 double; $285–$798 suite. Extra person $40. Children under 17 stay free in parent's room. AE, DC, DISC, MC, V. Valet parking $25. **Amenities:** Restaurant; bar; heated outdoor pool; exercise room; concierge; tour desk; gift shop; room service; babysitting; laundry; dry cleaning. *In room:* A/C, TV w/pay movies, dataport, minibar, coffeemaker, hair dryer, iron.

Dauphine Orleans Hotel ⭐ On a relatively quiet and peaceful block of the Quarter, the Dauphine Orleans Hotel is relaxed but not unkempt. It's just a block from the action on Bourbon Street, but you wouldn't know it if you were sitting in any of its three secluded courtyards. The hotel's back buildings were once the studio of John James Audubon, and the "patio rooms" across the street from the main building were originally built in 1834 as the home of New Orleans merchant Samuel Herrmann. At press time, the hotel was about to commence a thorough room remodel (previously nice enough, with marble bathrooms and semi-period furniture), which should be completed by the time you read this. A concierge was anticipated to return by the end of 2007.

415 Dauphine St., New Orleans, LA 70112. © **800/521-7111** or 504/586-1800. Fax 504/586-1409. www.dauphineorleans.com. 111 units. $149–$269 double; $149–$289 patio room; $179–$399 suite. Rates include continental breakfast and welcome-drink coupon. Extra person $20. Children under 17 stay free in parent's room. AE, DC, DISC, MC, V. Valet parking $18. **Amenities:** Bar; outdoor pool; small fitness room; Jacuzzi; babysitting; laundry; dry cleaning; guest library; Wi-Fi in public rooms. *In room:* A/C, TV, dataport, minibar.

The Garlands Historic Creole Cottages 𝒌𝒌

Here's a hidden gem across a side street from Armstrong Park, which makes it not the best location in town, though the inn itself is completely safe thanks to a good security fence. Still, you should exercise some caution coming home at night, and don't plan on venturing deeper into the Treme neighborhood. Please don't let our warning discourage you; this B&B is utterly charming, with some of the nicest accommodations in the city, set on the grounds of the former Claude Treme plantation. Creole cottages such as the three-room Queen Elizabeth feature big, sexy canopy beds, wide pine-board floors, exposed brick walls, a fireplace, a big oval soaking tub, and good-taste furniture. Some come with kitchens and small living rooms, while other rooms are smaller (since units vary in size, ask when booking), but all are impeccably maintained, and the whole place is set in small delightful Southern gardens. Some rooms now have dataports and/or Wi-Fi. Parking is plentiful, and the staff includes two sweet dogs.

1129 St. Philip St., New Orleans, LA 70116. © **800/523-1060** or 504/523-1372. Fax 504/523-1951. www.historicgarlands.com. 15 units. $115–$225 double; $355 2-bedroom cottage; higher rates during special events. Rates include breakfast. AE, MC, V. Parking $10. Pet-friendly (call ahead for specifics about your pet). **Amenities:** Jacuzzi; Wi-Fi. *In room:* A/C, TV.

Hotel Monteleone 𝒌𝒌

Opened in 1886, the Monteleone is the largest hotel in the French Quarter (and was home to Truman Capote's parents when he was born!), and it seems to keep getting bigger without losing a trace of its trademark charm. Because of its size, you can almost always get a reservation here, even when other places are booked. Everyone who stays here loves it, probably because it's a family hotel whose approach to business is reflected by the staff, among the most helpful in town. One guest who stayed here with a child with disabilities raved about the facilities.

All the rooms have been freshly renovated (Katrina winds broke windows) and look blandly pretty as a result, though there is still some difference in terms of size and style. Rooms in the 60s are near the ice machine; rooms from 56 to 59 are slightly bigger with old high ceilings; rooms in the 27s have no windows. Executive suites are just big rooms but have the nicest new furniture, including four-poster beds and Jacuzzis. One of the city's best-kept secrets is the renovated rooftop pool.

214 Royal St., New Orleans, LA 70130. (©) **800/535-9595** or 504/523-3341. Fax 504/561-5803. www.hotelmonteleone.com. 570 units. $199–$275 double; $360–$2,500 suite. Extra person $25. Children under 18 stay free in parent's room. Package rates available. AE, DC, DISC, MC, V. Valet parking $19 car, $25 small SUV. Pets allowed on certain floors, for a fee and deposit. **Amenities:** 3 restaurants; 2 bars (for info on the Carousel Bar & Lounge, see p. 191); heated rooftop swimming pool (open year-round); fitness center (understocked but w/fabulous views of the city and river); concierge; room service; babysitting; laundry. *In room:* A/C, TV, dataport, minibar, cof-feemaker, hair dryer, iron, safe.

Lafitte Guest House ⍟ Here you'll find the best of both worlds: antique living just blocks from Bourbon Street mayhem (though the Lafitte's cute little parlor seems almost antithetical to rowdy merriment). The three-story brick building, with wrought-iron balconies on the second and third floors, was constructed in 1849. Thanks to Katrina, a big hole in the roof sent water pouring down the walls, but it's been completely restored, and is better than ever. They took advantage of the situation to replace furniture (keeping the same visual idea), upgrade linens, and so forth. Each room has its own mostly Victorian flair, with thoughtful touches such as pralines on the pillow and even white-noise machines to handle Bourbon Street ruckus, which is an excellent idea. Some rooms have balconies over-looking Bourbon. Room no. 21 has its own sitting room, while gar-connière rooms are smaller and probably best for singles. Room no. 5 is in the old stables in back and has a tiny loft (the ceiling may be a little low for a tall person). Breakfast is delivered to wherever you want (your room, your balcony, the courtyard). The owners are committed to supporting their city and now only use products from local vendors.

1003 Bourbon St., New Orleans, LA 70116. (©) **800/331-7971** or 504/581-2678. Fax 504/581-2677. www.lafitteguesthouse.com. 14 units. $159–$229 double. Extra person $50. Rates include continental breakfast. AE, DISC, MC, V. Parking $20. **Amenities:** 24-hr. concierge. *In room:* A/C, TV, fridge in some rooms, hair dryers and irons available.

Maison Dupuy ⍟ Thanks to roof damage and some flooding, this hotel needed a complete renovation. It reopened in April 2006, looking essentially the same as it did before. That's a relief: We often forget to recommend this place, but that's a mistake. A little out of the main French Quarter action and a tad closer than some might like to dicey Rampart (though the hotel is entirely safe), the Maison Dupuy, with its seven town houses surrounding a good-size courtyard (and a heated pool), is still warm and inviting. While the rooms aren't remarkable, they are comfortable. Though floor space and balconies (with either courtyard or street views—the former is quieter) vary, the staff is most friendly and helpful, the courtyard of sufficiently pleasing ambience, and the location—a quieter end of the Quarter, near a bar with pool tables (a rarity in town)—puts it right in the middle of the "Oh, they've got rooms available? Why not?" category.

1001 Toulouse St., New Orleans, LA 70112. ✆ **800/535-9177** or 504/586-8000. Fax 504/525-5334. www.maisondupuy.com. 200 units. $99–$269 superior double; $149–$299 deluxe double with balcony; $329–$838 suite. AE, DC, DISC, MC, V. Valet parking $24 for cars, $28 for SUVs and trucks when available. **Amenities:** Restaurant; bar; heated outdoor saltwater pool; exercise room; concierge; room service; babysitting; same-day laundry/dry cleaning. *In room:* A/C, TV, minibar, dataport, hair dryer, iron, safe.

Omni Royal Orleans ✶✶ *Kids*   Despite being part of a chain, this is an elegant hotel that escapes feeling sterile and generic. This is only proper given that it is on the former site of the venerable 1836 St. Louis Exchange Hotel, one of the country's premier hostelries and a center of New Orleans social life until the final years of the Civil War. The original building was finally destroyed by a 1915 hurricane, but the Omni, built in 1960, which suffered no damage from Katrina, is a worthy successor, enjoying a prime location smack in the center of the Quarter. Truman Capote and William Styron have stayed here, and there is a Tennessee Williams suite. Furnishings in the guest rooms (which are quietly getting paint-and-wallpaper overhauls) have grave good taste, full of muted tones and plush furniture, with windows that let you look dreamily out over the Quarter. Suites are vast, making this a good choice for families despite the fancy appearance. Service is swift and conscientious and there are more amenities available here than in comparable properties.

621 St. Louis St., New Orleans, LA 70140. ✆ **800/THE-OMNI** in the U.S. and Canada, or 504/529-5333. Fax 504/529-7089. www.omniroyalorleans.com. 346 units. $169–$339 double; $339–$950 suite; $1,200–$1,600 penthouse. Children under 18 stay free in parent's room. AE, DC, DISC, MC, V. Valet parking $28. **Amenities:** Restaurant; 2 bars; heated outdoor pool; health club; concierge; business center; salon; barbershops; room service; massage; babysitting; emergency mending and pressing; florist; sundries shop and newsstand; complimentary shoeshine. *In room:* A/C, TV, Wi-Fi, dataport, minibar, coffeemaker, hair dryer, iron, safe.

St. Louis ✸   Right in the heart of the Quarter, the St. Louis is a small hotel that surrounds a lush courtyard with a fountain. But it's somewhat disappointingly dull for what ought to be a charming boutique hotel. Some third-floor rooms have private balconies overlooking Bienville Street, and all open onto the central courtyard. The exterior is looking a little battered, but the standard quality of the rooms seems better than ever thanks to the precipitous drop in price. Rooms got a pre-Katrina redo with new carpet, drapes, and furniture to help freshen up a slightly stodgy (and even shabby) decor. King rooms are smaller than doubles, though many of those are being converted to doubles as well (leaving queen-sizes for the single rooms). An additional wing with pricey units featuring parlors and kitchenettes is being added. The otherwise uninteresting bathrooms do have bidets.

730 Bienville St., New Orleans, LA 70130. ✆ **800/535-9111** or 504/581-7300. Fax 504/679-5013. www.stlouishotel.com. 98 units. $69–$179 double. Children under 18 stay free in parent's room. AE, DC, MC, V. Valet parking $19. **Amenities:** Restaurant; laundry; limited Wi-Fi service. *In room:* A/C, TV.

Westin New Orleans at Canal Place ✸   At the foot of Canal Street, the Westin is technically *in* the French Quarter—but not quite *of* it. It is literally *above* the Quarter: The grand-scale lobby is on the 11th floor of the Canal Place tower. At press time, the hotel was undergoing a shift from a Wyndham hotel to a Westin property. The guest rooms were in the process of total renovation to Westin standards, which will include all new furniture, new decor, and best of all, the Westin's trademarked Heavenly beds and Heavenly showers. This upgrade should be completed by spring 2008. This transition can only be a good thing, as the accommodations long hadn't lived up to the setting. The hotel provides some of the city's most expansive views of the river and the French Quarter; those rooms are clearly the most desirable.

100 Iberville St., New Orleans, LA 70130. ✆ **504/566-7006.** Fax 504/553-5120. www.starwood.com/westin. 438 units. $159–$309 double. Ask about packages and specials. AE, DISC, MC, V. Self-parking $20. **Amenities:** Restaurant; bar; heated pool; privileges at a nearby 18-hole golf course; concierge; tour desk; room service; laundry; dry cleaning; direct elevator access to Canal Place shopping center, where guests can use the health center free of charge, or visit the barbershop, salon, and stores. *In room:* A/C, TV, Wi-Fi, dataport, minibar, coffeemaker, hair dryer, iron, safe.

MODERATE

Bienville House ✸✸   A nice little Quarter hotel, better than most (thanks to a combo of location, price, and room quality) though not as good as some (owing to a lack of specific personality). It's generally sedate, except perhaps during Mardi Gras, when the mad gay revelers take over—as they do everywhere, truth be told. If you can score some of the lower-end prices, nab a spot here. Rooms mostly have high ceilings; kings have four-poster beds and slightly more interesting furniture than doubles. Some rooms have balconies overlooking the small courtyard that features a good pool for a dip (though the back gate looks out onto a busy street), and all have the standard amenities of a fine hotel.

320 Decatur St., New Orleans, LA 70130. © **800/535-7836** or 504/529-2345. Fax 504/525-6079. www.bienvillehouse.com. 83 units. $89–$119 double; $650 penthouse. AE, DC, DISC, MC, V. Parking $20, $25 for SUVs. **Amenities:** Restaurant; outdoor pool; room service. *In room:* A/C, TV, Wi-Fi, dataport, coffeemaker, hair dryer, iron.

Bourbon Orleans Hotel—A Wyndham Historic Hotel ☆

A lot of hotels claim to be centrally located in the French Quarter, but the Bourbon Orleans really is. And while many hotels *claim* to have an interesting history, this one actually does: The oldest part of the hotel is the Orleans Ballroom, constructed in 1815 as a venue for the city's masquerade, Carnival, and quadroon balls. Today the hotel occupies three buildings, but neither the lobby nor the French Regency–influenced rooms were hit by Katrina, which is a relief, because the hotel had just gotten a handsome $15.5-million face-lift before the storm. The rooms for the mobility-impaired are well designed. Some rooms have only armoires, no closets, and some have balconies. Rooms in the 17s have views up Bourbon Street, but if you want to escape noisy street excitement, ask for an interior room. Ceilings feel lower than the frequent high variety found around town, which may be an optical illusion. Beds are too firm, while bathrooms are long and narrow and feature Golden Door Spa toiletries. Small rooms are cozy but not unbearable, though if occupied by two people, they had better like each other. We are fond of the two-story town-house rooms, with exposed brickwork on the walls, and the beds upstairs in a romantic loft.

717 Orleans St., New Orleans, LA 70116. © **504/523-2222.** Fax 504/525-8166. www.bourbonorleans.com. 220 units. $139–$199 petite queen or twin; $189–$329 deluxe king or double; $239–$489 junior suite; $299–$599 town-house suite; $272–$482 town-house suite with balcony. Extra person $30. AE, DC, DISC, MC, V. Valet parking $30. **Amenities:** Restaurant; bar; outdoor pool; concierge; room service; same-day dry cleaning. *In room:* A/C, TV, fax, Wi-Fi, dataport, coffeemaker, hair dryer, iron, safe.

Bourgoyne Guest House *(Value*

This is an eccentric place with an owner to match. If you dislike stuffy hotels and will happily take things a little worn at the edges in exchange for a relaxed, hangout atmosphere, come here. Accommodations are arranged around a nicely cluttered courtyard, the right spot to visit and regroup before diving back out onto Bourbon Street (whose main action begins just a few feet away). Studios are adequate little rooms with kitchens and bathrooms that appear grimy but are not. The Green Suite is as big and grand as one would like, with huge, tall rooms, a second smaller bedroom, a bigger bathroom, and a balcony overlooking Bourbon Street. For price and location, it's a heck of a deal, maybe the best in the Quarter.

839 Bourbon St., New Orleans, LA 70116. ② **504/525-3983** or 504/524-3621. 5 apts. $92 studio double; La Petite Suite $120 double; Green Suite $130 double, $160 triple, $190 quad. AE, MC, V. *In room:* A/C, unstocked fridge, coffeemaker, iron.

Hôtel Provincial ☆ With flickering gas lamps, no elevators, no fewer than five patios, and a tranquil setting, this feels less like a hotel than a guesthouse. Both the quiet and the terrific service belie its size, so it seems smaller and more intimate than it is. It's also in a good part of the Quarter on a quiet street off the beaten path. For views of the river (plus higher ceilings), get a room on the third or fourth floor of the back building. Some rooms have half-tester beds (the furniture is a mix of antiques and reproductions). Regular rooms are dark but roomy. Finally, with such a pretty pool area, it's a shame there isn't much in the way of lounging or shade.

1024 Chartres St., New Orleans, LA 70116. ② **800/535-7922** or 504/581-4995. Fax 504/581-1018. www.hotelprovincial.com. 94 units. $79–$289 double. Packages available. AE, DC, DISC, MC, V. Valet parking $18. **Amenities:** Restaurant; bar; pool; Wi-Fi. *In room:* A/C, TV, dataport, hair dryer, iron.

Hotel St. Marie Just a little above Bourbon Street on an otherwise quiet street, this hotel could be on your list of "clean and safe backup places to stay if my top choices are full." Surrounding a pretty, foliage-and-light bedecked courtyard with a small pool (which you will bless the heavens for in summer), rooms are generic New Orleans, with dark colors and standard-issue, mock-European hotel furniture, and can smell moldy. Note that king rooms are more pleasant than doubles, and corner rooms are more spacious, which include the otherwise dinky bathrooms. Some rooms from the original town house have balconies overlooking the street and courtyard. Hallways are not numbered and can be dim, which could make a tipsy late-night return a challenge.

827 Toulouse St., New Orleans, LA 70112. ② **800/366-2743** or 504/561-8951. Fax 504/571-2802. www.hotelstmarie.com. 100 units. $49–$199 double, depending on season. AE, DC, DISC, MC, V. Valet parking $22. **Amenities:** Restaurant; bar; room service; laundry; dry cleaning. *In room:* A/C, TV, dataport, coffeemaker, hair dryer, iron.

Hotel Villa Convento ✦   Local tour guides say this was the original House of the Rising Sun bordello, so if you have a sense of humor (or theater), be sure to pose in your bathrobe on your balcony so that you can be pointed out to passing tour groups. With its rather small public spaces and the personal attention that its owners and operators, the Campo family, give to their guests, the Villa Convento has the feel of a small European inn or guesthouse and does a lot of repeat business. The building is a Creole town house; some rooms open onto the tropical patio, others to the street, and many have balconies. There is much to be fond of at this place—including free parking.

616 Ursulines St., New Orleans, LA 70116. ℂ **800/887-2817** or 504/522-1793. Fax 504/524-1902. www.villaconvento.com. 25 units. $89–$105 double; $155 suite. Extra person $10. Rates include continental breakfast. AE, DC, DISC, MC, V. *In room:* A/C, TV, hair dryer, iron.

Lamothe House ✦   Somehow, a shiny new hotel doesn't seem quite right for New Orleans. More appropriate is slightly faded, somewhat threadbare elegance, and the Lamothe House neatly fits that bill. The Creole-style plain facade of this 1840s town house hides the atmosphere you are looking for—a mossy, brick-lined courtyard with a fish-filled fountain and banana trees and rooms filled with antiques that are worn in the right places but not shabby. Despite recent interior upgrades, rooms can be dark and small, with clashing decor. Room no. 101 is a grand affair with lots of original plaster frills, though we wish there were good wood floors instead of that carpet. Room no. 117 nearly gets it right in terms of size and style. A continental breakfast is served in a second-floor dining room that just screams faded gentility. It's a short walk to the action in the Quarter and just a couple of blocks to the bustling Frenchmen scene in the Faubourg Marigny.

621 Esplanade Ave., New Orleans, LA 70116. ℂ **800/367-5858** or 504/947-1161. Fax 504/943-6536. www.lamothehouse.com. 36 units. $65–$199 double. Rates include breakfast. AE, DISC, MC, V. Self-parking $15. **Amenities:** Pool; newspaper in lobby; afternoon sherry. *In room:* A/C, TV, Wi-Fi, hair dryer, iron.

Le Richelieu Hotel ✦ *Kids*   First a row mansion, then a macaroni factory, then a hotel, and finally a Katrina victim—this building has seen it all, including part of its roof collapsing. But the latter mess allowed for some new paint (or textured wallpaper), carpet, drapes, and beds, and consequently Le Richelieu looks as good as it ever has (though some rooms still look rather motel-like, thanks to dated mirrored walls). Bathrooms are still the same, only fair, just like any old hotel. Le Richelieu is good for families (despite the surcharge for children), being away from the adult action and having a nice pool. Management is proudest of the enormous VIP suite—a sort of early-'70s-style apartment with three bedrooms, large bathrooms, a kitchen, a living room, a dining area, and even a steam room. Other rooms are standard high-end motel rooms. Many have balconies, and all overlook either the French Quarter or the courtyard. Le Richelieu is the only hotel in the French Quarter with free self-parking on the premises.

1234 Chartres St., New Orleans, LA 70116. © **800/535-9653** or 504/529-2492. Fax 504/524-8179. www.lerichelieuhotel.com. 86 units. $95–$180 double; $200–$550 suite. Extra person, including children, $15. Honeymoon and seasonal packages available. AE, DC, DISC, MC, V. Complimentary parking. **Amenities:** Restaurant; bar; outdoor pool; concierge; room service. *In room:* A/C, TV, Wi-Fi, unstocked fridge, hair dryer, iron.

Place d'Armes Hotel *(Finds)* *(Kids)*   Parts of this hotel seem a bit grim and old, though its quite large courtyard and amoeba-shaped pool are ideal for hanging out and may make up for it. Plus, it's only half a block from the Café du Monde. Rooms (all nonsmoking) are homey and furnished in traditional style; however, 32 of them do not have windows and can be cell-like—be sure to ask for a room with a window when you reserve. The location, just off Jackson Square, makes sightseeing a breeze.

625 St. Ann St., New Orleans, LA 70116. © **800/366-2743** or 504/524-4531. Fax 504/571-3803. www.placedarmes.com. 80 units. $59–$219, depending on season. Rates include continental breakfast. AE, DC, DISC, MC, V. Parking $22. **Amenities:** Outdoor pool; newspapers. *In room:* A/C, TV, Wi-Fi, coffeemaker, hair dryer, iron.

Prince Conti Hotel *(Finds)*   This tiny but friendly hotel is in a great location right off Bourbon and not generally noisy. Rooms are decorated with attractive reproduction antiques. They all have high ceilings, some with ceiling fans and exposed brick walls, and are bright and pretty. Flatscreen TVs are a bit incongruous with the antique decor. Bathrooms can be ultratiny, with the toilet virtually on top of the sink. Travelers with kids should stay at the hotel's sister location, the Place d'Armes (see above), because it is farther from Bourbon and has a pool.

830 Conti St., New Orleans, LA 70112. © **800/366-2743** or 504/529-4172. Fax 504/636-1046. www.princecontihotel.com. 53 units. $49–$199 double; $119–$299 suite. AE, DC, DISC, MC, V. Valet parking $20. **Amenities:** Restaurant; breakfast cafe; piano bar; limited laundry service. *In room:* A/C, TV, Wi-Fi (free), coffeemaker, iron.

INEXPENSIVE

New Orleans Guest House ⭑   This guesthouse is a little off the beaten path (just outside the French Quarter across N. Rampart St.), but it's painted a startling hot, Pepto-Bismol pink, so it's hard to miss. There are rooms in the old Creole main house (1848) and in what used to be the slave quarters. Roof damage flooded the top floor and rooms in the back, but all have been redone, mostly to fine, funky, and fun effect, all in a way that is classic NOLA guesthouse, in a manner that is being lost to generic good taste. Mainhouse rooms are dark-colored, sometimes with gaudy new bathrooms, but sweet, and room no. 8 has an outrageous Art Nouveau bedroom suite. The slave quarters are simpler but with interesting antiques and light colors. All rooms are nonsmoking. Some rooms have exposed brick walls, while others open directly on to the courtyard, a veritable tropical garden with a banana tree, more green plants than you can count, some intricately carved old fountains, and a fluffy cat.

1118 Ursulines St., New Orleans, LA 70116. ⓒ **800/562-1177** or 504/566-1177. Fax 504/566-1179. www.neworleans.com/nogh. 14 units. $59–$79 double; $69–$99 queen or twin; $89–$109 king or 2 full beds. Rates include continental breakfast. Extra person $25. AE, MC, V. Free parking. *In room:* A/C, TV, Wi-Fi, hair dryer, iron.

2 The Faubourg Marigny

The Faubourg Marigny is very distinct from the French Quarter, though they border each other and are just an easy walk apart. This arty and bohemian neighborhood may be better for a younger crowd who wants to be near the French Quarter without actually being in it. If you stay in the farther reaches of it, however, please either take a cab or be very cautious returning at night; the neighborhood has suffered from crime problems lately.

For hotels in this section, see the "Where to Stay in New Orleans" map on p. 40.

MODERATE

B&W Courtyards Bed & Breakfast ⭑⭑   The deceptively simple facade hides a sweet and very hospitable little B&B, complete with two small courtyards and a fountain. No two rooms are alike— you enter one through its bathroom. Another room is more like a small, two-story apartment with the bedroom upstairs and a virtually full kitchen downstairs. All are carefully and thoughtfully decorated. Rob (who designs jewelry, some of which has been worn by

Mary J. Blige and Oprah) and Kevin (a trained masseuse who can treat you in your room) are adept at giving advice—and strong opinions—not just about the city but about their own local favorites. Breakfast is light (fruit, homemade breads) but beautifully presented.

2425 Chartres St., New Orleans, LA 70117. © **800/585-5731** or 504/945-9418. Fax 504/949-3483. www.bandwcourtyards.com. 8 units. $99–$250 double. Rates include continental breakfast. AE, DISC, MC, V. Free parking available on street. **Amenities:** Hot tub; business center. *In room:* A/C, TV, Wi-Fi, coffeemaker, hair dryer, iron.

The Frenchmen ⊀   This is seen by some as a small, sweet, and slightly funky inn, very popular with in-the-know regular visitors who think of it as quintessential New Orleans. Some others think it's a total dump. The latter group may not be any more pleased by the all-new rooms, but we are. The hotel is just across from the Quarter and a block away from the main drag of the Frenchmen section of the Faubourg Marigny. Housed in two 19th-century buildings that were once grand New Orleans homes, the rooms vary in size considerably (rooms with two beds are quite large), and some are very small indeed. Each has its own rather eccentric, bright new paint color, plus old-timey prints or paintings, and new mattresses. They are a big improvement. First-floor rooms have tile floors, and some rooms have new large TVs. It still smells a bit musty, though, like old Quarter hotels. There is a small, newly cleaned-up pool and Jacuzzi in the inn's tropical courtyard. They have a carb-heavy (muffins, pastry, bagels) breakfast.

417 Frenchmen St. (at Esplanade Ave.), New Orleans, LA 70116. © **504/948-2166.** Fax 504/948-2258. www.frenchmenhotel.com. 27 units. $59–$210 double. Rates include breakfast. AE, DISC, MC, V. Parking $15. **Amenities:** Pool; Jacuzzi. *In room:* A/C, TV, Wi-Fi.

INEXPENSIVE
Royal Street Inn & R Bar ⊀   This is an offbeat, happening little establishment in a residential neighborhood with plenty of street parking and regular police patrols. It's loose but not disorganized, and there couldn't be a better choice for laid-back travelers. Breakfast isn't served, but the inn still bills itself as a B&B. That's because here B&B stands for bed-and-*beverage*—the lobby is the highly enjoyable **R Bar** (p. 193). You check in with the bartender, and as a guest, you get two complimentary cocktails.

New, enthusiastic owners are planning a long overdue, stripped-to-the-walls redo of the regular rooms, which should be completed by late 2007. Expect new furnishings and decor, fresh good bedding, and other upgraded amenities that will take advantage of the excellent bones of this establishment, and bring out more of a New Orleans vibe. Regular rooms are small but cute, like a bedroom in a real house but with doors that open directly to the street. The attic accommodations is a big room with sloping ceilings, pleasing for those with starving-artist-garret fantasies who don't like to give up good furniture. We love the smashing suite, with two large bedrooms (one does double duty as half the cavernous living room), each with beds so tall they require little step ladders, plus two free-standing fireplaces and even a floating arch. With a large balcony and plenty of gorgeous old New Orleans atmosphere, this is a great hangout/party space, perfect for two couples.

1431 Royal St., New Orleans, LA 70116. ℂ **800/449-5535** or 504/948-7499. Fax 504/943-9880. www.royalstreetinn.com. 5 units. $90–$250 double. Price includes tax; rates include bar beverage. AE, DISC, MC, V. Street parking available—purchase special permit from management. **Amenities:** Bar; complimentary bike rental. *In room:* A/C, TV, Wi-Fi, iPod docking station, DVD, coffeemaker, hair dryer, iron.

3 Mid-City/Esplanade

EXPENSIVE

The House on Bayou Road ✦✦✦   If you want to stay in a rural and romantic plantation setting but still be near the French Quarter, try The House on Bayou Road, quite probably the most smashing guesthouse in town. Just off Esplanade Avenue, this intimate Creole plantation home, built in the late 1700s for a colonial Spanish diplomat, has been restored by owner Cynthia Reeves, who oversees an operation of virtual perfection.

Each room has its own charm and is individually decorated to a fare-thee-well—slightly cluttered, not quite fussy but still lovingly done aesthetic. The Bayou St. John Room (the old library) holds a queen-size four-poster bed and has a working fireplace; the Bayou Delacroix has the same kind of bed and a wonderfully large bathtub. The large cottage has four rooms that can be rented separately or together (perfect for a large family). The private cottage has been rebuilt post-Katrina, and is even larger and better than before.

The unusually extensive grounds are beautifully manicured, despite losing about 22 trees to Katrina (mostly small ones, though), and there's an outdoor pool, Jacuzzi, patio, and screened-in porch. Expect a hearty plantation-style breakfast, and during the day and in the evening there's access to a minifridge filled with beverages.

2275 Bayou Rd., New Orleans, LA 70119. © 800/882-2968 or 504/945-0992. Fax 504/945-0993. www.houseonbayouroad.com. 8 units, 2 cottages. $155–$320 double. Rates include full breakfast. AE, DISC, MC, V. Free off-street parking. Children over 12 welcome. **Amenities:** Outdoor pool; Jacuzzi; massage. *In room:* A/C, Wi-Fi, dataport, minibar, hair dryer, iron, robes and slippers.

MODERATE

Ashton's Bed & Breakfast 𝄞𝄞   This charming guesthouse represents one of the gutsiest ventures in the city. Another Katrina victim, its chimney collapsed and 5,000 bricks tore a gaping hole in its top story, causing all kinds of mayhem inside. And yet, it's been fully restored and is a fine and worthy alternative to some of its more costly compatriots. There are pretty custom-paint treatments like shadow striping, on top of new molding and chandeliers, and other careful attention to detail. One room has a most inviting fluffy white bed, but its bathroom is contained in a curtained-off corner, while another room has merely partitioned off an area for the same. Those with personal-space and privacy issues might want to head to room no. 3, which is most grand, with a four-poster bed and the nicest bathroom in the guesthouse, complete with a claw-foot tub. All the rooms have wide wooden floorboards. A full breakfast is served. They sell artistic glassware (some featured on the breakfast table) and their excellent robes.

2023 Esplanade Ave., New Orleans, LA 70116. © 800/725-4131 or 504/942-7048. Fax 504/947-9382. www.ashtonsbb.com. 8 units. $99–$149 double; $199 for Mardi Gras; $239 during Jazz Fest. Rates include full breakfast and complimentary soft drinks. AE, DISC, MC, V. Free parking. *In room:* A/C, TV, Wi-Fi, hair dryer, iron, robes.

Block-Keller House 𝄞𝄞   This inn was extensively restored with an eye toward both guest comfort and preservation of the full Victorian aesthetic. It's a splendid choice for someone who wants both the classic Victorian B&B experience (look for period excess in the front rooms' gorgeous details) but also guiltily wants a room with modern amenities (Berber carpet, Jacuzzi tubs, and the like). If that's you, stay upstairs in the absurdly large top-floor rooms, as nice as any at the Ritz-Carlton. However, if you do desire traditional surroundings, the ground-floor rooms, with fireplaces and grand old beds, are for you. You'll find comfy communal sitting areas upstairs and in the bottom level. Room nos. 5 and 6 are large, while room no. 4 has a window seat. The hosts serve a continental breakfast. The gardens, wrecked under 6 feet of water, have been replanted and are spectacular. All in all, this place is perfect in looks, style, and service—plus, it's right on the new Canal streetcar line, making it an

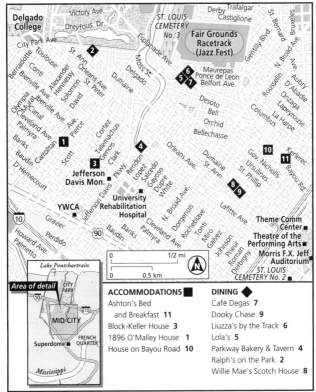

ACCOMMODATIONS ■

Ashton's Bed
and Breakfast **11**
Block-Keller House **3**
1896 O'Malley House **1**
House on Bayou Road **10**

DINING ◆

Café Degas **7**
Dooky Chase **9**
Liuzza's by the Track **6**
Lola's **5**
Parkway Bakery & Tavern **4**
Ralph's on the Park **2**
Willie Mae's Scotch House **8**

easy hop to either the Quarter or City Park. And say hello for us to sweet Milo, the black lab, and his best friend, Buster, the yellow lab. *Note:* At press time the inn was for sale, so it may be in different hands by the time you read this.

3620 Canal St., New Orleans, LA 70119. ℂ **877/588-3033** or 504/483-3033. Fax 504/483-3032. www.blockkellerhouse.com. 5 units. $110–$145 double. (Special events higher; seasonal rates lower.) Rates include breakfast. Special packages on website. AE, MC, V. **Amenities:** Coffee and tea service; fridge and microwave access; newspaper. *In room:* A/C, TV, Wi-Fi, hair dryer, iron.

The 1896 O'Malley House ⊛⊛ This (you guessed it) 1896 home flooded to a foot inside (post-K) but has been so beautifully restored that you can't tell. It's one of the most smashing B&Bs in the city, just a treasure inside, full of gorgeous antiques and repro furniture. The handsome, somewhat masculine rooms are each meticulously decorated, using clever touches such as vintage (at least appearing) oil paintings, Bali puppets, and European art to set specific moods. Second-floor rooms are larger, and most have Jacuzzi tubs. The third floor is a clever use of design and space, with formerly dull wood walls turned most striking by pickling the wood to a lighter color (ask to see the photos of the mysterious science equations found scrawled on one wall). These rooms are smaller and more garretlike, though they pale in desirability only if you really, *really* want that classic high-ceilinged look. There is an expanded breakfast with eggs, waffles, hot cinnamon rolls, and other fun items. Although it's located on a dull stretch of street and in a neighborhood gradually returning post-flood, the B&B is also mere minutes from a nice section of Canal and a streetcar ride to the Quarter.

120 S. Pierce St., New Orleans, LA 70119. © **866/226-1896** or 504/488-5896. www. 1896omalleyhouse.com. 9 units. $99–$155 double; $200 special events such as Mardi Gras and Jazz Fest. Rates include breakfast. AE, MC, V. *In room:* A/C, TV, Wi-Fi, dataport, hair dryer and iron on request.

4 Central Business District

For hotels in this section, please see the "Where to Stay in New Orleans" map on p. 40.

VERY EXPENSIVE

Harrah's ♠ New Orleans doesn't lack for impressive, grand hotels, but there is something so . . . *big* . . . about the Harrah's lobby that it passes right through grand and into something almost too immense to be truly elegant. Which isn't to knock the place; everyone did a good job. The rooms are sharp, if a touch generic, though photos by local artist Richard Sexton and splashes of Mardi Gras purple and gold help. Rooms are all pretty much the same size, except for the larger corner suites. Those don't offer enough extra to justify the price, however. Rooms ending in nos. 1 to 10 have romantic river views, while city views aren't anything special. There is an airy gym with a tall ceiling and windows, well stocked with a good mix of aerobic and weight machines.

228 Poydras St., New Orleans, LA 70130 © **800/VIP-JAZZ** or 504/533-6000. www. harrahs.com. 450 units. $149–$449 double. $30 additional person. AE, DC, DISC, MC, V. Valet and self-parking $30. **Amenities:** Restaurant (Riche, p. 110); 2 bars; gym; concierge; car service (w/fee); business center; room service; massage. *In room:* A/C, TV, Web TV, Wi-Fi ($12/day), CD player, fridge, coffeemaker, hair dryer, iron, safe, robes, umbrellas, newspaper, turndown.

Hilton New Orleans Riverside Hotel ⊀ *(Kids*   The Hilton is a self-contained complex of nearly a dozen restaurants, bistros, and bars; two gift shops; two pools; a full and exceptional racquet-and-health club; a huge exhibition space; and no fewer than 38 conference rooms. In addition, Harrah's Casino and the Riverwalk Marketplace are accessible from the hotel's lobby, which contains a nine-story atrium. Rooms are spacious (double-bedded rooms are smaller), but a tiny bit dull, though ongoing renovations, adding marble tops to some furniture, new white bedding, and plasma TVs will help. (Don't worry; the old rooms are still fine.) Parlor rooms have rather awesome Murphy beds complete with Hilton-brand mattresses! River views (usually with even-numbered rooms) are astonishing, though higher floors are always better. Given all that, this is a good choice for families, but not terrific for those with mobility issues, given the sheer size of the place.

2 Poydras St., New Orleans, LA 70140. ✆ **800/445-8667** or 504/561-0500. Fax 504/568-1721. www.neworleans.hilton.com. 1,600 units. $200–$450 double; $650–$2,000 suite. Special packages and some lower seasonal rates available. AE, DC, DISC, MC, V. Valet parking $31, self-parking $25. **Amenities:** 3 restaurants; 3 bars; concierge; airport transportation; business center; room service; laundry; dry cleaning and pressing service; eligibility for membership ($12/day, comped for Hilton club members) in the hotel's Rivercenter Racquet and Health Club. *In room:* A/C, TV, Wi-Fi ($12/day), minibar, coffeemaker, hair dryer, iron, turndown.

Hotel InterContinental ⊀   The red-granite Hotel InterContinental rises from the heart of the Central Business District within walking distance of the French Quarter and the Mississippi River attractions. It's a favorite of groups (including rock groups; the Rolling Stones have stayed here) and conventions. It's an old-fashioned business hotel, clearly targeting a certain kind of traveler who isn't impressed by the hip minimalists springing up everywhere. Rooms are done in dark-wood furniture (mattresses are nothing special) with similarly woodsy strong golds and reds; bathrooms can be small but dignified. Call it masculine in a slightly frilly way. All the rooms are decently sized, but the doubles (especially corner doubles) are somewhat larger, and "deluxe kings" are larger still, with patio balconies (overlooking office buildings, alas). Some rooms have balconies that overlook the courtyard, although said courtyard is modern and industrial in appearance.

444 St. Charles Ave., New Orleans, LA 70130. ✆ **800/327-0200** or 504/525-5566. Fax 504/585-4350. www.new-orleans.intercontinental.com. 479 units. $200–$429 double; $500–$2,500 suite. AE, DC, DISC, MC, V. Valet parking $29. **Amenities:** Restaurant; Pete's Pub serving lunch daily; coffee and sandwich bar; bar; outdoor

rooftop pool; health club; concierge; business center; gift shop; room service; laundry/dry-cleaning service; Wi-Fi (free) in lobby. *In room:* A/C, TV, Wi-Fi ($11/day), dataport, minibar, coffeemaker, hair dryer, iron, safe, robes.

JW Marriott Hotel New Orleans ♔

You can't fault the location on Canal right across from the Quarter (excellent for viewing Mardi Gras parades). But ultimately it's classy but boring—yes, we're spoiled—more for business travelers who don't plan on spending much time in their rooms. New NOLA-specific touches such as local photos and drawings are appreciated, as are the thickly made beds. The public areas are far more grand than the actual rooms. Bathrooms are dinky, though amenities are good. Corner "deluxe" king rooms have extra windows for an additional view, though higher up is best. The fitness center is decent-size, and there is a Don Shula Steakhouse on the property.

614 Canal St., New Orleans, LA 70130. ℂ 888/771-9067 or 504/525-6500. Fax 504/586-1543. www.jwmarriottneworleans.com. 494 units. $189–$355 double; $750–$1,000 suite. AE, DC, DISC, MC, V. Valet parking $28. **Amenities:** Restaurant; 2 bars; heated outdoor pool; health club; concierge; business center; gift shop; salon; room service; laundry; dry cleaning. *In room:* A/C, TV, Wi-Fi ($12/day), dataport, minibar, coffeemaker, hair dryer, iron, safe, newspaper, turndown.

Loft 523 ♔

Located in an old carriage and dry-goods warehouse in the Central Business District, each of the 18 lofts is a marvel of modern design, sort of a *Jetsons*-futuristic-meets-NYC-minimalist-fantasy. They are sleek and handsome, but those wanting plushy and overstuffed will be miserable as soon as they see the concrete floors. Beds are platforms, surprisingly comfortable with Frette linens (but just a chenille throw blanket over that; ask for the down comforters if the night brings a chill). A Sony CD/DVD Surround Sound system adds sonic warmth, and the bathrooms are big. But here's where they break from N.Y./L.A. detached cool: Throughout are reminders of the building's provenance—old wood planks form the floor downstairs, turn-of-the-20th-century tin ceiling tiles outfit the elevators, and columns from the old warehouse decorate the lounge.

523 Gravier St., New Orleans, LA 70130. ℂ 800/633-5770 or 504/200-6523. Fax 504/200-6522. www.loft523.com. 18 units (3 of them penthouses). $259–$359 double; $859–$1,100 suite. AE, DC, DISC, MC, V. Valet parking $30, SUVs $38. **Amenities:** Lounge; health club; babysitting; laundry/dry cleaning; computer in lobby. *In room:* A/C, TV, DVD, Wi-Fi, remote-control stereo system, coffeemaker, hair dryer, iron, safe.

Windsor Court ♔♔♔

The Windsor Court is mighty fine—possibly the finest in town. The unassuming, somewhat office-building exterior is camouflage for the quiet but posh delights found within.

Spending the Night in Chains

For those of you who prefer the predictability of a chain hotel, there's a perfectly okay **Marriott** ⓡ at 555 Canal St., at the edge of the Quarter (ⓒ **800/654-3990** or 504/581-1000). A **Sheraton** at 500 Canal St. (ⓒ **504/525-2500**) is also a good bet.

In the Central Business District (CBD), check out the **Holiday Inn Express,** 221 Carondelet St. (ⓒ **504/962-0800**), or consider the slightly spiffier **Cotton Exchange** next door at 231 Carondelet St. (which is now part of the Holiday Inn), in the historic building of the same name (ⓒ **504/962-0700**). **Residence Inn by Marriott** ⓡ, 345 St. Joseph St. (ⓒ **800/331-3131** or 504/522-1300), and **Courtyard by Marriott** ⓡ, 300 Julia St. (ⓒ **888/703-0390** or 504/598-9898), are both a couple of blocks from the convention center. The **Homewood Suites,** at 901 Poydras St., is pretty dazzling, in a cookie-cutter way (ⓒ **800/225-4663** or 504/581-5599), while the **Quality Inn,** at 210 O'Keefe Ave., seems clean and fine (ⓒ **877/525-6900** or 504/525-6800).

Here's a bunch more, all more or less CBD or adjacent: **Comfort Suites** (346 Baronne St.; ⓒ **800/524-1140** or 504/524-1140), **Country Inn and Suites by Carlson** (315 Magazine St.; ⓒ **800/456-4000** or 504/324-5400), **Embassy Suites** (315 Julia St.; ⓒ **504/525-1993**), **Hampton Inn and Suites** (1201 Convention Center Blvd.; ⓒ **866/311-1200** or 504/566-9990), **La Quinta Inn and Suites** (301 Camp St.; ⓒ **800/531-5900** or 504/598-9977), and **SpringHill Suites by Marriott** (301 St. Joseph St.; ⓒ **800/287-9400** or 504/522-3100).

Two corridors downstairs are minigalleries that display original 17th-, 18th-, and 19th-century art, and a plush reading area with an international newspaper rack is on the second floor. Everything here is very, very traditional and serene, though not unwarm. It's not too stiff for restless children, though it still feels more like a grown-up hotel. The level of service is extraordinarily high.

The accommodations are exceptionally spacious, with classy, not flashy, decor. Almost all are suites (either really big or downright huge) featuring large bay windows or a private balcony overlooking the river or the city, a private foyer, a large living room, a bedroom with French doors, a large marble bathroom with particularly luxe amenities, two dressing rooms, and a "petite kitchen." You aren't going to get better traditional hotel accommodations anywhere else in New Orleans, though some of the aged furnishings will benefit from ongoing gradual renovations. The club level provides continental breakfast, plus access to a stylish lounge with beverage service during the day, and cocktails and snacks in the evening.

300 Gravier St., New Orleans, LA 70130. ⓒ **800/262-2662** or 504/523-6000. Fax 504/596-4749. www.windsorcourthotel.com. 324 units. $149–$350 standard double; $169–$400 junior suite; $199–$450 full suite. Children under 12 stay free in parent's room. Packages available. AE, DC, DISC, MC, V. Valet parking $28. **Amenities:** The New Orleans Grill Room restaurant (p. 106); Polo Club Lounge; health club w/resort-size pool and hot tub; concierge; suite service (much more than your average room service); in-room massage; laundry; dry cleaning. *In room:* A/C, TV, Wi-Fi, dataport, minibar, hair dryer, iron, safe, robes.

W New Orleans 🐦🐦   There are certainly no more-playful rooms in town, done up as they are in black, plum, and white—frosty chic, to be sure, but oh, so comfortable, thanks to feather everything (pillows, comforters, beds—and yes, allergy sufferers, they have foam alternatives). There are nifty amenities and gewgaws galore; suites offer little different from the rooms except more space and, indeed, more of everything (two TVs, two DVD players, two bathrooms, one Ouija board). Not all rooms have views, but the ones that do, especially those of the river, are outstanding.

333 Poydras St., New Orleans, LA 70130. ⓒ **800/522-6963** or 504/525-9444. Fax 504/581-7179. www.whotels.com. 423 units. $179–$469 double. AE, DC, DISC, MC, V. Valet parking $28. **Amenities:** Restaurant; bar; swimming pool; fitness center; concierge; business services; room service; massage. *In room:* A/C, TV/VCR/DVD, CD player, dataport, minibar, coffeemaker, hair dryer, iron, safe.

EXPENSIVE

Astor Crowne Plaza: The Alexa   This boutique-hotel wannabe is connected to the larger and more traditionally elegant Astor Crown Plaza by a series of corridors and elevators, which makes for confusion if no one at the front desk warns you about this or lets you know that all the major facilities—such as the business center, health club, and pool—are over at the sister property. Then why, you may ask, should you stay here rather than there? It's cheaper. Rooms are narrow and small, though the exposed brick wall and period-style furniture help, as does the pretty dark marble in the petite bathrooms. Rooms also contain a desk with a comfortable executive's chair, and guests have access to a good restaurant, making this hotel a smart bet for the solo business traveler with no claustrophobia issues.

119 Royal St., New Orleans, LA 70130. © **888/884-3366** or 504/962-0600. Fax 504/962-0601. www.astorneworleans.com/alexaquarters. 192 units. $149–$249 double; $350 suite. AE, DC, DISC, MC, V. **Amenities:** Bourbon House Seafood restaurant (p. 86); bar; swimming pool; fitness room; concierge. *In room:* A/C, TV, dataport, hair dryer, iron, safe-deposit box.

Hilton St. Charles   The site of the old Masonic Temple, and the second skyscraper in the city, this establishment was taken over by Hilton in 2007, and it keeps making improvements and upgrades. It's a lot more memorable than the other Hilton in town. Rooms have some pizazz in the form of wild prints and designs, plus black marble vanities in the spacious bathrooms (tubs are small, though), fresh new bedding, flatscreen TVs, and Lavazza coffee. Corner-room doubles have extra space, perfect for non-couple traveling partners. The smashing new wood deck that overlooks the city is sure to become a nighttime hot spot, and the wedding chapel (the only hotel-based one in town) still carries its Masonic roots.

333 St. Charles Ave., New Orleans, LA 70130. © **504/524-8890.** www.hhnew orleansstcharles.com. 250 units. $109–$389 double. AE, DC, DISC, MC, V. Valet parking $29. **Amenities:** Restaurant; bar; indoor pool; health club; concierge; business center; room service; babysitting; laundry/dry cleaning; wedding chapel; Wi-Fi in public spaces. *In room:* A/C, TV, dataport, MP3 player, coffeemaker, hair dryer, iron, safe, newspaper, turndown.

International House   The International House sets the local standard for modern hotels with its creative design and meticulous attention to detail. Here, a wonderful old Beaux Arts bank building has been transformed into a modern space that still pays tribute to its locale. Consequently, in the graceful lobby, classical pilasters stand next to modern wrought-iron chandeliers.

Interiors are the embodiment of minimalist chic. Rooms are simple with muted, monochromatic tones, tall ceilings and ceiling fans, up-to-the-minute bathroom fixtures, but also black-and-white photos of local musicians and characters, books about the city, and other clever decorating touches that anchor the room in its New Orleans setting. The big bathrooms boast large tubs or space age glassed-in showers and come off as a bit industrial. But compensations include cushy touches such as feather pillows, large TVs, your own private phone number in your room, and CD players with CDs. Room service should be back by the time you read this.

221 Camp St., New Orleans, LA 70130. © **800/633-5770** or 504/553-9550. Fax 504/553-9560. www.ihhotel.com. 117 units. $149–$379 double; $369–$1,799 suite. AE, DC, DISC, MC, V. Valet parking $30 cars, $35 SUV. **Amenities:** Bar; health club; concierge; dry cleaning. *In room:* A/C, Wi-Fi, dataport, CD player, minibar, hair dryer, iron.

Le Cirque   A smart, sharp, and chic version of the generic business hotel—sort of like a Crowne Plaza, if it was done up in chartreuse and that new misty gray-blue that's all the rage. Oddly, it's not set up as a business hotel, lacking amenities such as separate dataports and even room service, but it does offer 4,000 square feet of meeting space. Rooms are average size; the ones with king-size beds are a bit cramped thanks to all the furniture jammed in along with it (chair, desk, TV). Queen rooms are even smaller.

936 St. Charles Ave., New Orleans, LA 70130. © **888/211-3447** or 504/962-0900. Fax 504/962-0901. www.neworleansfinehotels.com/hotellecirque. 138 units. $69–$299 double. AE, DC, DISC, MC, V. **Amenities:** Concierge; babysitting; laundry; dry cleaning. *In room:* A/C, TV, Wi-Fi, hair dryer, iron, safe.

Loews New Orleans Hotel 𝕲𝕲   The stylish, swanky Loews is a sharp-dressed combo of modern and *moderne,* with judiciously applied sprinkles of New Orleans flavor. Maybe it's the relative newness of the place or that the front desk has a photo-tile collage featuring black-and-white shots of iconic local images. Whatever it is, we are quite smitten. The rooms are all spacious, starting with the "Luxury" rooms, at 346 square feet—bright and decorated with art by a local photographer, with goose-down comforters and pillows. Bathrooms are small, but granite and wood vanities make up for the lack of space. "Grand Luxury" rooms and bathrooms are bigger. Views vary from river to partial river plus piazza to New Orleans city skyline, which get better the higher up you go. Note that the hotel's lowest floor is the 11th, so this is not the choice for those with vertigo or other high-floor issues. Loews has a company-wide "Loews Loves Pets" policy, which practically encourages Fido to come join in the fun.

300 Poydras St., New Orleans, LA 70130. © **800/23-LOEWS** (800/235-6397) or 504/595-3300. www.loewshotels.com. 285 units. Luxury units $129–$279; Grand Luxury $159–$319. AE, DC, DISC, MC, V. Valet parking $29. Pets allowed (no deposit). **Amenities:** Restaurant; bar; pool; workout room; spa; concierge; business center; room service; babysitting; dry cleaning; laundry; Wi-Fi in lobby. *In room:* A/C, TV, dataport, CD player, video games, minibar, hair dryer, iron, safe, umbrella.

The Pelham   The Pelham—a boutique hotel—feels like an upscale apartment building. Centrally located rooms are generally less bright than those on the exterior of the building; all have been recently renovated. Some rooms have sitting areas, some have four-poster kings and old-fashioned art on the walls, most have high ceilings, and all have boring bathrooms. There is potential, so we have hopes that the redo will make this feel newer and justify the sometimes very high prices. The staff is nice, so it's worth considering if you can get the low-end price.

444 Common St., New Orleans, LA 70130. © **888/211-3447** or 504/522-4444. Fax 504/539-9010. www.thepelhamhotel.com. 60 units. $79–$399 double. AE, DC, DISC, MC, V. Valet parking $25. **Amenities:** Concierge; laundry service; newspaper. *In room:* A/C, TV, Wi-Fi, dataport, coffeemaker, hair dryer, iron, safe for additional fee.

Renaissance Arts Hotel ⦅✦⦆   The Renaissance brand is the Marriott's attempt at a hip, W-style hotel, a place for younger business travelers to feel a bit better about themselves. Don't expect painters in the lobby, splattering like Pollock or staging suspicious performance-art gags. What "arts" here means is that the designers made a concerted effort to incorporate art, specifically local art, into the decor. But the theme gets stronger once you enter the hallways, and comes into stronger focus in the rooms, which are hung with the works of several Louisiana artists. The rooms are well sized (look for a connecting room to get extra square footage) and include down pillows and covers. The hotel has a dull rooftop pool with a view of industrial New Orleans, and a health club with adequate elbowroom.

700 Tchoupitoulas St., New Orleans, LA 70130. © **504/613-2330.** Fax 504/613-2331. www.marriott.com. 217 units. $189 double. AE, DC, DISC, MC, V. Valet parking $28. **Amenities:** Restaurant; bar; pool; health club; concierge; business center; gift shop; room service; babysitting; laundry; dry cleaning; newspaper delivery. *In room:* A/C, TV, high-speed Internet access, minibar, coffeemaker, hair dryer, iron, safe.

St. James Hotel ⦅✦⦆   A fine preservation job has given what could have been an eyesore derelict (if historic) building a new useful function. Actually, this is two different buildings, one of which used to be—get this!—the St. James Infirmary, sung about so memorably by many a mournful jazz musician. This gives the place a touch more style than the fresh white-bed generic look popping up all over town. Look for parrots, palm trees, and even monkey-shaped pull chains on the lamps. Because the restorers had to make do with a nonuniform space, rooms vary in size and style, and a few lack windows. You want high ceilings? Ask for a room in the back building. Rooms have either painted texture or, on the top floor, exposed brick and wood. All rooms have feather beds, soft towels, and marble bathrooms. Two suites and a room share a small, private brick courtyard with a fountain—a nice setup for a small group. There is a teeny-weeny pool.

330 Magazine St., New Orleans, LA 70130. © **888/211-3447** or 504/304-4000. www.saintjameshotel.com. 86 units. $150–$250 double. AE, DC, DISC, MC, V. Valet parking $25. **Amenities:** Pool; concierge; laundry; dry cleaning. *In room:* A/C, TV, Wi-Fi, CD player, coffeemaker, hair dryer, iron, safe.

The Whitney—A Wyndham Historic Hotel ⟨⋆⟩   A grand old bank building has been converted into a fine modern hotel. The unique results include gawk-worthy public spaces; be sure to look up at all the fanciful, wedding-cake-decoration old plasterwork and help us wonder how the heck safecrackers got past those thick slabs of doors. Best of all is the imposing lobby, full of stately pillars, now part restaurant but also still part working bank—it puts other swellegant establishments in town to shame.

Rooms are a little too stately to classify as true business efficient but also a little too generic to make this a proper romantic getaway. Having said that, there are recent room upgrades, including new paint and carpet, new fresh bedding on Wyndham beds, and good amenities in the bathrooms. Overall, The Whitney has more character than your average upscale chain, so it ultimately gets a positive vote. If you are a hoity-toity businessperson, you will probably like it a lot. And if you are a preservationist, you will probably like it even more.

610 Poydras St., New Orleans, LA 70130. ⟨©⟩ **504/581-4222.** www.wyndhamnew orleanshotels.com. 93 units. $79–$399 double. AE, DC, DISC, MC, V. Valet parking $25. **Amenities:** Lobby bar; private dining room; fitness center; computer in lobby. *In room:* A/C, TV, dataport, CD player, coffee- and tea-making facilities, hair dryer, iron.

MODERATE

Drury Inn & Suites ⟨⋆⟩ ⟨Value⟩   This family-owned chain looks all too generic outside, but inside is a pleasant surprise, with grander-than-expected public spaces and rooms that are fancier than those in the average chain, not to mention new beds. All have high ceilings (except for those on the fifth floor) and a decent amount of square footage, though rooms on the first floor can be dark with zero views. Bathrooms are small with sinks in the dressing area. There is a nice little heated rooftop pool plus a small exercise room. Free popcorn and sodas are offered from 3 to 10pm, and a nachos and wine snack service goes from 5:30 to 7pm. Look for more specials, like 1 hour of free long distance calling per night.

820 Poydras St., New Orleans, LA 70112-1016. ⟨©⟩ **800/DRURY-INN** (800/378-79466) or 504/529-7800. Fax 504/581-3328. www.druryhotels.com/properties/neworleans. cfm. 156 units. $109 regular room; $139 suite. Rates include full breakfast and weekday evening cocktails. AE, DC, DISC, MC, V. Parking $15. **Amenities:** Heated pool; exercise room; laundry/dry cleaning services; washer-dryer. *In room:* A/C, TV, Wi-Fi, dataport, minifridge, microwave, coffeemaker, hair dryer, iron, some suites have whirlpool tubs.

Le Pavillion Hotel *ẞẞ*   Le Pavillion feels like elegant old New Orleans in a way that so few places sadly now do. The lobby is stunning, just what you want in a big, grand hotel, with giant columns and chandeliers. The standard guest rooms are all rather pretty and have similar furnishings, but they differ in size. Deluxe rooms have ceiling fans, detailed ceiling painting, and black marble bathrooms. "Bay Rooms" are standard with two double beds and bay windows. Suites are actually hit-or-miss in terms of decor, with the nadir being the mind-bogglingly ugly Art Deco Suite. Much better is the Plantation Suite, decorated in—you guessed it—antiques including pieces by Mallard, C. Lee, Mitchell Rammelsberg, Belter, Badouine, and Marcotte. The Honeymoon Suite has "Napoleon's" marble bathtub and is a riot of fantasy hilarity. Late-night peanut-butter-and-jelly sandwiches, one of New Orleans's sweetest traditions, are offered in the lobby.

833 Poydras St., New Orleans, LA 70112. ℂ **800/535-9095** or 504/581-3111. Fax 504/522-5543. www.lepavillon.com. 226 units. $149–$299 double; $199–$1,695 suite. AE, DC, DISC, MC, V. Valet parking $28. **Amenities:** Restaurant; bar; heated outdoor pool; fitness center and whirlpool spa; concierge; room service; babysitting; laundry; dry cleaning; spa service. *In room:* A/C, TV, Wi-Fi, dataport, minibar, coffeemaker on request, hair dryer, iron, robes, turndown, newspaper.

INEXPENSIVE

The Depot at Madame Julia's *ẞ* *(Finds*   The Depot takes up part of a whole complex of buildings dating from the 1800s and is an alternative to more commercial hotels in the Central Business District. Then again, it may be full of volunteer groups helping to rebuild the city when you call. Low prices and a guesthouse environment mean a number of good things, but it also means shared bathrooms, rooms on the small and cozy side, and a location that, although quiet on the weekends, can get noisy in the mornings as the working neighborhood gets going. Still being gentrified, the neighborhood is hit-or-miss, but more of the former than the latter thanks to artsy Julia Street. A mere 7 blocks (safe in the daytime) from the Quarter, it's a quick walk or a short streetcar/bus ride. The budget-conscious and those who prefer their hotels with personality will consider this a find.

748 O'Keefe St., New Orleans, LA 70113. ℂ **504/529-2952.** Fax 504/529-1908. 25 units, all with shared bathrooms. $65–$85 double. Rates include continental breakfast. Cash or personal checks only (if paid in advance). Off-street parking available. *In room:* A/C, Wi-Fi.

5 Uptown/The Garden District

For hotels in this section, see the "Where to Stay & Dine Uptown" map on p. 73 or the "Where to Stay in New Orleans" map on p. 40.

EXPENSIVE

The Grand Victorian Bed & Breakfast *𝒜𝒜*   Owner Bonnie Rabe confounded and delighted her new St. Charles neighbors when she took a crumbling Queen Anne–style Victorian mansion right on the corner of Washington (2 blocks from Lafayette cemetery and Commander's Palace with a streetcar stop right in front) and, over the course of many arduous months, resurrected it into a showcase B&B. The location makes its porches and balconies a perfect place to view Mardi Gras parades.

The stunning rooms are full of antiques (each has an impressive four-poster or wood canopy bed—though a couple are small thanks to their vintage) with the slightly fussy details demanded by big Victorian rooms. Linens, pillows, and towels are ultraplush, and some bathrooms have big Jacuzzi tubs. The largest room overlooks the street corner (and has its own St. Charles–view balcony) and so is potentially noisy. You can always request one toward the back. A generous continental breakfast is served.

2727 St. Charles Ave., New Orleans, LA 70130. *℗* **800/977-0008** or 504/895-1104. Fax 504/896-8688. www.gvbb.com. 8 units. $150–$350 double. Rates include continental breakfast. AE, DISC, MC, V. *In room:* A/C, TV, Wi-Fi, dataport, hair dryer, iron.

Magnolia Mansion *𝒜𝒜*   This hilarious and alluring bed-and-breakfast features huge public rooms splashed with plaster curlicues and Victorian furniture, while the theatrical guest rooms are the owner's imagination run amok. With the exception of the appropriately named Napoleon's Retreat, downstairs rooms are bigger, with 15-foot ceilings and elaborately explored decor. The black, blood red, and green Vampire's Lair is your Gothic fantasy, while the front bridal room is the largest. Upstairs rooms are smaller and not quite as over-the-top, and many have extra twin beds. Consequently, even as the downstairs accommodations are ripe for wedding-night romance, the upstairs could work perfectly for a girls' night out.

2127 Prytania St. (at Jackson), New Orleans, LA 70130. *℗* **504/412-9500**. Fax 504/412-9502. www.magnoliamansion.com. 10 units. $125 and up double, depending on time of year. Rates include breakfast. AE, DISC, MC, V. Guests must be 21 or older; no children. *In room:* A/C, TV w/VCR or DVD, hair dryer, iron, robes.

Where to Stay & Dine Uptown

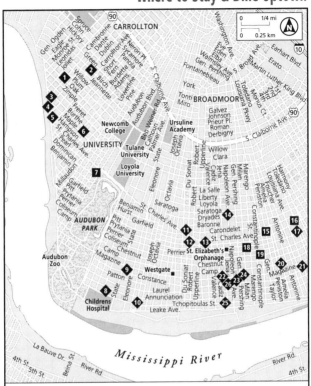

ACCOMMODATIONS ■

Chimes B&B **19**
The Columns **15**
Hampton Inn Garden District **16**
Maison Perrier Bed & Breakfast **18**
Park View Guest House **7**

DINING ◆

Bluebird Cafe **17**
Brigtsen's **3**
Camellia Grill **5**
Casamento's **23**
Clancy's **8**
Dante's Kitchen **4**
Dick & Jenny's **25**
Franky & Johnny's **10**
Gautreau's **11**
Iris **2**
Jacques-Imo's **1**
La Boulangerie **22**
La Crêpe Nanou **12**
La Divinia Gelateria **26**
La Petite Grocery **24**

Lilette **20**
Martinique Bistro **9**
Pascal's Manale **14**
PJ's Coffee &
  Tea Company **6**
Slim Goodies Diner **21**
Upperline **13**

Maison Perrier Bed & Breakfast 🎔🎔 This place has had a couple of owners over time, but the current one has given it a solid upgrade, adding more antique elements to the splashy good-looking rooms and attending to other details that make it as likable as it's ever been. Some rooms have light color schemes, others have dark; we are partial to the latter, particularly the Jasmine room. The rooms have good beds with high-quality linens and well-appointed bathrooms, and nearly all have whirlpool tubs. The Lillian suite is quite spacious and includes a Jacuzzi tub built for four or more. The least impressive room is also the cheapest, a modest space just off the kitchen. A hearty cooked breakfast is offered by the resident chef, and there is a fully stocked honor bar, along with a weekend wine-and-cheese party and daily snacks like fresh-baked brownies.

4117 Perrier St. (2 blocks riverside from St. Charles Ave., 3 blocks downtown from Napoleon Ave.), New Orleans, LA 70115. ✆ **888/610-1807** or 504/897-1807. Fax 504/897-1399. www.maisonperrier.com. 14 units. $130–$260 double. Rates include breakfast. AE, DISC, MC, V. Parking available on street, limited on-site parking as well. **Amenities:** Concierge; business center; laundry service. *In room:* A/C, TV/DVD, CD player, Wi-Fi, dataport, minibar, hair dryer, iron.

The McKendrick-Breaux House 🎔🎔 This is one of the best B&Bs in town. The rooms are done in impeccable good taste (barely storm-touched—they reopened 3 weeks later, housing FEMA types!), with high-quality mattresses and pillows, and each has its own style; the ones in the main house have claw-foot tubs and (sadly nonworking) fireplaces. Room no. 36 is the largest but also has the most traffic noise. Third-floor rooms evoke classic garret quarters, with exposed brick walls and less of that traffic noise, thanks perhaps to lower ceilings and fewer windows (we swoon over room no. 38). Rooms in the second building are somewhat larger; the first-floor units are slightly more modern in appearance (but have large bathrooms), which is probably why we like the ones on the second floor (especially the front room, and the deep-purple walls and bright-green bathroom wainscoting of the Clio room). A full breakfast has been added.

1474 Magazine St., New Orleans, LA 70130. ✆ **888/570-1700** or 504/586-1700. Fax 504/522-7134. www.mckendrick-breaux.com. 9 units. $145–$235 double. Rates include tax and breakfast. AE, DC, DISC, MC, V. Limited free off-street parking. **Amenities:** Jacuzzi in courtyard. *In room:* A/C, TV, Wi-Fi, dataport, hair dryer, iron.

MODERATE

Chimes B&B 🎔🎔🎔 *Finds* This is a real hidden gem, one that truly allows you to experience the city away from the typical tourist experience. Your hosts, Jill and Charles Abbyad, have run this B&B

(located in the old servants' quarters behind their house, surrounding a small, sweet courtyard) for 22 years, and their experience shows. The Chimes opened days after Katrina as the home base for Reuters, who are still a presence.

Rooms vary in size from a generous L-shape to a two-story loft type (with a very small bathroom) to some that are downright cozy. All have antiques but are so tastefully underdecorated, particularly in contrast to other B&Bs, that they are positively Zen. An ambitious continental breakfast is served in the hosts' house. The Chimes has recently made improvements designed for the business traveler, and all we need to say is laptop + courtyard = working bliss. The Abbyads know and love their city, and their friendliness and charm are among the reasons they have so many loyal, repeat customers.

1146 Constantinople St., New Orleans, LA 70115. ⓒ **504/899-2621** or 504/453-2183 (owner's cell). Fax 504/899-9858. www.chimesneworleans.com. 5 units. $130–$155 double in season; $86–$140 double off season. Rates include breakfast. Look for rates, availability, and featured specials online. AE, MC, V. Limited off-street free parking. Well-behaved pets accepted. **Amenities:** Small business center. *In room:* A/C, TV, Wi-Fi, dataport, coffeemaker, hair dryer, iron.

The Columns ⚲   New Orleans made a mistake when it tore down its famous bordellos. If somebody had turned one of the grander ones into a hotel, imagine how many people would stay there! The next best thing is The Columns, whose interior was used by Louis Malle for his film about Storyville, *Pretty Baby.* Built in 1883, the building is one of the city's greatest examples of a late-19th-century Louisiana residence. The grand, columned porch is a highly popular evening scene thanks to the bar inside. The immediate interior is utterly smashing; we challenge any other hotel to match the grand staircase and stained-glass-window combination.

The Columns is another hotel that benefited from Katrina. The building lost part of its roof during the storm, creating a waterfall effect inside. The resulting new carpets, drapes, paint, and bedspreads have freshened up a musty place that sorely needed it. We wish still more had been done to make the upstairs match that smashing downstairs; it's still a bit too dark and the color schemes not that great. The totally renovated third floor looks more modern, mostly to good and comfortable effect. The Pretty Baby room has no discernable nods to its ostensible theme (nor does the Bellocq), but it does have a nice garret sitting area. We particularly like room no. 16, with its grand furniture and floor-to-ceiling shutters that lead out to a private, second-story porch.

3811 St. Charles Ave., New Orleans, LA 70115. ✆ **800/445-9308** or 504/899-9308. Fax 504/899-8170. www.thecolumns.com. 20 units. $120–$173 double Mon–Thurs; $160–$230 double Fri–Sun. Rates include full breakfast. AE, MC, V. Parking available on street. Pet-friendly. **Amenities:** Bar; newspaper. *In room:* A/C, TV, Wi-Fi, hair dryer, iron.

Hampton Inn Garden District   This is a top choice for a chain hotel, if you don't mind being a bit out-of-the-way. (We don't—it's quite nice up here on St. Charles in a grand section of town that is generally not overly touristed but is right on the Mardi Gras parade route.) The public areas are slightly more stylish than those found in other chains, and there are welcome touches like free coffee in the lobby and complimentary cheese and tea served daily from 6 to 7pm. The style does not extend to the rooms, however, which are pretty mundane. But they're not *that* bad (the bedspreads and mustard-colored walls excepted). There are all kinds of personality-enhancing details (decent photos for artwork, ever-so-slight Arts and Crafts detailing on furniture, and big TVs) hidden in that bland color scheme.

3626 St. Charles Ave., New Orleans, LA 70115. ✆ **800/426-7866** or 504/899-9990. Fax 504/899-9908. www.neworleanshamptoninns.com. 100 units. $119–$179 double. Rates include continental breakfast with hot items, free local calls, and free incoming faxes. AE, DC, DISC, MC, V. Free parking. **Amenities:** Small outdoor lap pool; laundry; dry cleaning. *In room:* A/C, TV, Wi-Fi (free), coffeemaker, hair dryer, iron.

INEXPENSIVE

Park View Guest House ✿   Built in the late 1800s as a boardinghouse for the World Cotton Exchange, this is an inn crossed with a B&B, which means a front desk staffed 24/7 and proper public areas. But it's far uptown, so if you can't live without Bourbon Street and bars mere steps from your hotel entrance, then this is not the place for you. The stunning location on St. Charles (with a streetcar stop right opposite, so it's easy to get to and from the Quarter), with views right across to Audubon Park, makes it well worth considering. Still, we wish they were more careful with their decor, a mix of antiques and sometimes truly bad modern furniture—witness no. 19, a spacious room with a balcony, claw-foot tub, and fireplace with glazed tiles, and some godawful 1980s motel room furniture. If this sort of aesthetic mistake bothers you as much as it does us, you are better off with no. 9 (two antique wood beds, nice old fireplace, large balcony, new bathroom) or no. 17 (bigger bathroom, better furniture). Most of the rooms are spacious, and those downstairs, while just off the public areas, are grander still. New bathrooms mean only a few shared ones remain.

7004 St. Charles Ave., New Orleans, LA 70118. ℂ **888/533-0746** or 504/861-7564. Fax 504/861-1225. www.parkviewguesthouse.com. 22 units, 19 with private bathroom. $99–$159 double. (Special-event rates higher.) Rates include continental breakfast. Extra person $10. AE, DISC, MC, V. Parking available. **Amenities:** Coffee available throughout the day; newspaper in dining room. *In room:* A/C, TV, Wi-Fi, hair dryers available, iron/ironing board available.

Prytania Park Hotel   This 1840s building (which once housed Huey Long's girlfriend) is now equal parts motel and funky simulated Quarter digs. Rooms vary: Some have been redone to the owner's pride (adding darker wood tones and four-poster beds plus bathrooms that still have a Holiday Inn feel), but we kind of prefer the older section with its pine furniture, tall ceilings, and nonworking fireplaces. All rooms have lots of good reading lights. Some units have balconies or loft bedrooms (accessible by spiral staircases). Those without the loft can be small, and the dark-wood furniture makes it a bit ponderous. The hotel is currently remodeling all of the rooms; new paint, curtains, furnishings, and mattresses will be the result. Rooms closer to the lobby have better Wi-Fi reception.

1525 Prytania St. (enter off Terpsichore St.), New Orleans, LA 70130. ℂ **800/862-1984** or 504/524-0427. Fax 504/522-2977. www.prytaniaparkhotel.com. 62 units. $80–$90 double. Extra person $10. Rates include continental breakfast. Children under 12 stay free in parent's room. Seasonal rates and special packages available. AE, DC, DISC, MC, V. Off-street parking available. *In room:* A/C, TV, Wi-Fi, fridge, microwave.

St. Charles Guesthouse ♠   Our first choice for budget travelers or the less-than-picky folks who have spent time in European pensions and aren't looking for the spick-and-span hotel experience. This was the first such accommodations in the Garden District, and it has remained a friendly place to stay for the past 25 years. You can't beat the quiet, pretty location, especially for first-time New Orleans visitors, simply because it gets you out of the engulfing Quarter and into a different part of town. Rooms are plain and vary wildly in size—from reasonably spacious to "small and spartan" (the management's words)—and also range from low-end backpacker with no air-conditioning to larger chambers with air-conditioning and private bathrooms. Roof damage has resulted in new carpeting and some linen and bed upgrades. Room no. 5, with twin beds in a separate room, is perfect for a family. A bonus is the banana-tree-lined courtyard with a pool, featuring a daily continental breakfast with a variety of carbs and fresh juices. While it's still a little musty smelling, here you can pay very little for a good-size room with a mix of antiques and new furnishings and humble bathrooms with bright green or yellow tile. It's a little crumbly in places (some thin walls and unreliable plumbing), but it's still one of the best values in town, an old-style NOLA guesthouse that is rapidly disappearing from a revamped marketplace.

1748 Prytania St., New Orleans, LA 70130. © **504/523-6556.** Fax 504/522-6340. www.stcharlesguesthouse.com. 35 units, 23 with private bathroom. $55–$95 double. Rates include continental breakfast. No credit cards. Parking available on street. **Amenities:** Outdoor pool. *In room:* Wi-Fi, no phone.

4

Where to Dine

New Orleans restaurant matriarch Miss Ella Brennan says that whereas in other places, one eats to live, "In New Orleans, we live to eat." Never was that more apparent than when the first high-profile restaurant—as it happens, a Brennan family restaurant called Bacco—reopened in the French Quarter post-Katrina. You can only imagine what that meant for the spirits and souls of the intrepid locals. Each returning restaurant is greeted with cries of pleasure and relief, and the opening of every new place—a startling number, as it happens—is seen as an act of bold defiance that must be supported. Together, they indicate that normalcy and good times are returning to the city. But beyond that, they signify the return of family. Returning restaurants are often packed. And by nonscientific count, there are more restaurants in the non-flooded, basic tourist areas than there were pre-Katrina.

While it's wonderful when the high-profile folks return, New Orleans cuisine is not just about old-line fancy-pants places. It's also about the corner po' boy shops, and Miss Willie Mae's Scotch House, home to fried chicken so heavenly she was celebrated by a major culinary organization not long before the floodwaters destroyed her restaurant. In one of the shows of grace that emerge from adversity, local restaurateurs and others banded together to help her rebuild, with one vowing he wouldn't rest until that first plate of chicken was served. That's the kind of dedication to food and community that makes New Orleans special.

You are going to want to eat a lot here. And then you are going to want to talk about it. After being in New Orleans for just a short amount of time, you will find yourself talking less about the sights and more about the food—if not constantly about the food: what you ate already, what you are going to be eating later, what you wish you had time to eat. We are going to take a stand and say to heck with New York and San Francisco: New Orleans has the best food in the United States. (Some natives will gladly fight you if you say otherwise.)

Where to Dine in New Orleans

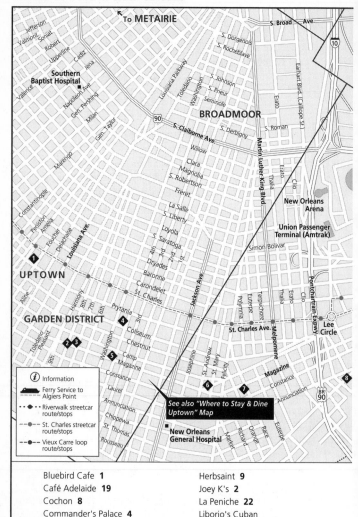

Bluebird Cafe **1**
Café Adelaide **19**
Cochon **8**
Commander's Palace **4**
Cuvee **15**
Elizabeth's **27**
Emeril's **10**
Ernst's Café **21**
Feelings Cafe D'Aunoy **26**

Herbsaint **9**
Joey K's **2**
La Peniche **22**
Liborio's Cuban
  Restaurant **17**
Lüke **12**
Marigny Brasserie **24**
Mona's **25**
Mother's **13**

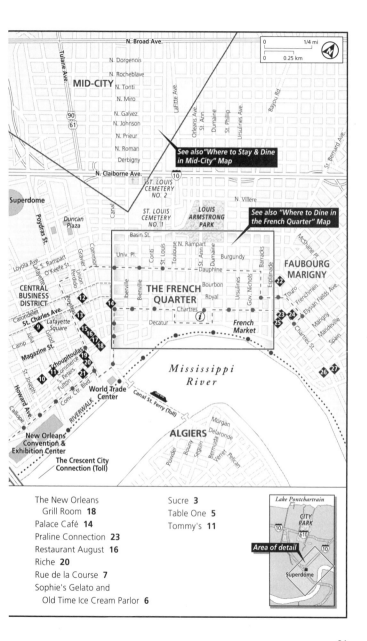

The New Orleans
  Grill Room **18**
Palace Café **14**
Praline Connection **23**
Restaurant August **16**
Riche **20**
Rue de la Course **7**
Sophie's Gelato and
  Old Time Ice Cream Parlor **6**

Sucre **3**
Table One **5**
Tommy's **11**

We have to admit that neither the cuisine nor the cooking of New Orleans is all that innovative, with some exceptions. Many places are variations on either Creole or Italian (or both), and a certain sameness, if you are paying attention, can creep on to menus. Further, there is a longtime citywide tradition wherein on those occasions when a new dish does arrive, once it gains enough local credence, it becomes a "standard"—in other words, you can count on seeing it all over the place. This accounts for the omnipresence of shrimp rémoulade on fried green tomatoes, white-chocolate bread pudding, and a few other new "classics."

This may sound like we are denigrating the food of New Orleans. Believe us. We don't do that. It will take you a while to notice any menu repetition, about the same amount of time it will take you to emerge from a coma that is brought on by equal parts butter sauce and pleasure.

This is the city where the great chefs of the world come to eat—if they don't work here already. Many people love to do nothing more than wax nostalgic about great meals they have had here, describing entrees in practically pornographic detail. It is nearly impossible to have a bad meal in this town; at worst, it will be mediocre, and with proper guidance, you should even be able to avoid that.

Please keep in mind that all times and prices in the following listings are subject to change as restaurants may still have issues with staffing or other economic ups and downs that may cause them to change hours on a whim. You should call in advance to ensure the accuracy of anything significant to you.

While it is true that the New Orleans food scene is dominated by places like Commander's Palace, it is also true that New Orleans food is a classic shrimp or hot sausage po' boy, dressed, of course, and a nectar snoball from a local family that has been making those things for generations. Places like that are brave to make a comeback, so if you see one open, take a chance and stop in. Tell them you are glad they are there. Ask 'em where you ought to eat next.

1 The French Quarter
EXPENSIVE
Antoine's CREOLE   Owned and operated by the same family for an astonishing 160 years, Antoine's sustained some of the most dramatic Katrina damage in the otherwise relatively untouched Quarter; a 30×40-foot portion of an exterior wall on the second and third

Where to Dine in the French Quarter

Acme Oyster House **2**

Angeli on Decatur **37**

Antoine's **19**

Arnaud's **9**

Bacco **13**

Bayona **22**

Bourbon House Seafood **3**

Brennan's **20**

Broussard's **21**

Café Beignet **11**

Café du Monde **33**

Café Giovanni **4**

Café Maspero **29**

Clover Grill **32**

Court of Two Sisters **26**

Dickie Brennan's Steakhouse **2**

Dominique's **24**

EnVie **38**

Felix's Restaurant &
   Oyster Bar **7**

Galatoire's **6**

Irene's Cuisine **35**

Johnny's Po Boys **16**

K-Paul's Louisiana Kitchen **15**

Louisiana Pizza Kitchen **39**

Mr B's Bistro **8**

Muriel's **30**

Napoleon House **17**

Nola **14**

The Pelican Club **12**

Peristyle **25**

Petunia's **23**

Port of Call **40**

Ralph & Kacoo's **28**

Red Fish Grill **1**

Remoulade **10**

Rib Room **18**

Royal Blend Coffee
   and Tea House **27**

Sekisui Samurai **5**

Stanley **31**

Stella! **36**

Tujague's **34**

83

floors crumbled, poignantly exposing the inside of the restaurant. Because of that wall collapsing, a beam was weakened and gave way in the main dining room. That's being worked on as we write this. But that's okay—they have 14 other dining rooms, at least 7 of which had reopened by late summer 2006. Because we are sentimental, we have a serious soft spot for Antoine's. We love that Thomas Wolfe said he ate the best meal of his life here, and that author Frances Parkinson Keyes immortalized it in her mystery *Dinner at Antoine's*. We love that we took a friend, a multigeneration New Orleanian, and that she reminisced happily about her grandfather's regular visits and favorite dishes.

But we also like to eat, and consequently we can't help but notice that when asked for New Orleans restaurant recommendations, we never think of Antoine's. The food is as classic New Orleans dining as you can get, but if that were your introduction to same, you may well wonder what all the fuss is about. Still, it's hard to ignore a legend, and so with some caution you may wish to investigate for yourself. Locals—loyal customers all, mind you—will advise you to focus on starters and dessert and skip the entrees. You might order a side of creamed spinach, which is classic comfort food. Oysters Rockefeller (served hot in the shell and covered with a mysterious green sauce—Antoine's invented it and still won't give out the recipe) will live up to its rep, and the infamous football-size (and football-shaped) baked Alaska is surely the most frivolous dessert ever.

713 St. Louis St. ℂ 504/581-4422. www.antoines.com. Reservations not required. No shorts, sandals, or T-shirts, but jackets no longer required. Main courses $24–$40. AE, DC, MC, V. Mon and Thurs–Sat 5:30–9:30pm; Sun 11:30am–2:30pm.

Arnaud's 𝕲𝕲 CREOLE   Arnaud's seems to have the lowest profile of all the classic old New Orleans restaurants, but undeservedly so, since it tops them in quality. You need to try at least one venerable, properly New Orleans atmospheric establishment, and that one should be Arnaud's, which post-Katrina is doing some of the best culinary work it has in years. Apart from the signature appetizer, shrimp Arnaud (boiled shrimp topped with a spicy rémoulade sauce), we love the crabmeat Ravigotte (generous amounts of sweet lump crabmeat tossed with a Creole mustard–based sauce, hearts of palm, and other veggies), and the charbroiled oysters, all smoky and buttery flavor. It's hard to find a better turtle soup. Delicious fish dishes include snapper or trout Pontchartrain (topped with crabmeat), the spicy pompano Duarte, and pompano David and tuna Napoleon, good choices for those watching waistlines. Any filet mignon entree is superb (the meat is often better than what's served in most steakhouses in town). Desserts aren't quite as magnificent, but the bananas Foster are spot on, and one crème brûlée fan said Arnaud's was the best she'd ever had.

Arnaud's also operates a less formal, less expensive brasserie, **Rémoulade** (p. 95), right next door.

813 Bienville St. ℂ **866/230-8892** or 504/523-5433. www.arnauds.com. Reservations requested. Business casual. Main courses $21–$40. AE, DC, DISC, MC, V. Sun–Thurs 6–10pm; Fri–Sat 6–10:30pm; Sun brunch 10am–2:30pm.

Bacco ℱ ITALIAN/CREOLE   Any affection we already had for Bacco increased exponentially the day, about a month after Katrina, it became the first major Quarter restaurant to reopen. Did it matter the menu was limited to five items, all grilled and served on plastic dinnerware? Heck, no. It was New Orleans food, again, and even taking obvious joyful bias into account, it was delicious. At night it's romantic and candlelit, at lunchtime it's more affordable and casual, with particularly well-priced lunch specials (three courses for around $15). Don't expect spaghetti and marinara sauce here. The menu changes regularly, but our latest trip produced a superior take on New Orleans BBQ shrimp (with a spicy finish) and terrific hickory smoked redfish. Skip the crawfish ravioli, but other pasta dishes are probably sure things. Mrs. Ralph's ice cream sandwich—moist chocolate cake layered with Louisiana strawberry ice cream—made up for the disappointing espresso cupcake.

310 Chartres St. ℂ **504/522-2426.** www.bacco.com. Reservations recommended. Main courses $18–$31. AE, DC, DISC, MC, V. Daily 11:30am–2:30pm; Sun–Thurs 6–9:30pm; Fri–Sat 6–10pm.

Bayona ℱℱ INTERNATIONAL   Chef-owner Susan Spicer is a local treasure, and certainly her grit in reopening her business—she lost her house as did her co-manager, business manager, and assistant, and Spicer regularly commuted from her temporary digs in Jackson, Mississippi, during the early days of her restaurant's return—has only increased that affection. Happily, Bayona's lovely courtyard came through the storm just fine and was blooming like crazy by summer 2006.

Be sure to begin with the outstanding cream of garlic soup, a perennial favorite. Appetizers include grilled shrimp with cilantro sauce and black-bean cakes, and delicate, flavorful veal sweetbreads sautéed with scallions and diced potatoes in sherry vinaigrette. Knockout entrees have included medallions of lamb loin with a lavender honey aioli (a mayonnaise-based sauce) and a zinfandel demi-glace; a perfectly grilled pork chop with a stuffing of fontina cheese, fresh sage, and prosciutto; and yet another lamb dish, this one topped with goat cheese, that may have been the best lamb we've ever tasted. Heaven.

430 Dauphine St. © 504/525-4455. www.bayona.com. Reservations required at dinner, recommended at lunch. Main courses $9–$15 lunch, $22–$28 dinner. AE, DC, DISC, MC, V. Tues–Thurs 6–9:30pm; Fri–Sat 6–10pm; Wed–Fri 11:30am–2pm; Sat noon–3pm.

Bourbon House Seafood 🐟🐟 SEAFOOD   The latest entry from Dickie Brennan, this is a modern take on the classic New Orleans fish house, both aesthetically and gastronomically. It's a big, cheerful room with balcony seating perfect for spying or canoodling. The menu features all kinds of fish, from platters of fresh boiled or raw seafood to entrees like baked fish Grieg (a soft, tender fish in a meunière sauce that is neither overpowering nor overly buttery) and grilled Gulf fish on a ragout of local legumes. This is the place for some fine seafood appetizers, including commendable versions of oysters Rockefeller, a lovely (and not overly biting) rémoulade sauce, marinated seafood salads, and more. Check out fresh blueberry mojitos, orange cosmos, and pomegranate champagne, not to mention the restaurant's natural deep commitment to all things bourbon. If there is a wait for a table, you can order from the dinner menu at the bar and watch the oyster men shuck away.

144 Bourbon St. © 504/522-0111. www.bourbonhouse.com. Reservations suggested. Main courses $5.25–$20 breakfast, $8.50–$30 lunch, $16–$32 dinner. AE, DISC, MC, V. Sun–Thurs 11am–10pm; Fri–Sat 11am–11pm.

Brennan's 🐟 FRENCH/CREOLE   For more than 40 years, breakfast at Brennan's has been a New Orleans tradition, a feast that has surely kept many a heart surgeon busy. Reopened in late April 2006 after a lengthy post-K renovation, in time to celebrate their 60th anniversary, Brennan's is a lesson in New Orleans survival, and, of course, diet. Don't expect any California health-conscious fruit-and-granola options here; this multicourse extravaganza is unabashedly sauce- and egg-intensive. It's also costly—it's not hard to drop $50 on breakfast—so you might be better off sticking with the fixed-price meal (though it often limits your choices). This is Special Event Dining, for Grandma's birthday or to celebrate an engagement, when it seems right to dress up in suits and even hats, and eat classically prepared eggs Benedict or eggs Portuguese (poached on top of a tomato concoction, served in a puff pastry with hollandaise ladled over the whole), very fine turtle soup, and the superb onion soup made with a roux. You can justify the outlay of cash by making this your main meal of the day. Breakfast and lunch are quite crowded; dinner is less so (head straight to the gas-lamp-lined balcony for dinner), probably due to a less-solid reputation for that meal. Even with a reservation, expect a wait.

417 Royal St. ⓒ **504/525-9711.** www.brennansneworleans.com. Reservations recommended. Main courses $20–$39; fixed-price lunch $36; fixed-price 4-course dinner $48. AE, DC, DISC, MC, V. Thurs–Mon 9am–1pm and 6–9pm. Closed for dinner on Christmas Eve and all day Christmas Day.

Broussard's ⓡ CREOLE Unfairly dismissed as a tourist trap (which, in truth, it was for some years), Broussard's is a perfectly fine alternative to some of its similarly well-established peers. And you have to love their post-storm attitude: "We will open up and serve jambalaya if we have to!" vowed owner Gunther Preuss in a CNN interview. "Gunther has a way with crab," claims his press material, and once we stopped giggling over that turn of phrase, we had to admit it was true. We suggest the appetizer of crabmeat Florentine, which includes spinach and is covered in a brie sauce. Another of our favorites is the baked filet of redfish Herbsaint (a local anise-flavored liqueur), clever and delicious in its components, which include impossibly sweet crabmeat and lemon risotto. Many of the desserts are happily heavy and creamy.

819 Conti St. ⓒ **504/581-3866.** www.broussards.com. Reservations recommended. No jeans, shorts, sneakers, or T-shirts. Main courses $22–$36. AE, MC, V. Daily 5:30–10pm.

Café Giovanni ⓡ ITALIAN Though chef Duke LoCicero has been winning culinary awards right and left, Café Giovanni is kind of a mixed bag, thanks to a combo of fine food, lackadaisical service even before Katrina, and—of course—the dreaded (or highly enjoyable, depending on your conversational needs during dinner and your love of schmaltz) strolling opera singers (to be found Wed, Fri, and Sat nights, singing with all their might). Though chef Duke is renowned for his pastas, including a duck-and-rabbit ragout over pappardelle (the duck overpowered the rabbit in this rich dish) and pasta Gambino, which tosses shrimp, garlic, cream, and other tidbits together, these may not be all that much better than the pastas found over at Irene's Cuisine (p. 92).

117 Decatur St. ⓒ **504/529-2154.** www.cafegiovanni.com. Main courses $15–$33. AE, DC, DISC, MC, V. Mon–Sat 5:30–10pm.

Court of Two Sisters *(Overrated)* CREOLE   This is probably the prettiest restaurant in town (thanks to a huge, foliage-filled court-yard located in a 2-centuries-old building, both spared any storm-related issues), but even major ambience can't obscure the problems with the food. You'll find the only daily jazz brunch in town here (remarkable that they are still doing it, under the circumstances), but it suffers from the typical buffet problem—too many dishes, none of which succeed except maybe the made-to-order items such as eggs Benedict. Avoid the vinegary seviche, but try the seafood slaw (we give it a thumbs up). Dinner may be even worse; apart from a Caesar salad (made in the traditional style, at tableside), there is little, if anything, to recommend. It's a pity, because you can't ask for a better setting.

613 Royal St. ⓒ 504/522-7261. www.courtoftwosisters.com. Reservations recommended for dinner and brunch. Main courses $24–$28; brunch $25. AE, DC, DISC, MC, V. Mon–Fri 11am–3pm; Sat–Sun 9am–3pm; Mon and Thurs–Sat 5:30–9pm.

Dickie Brennan's Steakhouse *⚹⚹* STEAK   This is one of the few restaurants that received serious physical damage from Katrina. Nonetheless, aficionados won't be able to tell the difference in this handsome steakhouse, thanks to a laborious reconstruction. It looks gorgeous, but not as much so as its prime steaks. We are hard-pressed to choose our favorite between the 14-ounce rib-eye, the 16-ounce cast-iron-seared filet, or the house filet topped with béarnaise sauce, flash-fried oysters, and creamed spinach. Prime rib is less impressive, as it's a bit pallid compared to a hearty aged steak. And even fish entrees are entirely successful, particularly the grilled red fish topped with lemon beurre blanc sauce and the terrific crab cake appetizer, which tastes like all crab and no filling. Save room for desserts such as the family's Creole cream cheese cheesecake (not an ordinary cheesecake by any means), bananas Foster bread pudding (a new twist on an old faithful dish), coconut cake, and a chocolate-café mousse.

716 Iberville St. ⓒ 504/522-2467. www.dickiebrennanssteakhouse.com. Reservations recommended. Main courses $13–$34 lunch, $29–$40 dinner. AE, DISC, MC, V. Sun–Thurs 5:30–10pm; Fri–Sat 5–10pm. (The bar serves food until 10:30pm.)

Dominique's *⚹* INTERNATIONAL   Though it's been around for a few years, Dominique's seems to have struggled to achieve a significant profile among New Orleans restaurants. Perhaps that's the reasoning behind some reconceptualizing of the cuisine. Currently, it's French-Caribbean, and although it may have the prettiest presentations in town, the dishes are too busy, with hit-or-miss results. "L.A. visuals with New Orleans–size portions," said one guest, and that about sums it up. Hits include blue crab and coconut soup served in the actual shell (why doesn't everyone do that?), cured wild salmon on blue-crab claw meat on a brioche, an entree of pan-seared shrimp with a bonito and rock-shrimp croquette, and best of all, citrus-spiced crusted pheasant breast stuffed with veal cheeks (you can see what we mean about the needless complexity of certain dishes) with sweet potato gnocchi.

In the Maison Dupuy Hotel, 1001 Toulouse St. ℂ 504/522-8000. www.dominiques restaurant.com. Reservations suggested. Main courses $23–$34. AE, DC, DISC, MC, V. Tues–Sat 6–10:30pm.

Galatoire's ⊛ FRENCH   The venerable Galatoire's causes heated discussions among local foodies: the best restaurant in New Orleans or past its prime? This conversation was rendered almost irrelevant when it reopened after Katrina. Walking into its classic green-wall-paper interior, exactly as it used to be, complete with favorite waiter John, at his post for 35 years and counting, despite the loss of his home to flooding, was such a relief, such a return to normalcy that any gastronomic inadequacies are easy to overlook. Or even welcomed; really, you don't come to Galatoire's for cutting-edge cuisine. You come here to eat a nice piece of fish, perfectly sautéed or broiled, topped with fresh crabmeat. Or you have a seafood dish with a gloopy white sauce, because that's what you've been eating at your regular Sunday-evening dinners, where all the old waiters know your name, for years. Galatoire's, where in *A Streetcar Named Desire*, Stella took Blanche to escape Stanley's poker game, is New Orleans tradition, and a symbol of everything else we could have lost, and that alone makes it worth the trip. You may not have the same experience as a knowledgeable local unless you get a waiter who can really guide you (ask for John; everyone else does). We love the lump crabmeat appetizer (think coleslaw, only with crab instead of cabbage), the shrimp rémoulade, and the oysters Rockefeller. For an entree, get the red snapper or redfish topped with sautéed crabmeat meunière (a delightful butter sauce)—it will probably be one of the finest fish dishes you'll have during your stay. Don't miss out on the terrific creamed spinach and the puffy potatoes with béarnaise sauce, which will make you swear off regular french fries forever.

209 Bourbon St. ℂ 504/525-2021. www.galatoires.com. Reservations accepted for upstairs. Jackets required after 5pm and all day Sun. Main courses $20–$31. AE, DC, DISC, MC, V. Tues–Sat 11am–10pm; Sun noon–10pm. Closed Memorial Day, July 4th, Thanksgiving, and Christmas.

K-Paul's Louisiana Kitchen ✸ CAJUN/CREOLE   Paul Prud-homme was at the center of the Cajun revolution of the early 1980s, when Cajun food became known throughout the world. His reputation and his line of spices continue today, while Chef was a culinary hero during the disaster. His establishment cooked for volunteers, firemen, troops, displaced locals, and more, serving tens of thousands of meals. Unfortunately, although the American regional food is still good (our last meal here was really quite good, in fact), it's not spectacular and certainly is not worth the wait (upwards of 1½ hr. at its peak) or the high cost. Different menu items are offered daily, but you can't go wrong with duck *boudin,* blackened beef tenders with debris, or blackened drum with sautéed crabmeat chipotle. A Paul-level of spicy bronzed salmon is just so-so.

416 Chartres St. ✆ 504/524-7394. www.kpauls.com. Reservations recommended. Main courses $26–$40. AE, DC, DISC, MC, V. Mon–Sat 5:30–9:30pm.

Muriel's ✸✸ CREOLE/ECLECTIC   Conventional wisdom would have it that any restaurant this close to tourist-hub Jackson Square—as in, across the street from it—would have to serve overpriced, mediocre food. But then conventional wisdom notes the Gothic-parlor look to the dining rooms in Muriel's and decides to sit down just to be polite. Then conventional wisdom eats excellent duck confit, a charcuterie plate with chunky pâté, poached oysters in a rosemary cream sauce, and rather sumptuous creamy goat cheese and shrimp crepes—skipping the beet salad, which was a little weird, to be honest—following it up with a perfect double cut sugar-cane apple-glazed pork chop, and equally good wood-grilled tuna (on top of risotto) and redfish. It then has a "dome" of peanut butter mousse with a chocolate shell. Sated and fully satisfied, conventional wisdom then floats upstairs and has a drink. Possibly a canoodle with its dining companion. Conventional wisdom is reminded that rules are made to be broken and vows to tell everyone to come here.

801 Chartres (at St. Ann). ✆ 504/568-1885. www.muriels.com. Reservations suggested. Main courses $13–$18 lunch, $15–$20 brunch, $24–$37 dinner. AE, DISC, MC, V. Wed–Sat 11:30am–2:30pm; Sun jazz brunch 11am–2pm; daily 5:30–10pm.

Nola ✸ CREOLE/NEW AMERICAN   This modern two-story building with a glass-enclosed elevator is the most casual of Chef Emeril Lagasse's three restaurants, and the most conveniently located for the average tourist. Unlike Lagasse's other restaurants, the dining experience here can be a bit hit-or-miss. Whatever variation on duck pizza they're serving (confit and fried egg with truffle oil on a recent visit) is always a sure thing, as are soups such as a nearly fork-able thick roasted garlic-Reggiano Parmesan with basil pesto. But while a recent garlic-crusted redfish topped with a bacon and beurre rouge sauce was an excellent combination of flavors, a pork porterhouse was just a blah hunk of meat, while the shrimp with grits rather dull compared to other versions around town. It's also a particularly noisy space in a town not known for hushed dining.

534 St. Louis St. (℗ **504/522-6652.** www.emerils.com. Reservations recommended. Main courses $25–$38. AE, DC, DISC, MC, V. Wed–Mon 6–10pm; Sat 11:30am–2pm.

The Pelican Club ℱ NEW AMERICAN   Just a short stroll from the House of Blues, The Pelican Club is worth investigating. The appetizers are a bit more inventive than the entrees, but everything is quite tasty. Escargots come in a tequila garlic butter sauce, topped with tiny puff pastries. Oysters are garnished with apple-smoked bacon—even oysterphobes won't have a problem with these babies. Special salads are served each evening; a recent visit found arugula, Gorgonzola, and apple in balsamic dressing. Tender lamb comes coated in rosemary-flavored bread crumbs with a spicy pepper jelly, and fish is cooked to perfection. The desserts are certainly stand-outs. Try the flat (rather than puffy) white-chocolate bread pudding, creamy chocolate pecan pie, or amazing profiteroles filled with coffee ice cream and topped with three sauces.

615 Bienville St., entrance in Exchange Alley. (℗ **504/523-1504.** www.pelicanclub. com. Reservations recommended. Main courses $25–$34. AE, DC, DISC, MC, V. Daily 5:30–10pm. Closed July 4th.

Peristyle ECLECTIC   When Anne Kearney gave up her seminal restaurant, local foodies went into mourning. Peristyle was regarded by many as the best in New Orleans, so this was a blow. Still, locals took heart, because new chef-owner Thomas Wolfe was behind the well-regarded Wolfe's in Metairie. Different Peristyle it would be, but still worthy. Unfortunately, those optimistic expectations haven't yet been borne out. Visits keep producing largely mediocre food. Perhaps it was our fault for not realizing that champagne–vanilla bean poached oysters wouldn't work. Lump crabmeat and roasted beets was a better combination, but the pickled red onions were an erroneous tart touch. As for entrees, roast chicken topped with apricots was juicy (not always the case in restaurants) but dumped on tasteless, dry, and pointless oven-baked crispy spaetzle (dumplings). Pan-seared tuna suffered from similar careless presentation. A repeat trip for the prix-fixe lunch produced a split decision; one set of appetizers and entrees tasted strangely fishy (the fish in question may have been frozen), while the other combination was fine. Wolfe's in Metairie was a casualty of Katrina, and we are sorry, but perhaps that means Chef will begin to shine here at last.

1041 Dumaine St. ℂ **504/593-9535**. www.peristylerestaurant.com. Reservations recommended. Main courses $24–$28. DC, DISC, MC, V. Tues–Sat 6–9:30pm.

Rib Room ℱ SEAFOOD/STEAK   One of the first restaurants in the Quarter to reopen post-Katrina, this is where New Orleanians come to eat beef. And who can fault their choice of surroundings? The solid and cozy Old English feel of this room is complete with natural-brick and open ovens at the back. But while the meat is good, it is not outstanding, and the acclaimed prime rib is just a bit tough and more than lacking in flavor. There are also filets, sirloins, brochettes, tournedos, and steak au poivre, plus some seafood dishes. Carnivores, landlubbers, and ichthyophobes will be happier here than at one of the city's Creole restaurants, but it is not the must-do that its reputation would have you believe.

In the Omni Royal Orleans hotel, 621 St. Louis St. ℂ **504/529-7045**. www.omni hotels.com. Reservations recommended. Main courses $24–$38. AE, DC, DISC, MC, V. Daily 6:30–10:30am, 11:30am–2pm, and 6–9pm.

Stella! ℱℱ INTERNATIONAL   We are now very fond of this charming Quarter restaurant, whose newly redone room glows with real and faux candlelight, making it instantly warm and appealing. The clever, arty food is heavy on design and construction, with some combinations more successful than others. The menu changes frequently, and it will always be interesting to see what Chef might be experimenting with, and a pleasure to participate in something that isn't afraid to depart from the New Orleans culinary norm. A recent foray produced the following: for appetizers, a foie gras and duck pâté BLT, a decadently stacked, heady combo; shark's fin soup garnished with 24-carat gold leaves, a tricked-out version of an Asian staple. The almond- and herb-crusted rack of lamb paired with boneless lamb rib-eye is meltingly tender. There is always an interesting pastry chef at work, and the restaurant always has laudable homemade ice-cream treats. See later in this chapter for the owner's excellent inexpensive cafe, Stanley.

1032 Chartres St. (in the Hotel Provincial). ℂ **504/587-0091**. www.restaurant stella.com. Reservations recommended. No shorts or tank tops; business casual. Main courses $28–$36. AE, DC, DISC, MC, V. Thurs–Mon 5:30–10:30pm.

MODERATE

Irene's Cuisine ℱℱ FRENCH/ITALIAN   Irene's is somewhat off the regular tourist dining path, and locals would probably prefer to keep it that way—waiting upwards of 90 minutes for a table at Irene's is something you can count on. But those same locals feel the French provincial and Italian food is worth it, and you may as well. Once you do enter, you will find a dark, cluttered, noisy tavern, with ultrafriendly waiters who seem delighted you came and who keep the crowds happy with prompt service.

On a recent visit, we were thrilled by soft-shell-crab pasta, an entirely successful Italian/New Orleans hybrid consisting of a whole fried crustacean atop a bed of pasta with a cream sauce of garlic, crawfish, tomatoes, and wads of whole basil leaves. The panned oysters and grilled shrimp appetizer can be magnificent, and don't forget the *pollo rosemarino*—five pieces of chicken marinated, partly cooked, marinated again, and then cooked a final time. Desserts, alas, are the usual dull New Orleans suspects (repeat after me: crème brûlée, bread pudding, chocolate torte . . .). *Note:* Irene's longtime partner, Tommy, opened up his own place, which is more or less Irene's all over again, with one crucial detail: It takes reservations (see review later in this chapter).

539 St. Philip St. © 504/529-8811. Limited reservations accepted if space is available. Main courses $17–$23. AE, MC, V. Mon–Sat 5:30–10pm. Closed New Year's Day, July 4th, Labor Day, Thanksgiving, and Christmas.

Mr. B's Bistro ⭐⭐ CONTEMPORARY CREOLE   This deceptively simple place had major storm damage requiring about 18 months of laborious renovations. Regulars, who counted on having lunch here several days a week, are thrilled to have their restaurant back.

The food, mostly modern interpretations of Creole classics, is simple but peppered with spices that elevate the flavors into something your mouth really thanks you for. The crab cakes are about as good as this dish gets. Superb, too, is the not-too-spicy andouille sausage—get it in everything you can. Gumbo Ya Ya is a hearty, country-style rendition with chicken and sausage, perfect for a rainy day. The Cajun barbecued shrimp are huge and plump, with a rich, thick, buttery sauce. It's so tasty it makes you greedy for every drop of sauce, completely oblivious to the silly bib they make you wear, and it's our favorite version of one of our favorite dishes.

201 Royal St. © 504/523-2078. www.mrbsbistro.com. Reservations recommended. No shorts or tank tops; business casual. Main courses $14–$20 lunch, $18–$30 dinner. AE, DC, DISC, MC, V. Mon–Sat 11:30am–2:30pm and 5:30–9:30pm.

Port of Call ⭐⭐ HAMBURGERS   Sometimes you just need a burger—particularly when you've been eating many things with sauce. Locals feel strongly that the half-pound monsters served at the cozy (and we mean it) Port of Call are the best in town. We are going to take a stand and say that, yes, they are certainly terrific, but all that meat may be too much of a good thing. The brawny hamburgers come with an enormous baked potato (because you might not have gotten enough food), and there are also excellent filet mignon, rib-eye steaks, and New York strip steaks. Because businesspeople come here from all over the city, it's often jammed at regular eating hours, so try it before 7pm, when people who work in the Quarter begin to gather here. They have their own signature drink, the Monsoon, a citrus-laden rum combo that is refreshing and unexpectedly potent.

838 Esplanade Ave. ✆ **504/523-0120.** www.portofcallneworleans.com. Main courses $9–$25. AE, MC, V. Sun–Thurs 11am–midnight; Fri–Sat 11am–1am.

Ralph & Kacoo's CREOLE/SEAFOOD   This is a satisfying, reliable place for seafood, nothing we would consider writing home about, but a decent backup place. The Creole dishes are quite good, portions are more than ample, prices are reasonable, and the high volume of business means everything is fresh. Start with fried crawfish tails or the killer onion rings, and if you're adventurous, give the blackened alligator with hollandaise a try. For those on restricted diets, there's a special "heart-healthy" menu. Be sure to try the Godiva chocolate cheesecake for dessert.

519 Toulouse St. ✆ **504/522-5226.** www.ralphandkacoos.com. Reservations suggested. Main courses $14–$40. AE, DC, DISC, MC, V. Mon–Thurs 4–10pm; Fri 4–11pm; Sat noon–11pm; Sun noon–9pm.

Red Fish Grill ✿ SEAFOOD   Red Fish is far better than anything else in its price range on Bourbon Street, and—surprise!—it's another Brennan restaurant. Ralph Brennan's place (one of the first Quarter restaurants to reopen after Katrina) serves many New Orleans specialties with an emphasis on—surprise again—fish. Skip the dull salads in favor of appetizers like shrimp rémoulade napoleon (layered between fried green tomatoes) or grilled shrimp and shiitake-mushroom quesadillas. For your entree, go right to the fish they do so well. Whatever you have will be light and flaky with flavors that complement one another, rich (it *is* New Orleans) but not overly so. The signature dish is a pan-seared catfish topped with sweet-potato crust and an andouille cream drizzle. It's so outstanding, we asked for the recipe so we could try to re-create it at home. (We couldn't really, but it was fun trying.) Also splendid is the grilled Gulf fish with a pecan butter sauce.

115 Bourbon St. ☎ **504/598-1200.** www.redfishgrill.com. Reservations limited. Main courses $8.75–$16 lunch, $16–$29 dinner. AE, DC, DISC, MC, V. Daily 11am–3pm; Sun–Thurs 5–10pm; Fri–Sat 5–11pm. Oyster bar Sun–Thurs 11am–10pm; Fri–Sat 11am–11pm.

Rémoulade CREOLE/CAJUN/AMERICAN   An informal cafe offshoot of the venerable Arnaud's (p. 84), Rémoulade is certainly better than the otherwise exceedingly tourist-trap restaurants on Bourbon Street (Red Fish Grill being the exception), offering average but adequate local food at reasonable prices. You are best off ignoring the undistinguished jambalayas, gumbos, and so forth in favor of trying some of the Arnaud's specialties featured here—particularly the fine turtle soup and shrimp rémoulade. Burgers and pizza fill out the menu. This is one of the few places in town that serves Brocato's Italian ice cream.

309 Bourbon St. ☎ **504/523-0377.** www.remoulade.com. Main courses $8–$20. AE, DISC, MC, V. Daily 11:30am–midnight.

Sekisui Samurai ✦ JAPANESE   Lord knows we love a cream sauce as much as, and probably more than, the next person, to say nothing of our deep commitment to deep-fried anything, but sometimes something's gotta give (like our waistbands), and that's why, if we can't get our hands on a plain green salad, we end up eating sushi. If you find yourself needing a similar break, you could do worse than trying out this French Quarter sushi place, which also delivers both in the Quarter and the Central Business District. While the crawfish-tail sushi is hit-or-miss, the Crunchy Roll (a California roll topped with tempura—see, we always come back to deep-fried) and the spicy tuna roll are worth checking out, as is the enjoyably named Flying Fish Roll. They also have teriyaki and so forth. And it is interesting to see how a town known for fish does it raw. The website often has coupons for discounts and specials.

239 Decatur St. ☎ **504/525-9595.** Sushi $3.50–$7.50 for pieces/rolls; lunch specials $6.75–$15; dinner $14–$26. AE, DC, DISC, MC, V. Daily 11:30am–10pm.

Tujague's ✦ CREOLE   Dating back to 1856, Tujague's (pronounced *Two*-jacks) is every bit as venerable and aged as the big-name New Orleans restaurants (heck, the mirror in the bar has been in place for 150 years!), and yet no one ever mentions it—which is a shame. It may not be a knockout, but it's authentic and solid.

Tujague's does not have a menu; instead, each night it offers a set six-course (it seems one course is coffee) meal. You will eat what they cook that night. Don't expect fancy or nouvelle: This is real local food. Meals start with a sinus-clearing shrimp rémoulade, heads to a fine gumbo, then on to a sample of a so-tender-you-cut-it-with-a-fork brisket, and then on to whatever is happening for an entree. There's likely to be filet mignon for sure, but skip it (it's ordinary) in favor of items such as stuffed shrimp or perfect fettuccine or Bonne Femme chicken, a baked garlic number from the original owner's recipe (the restaurant has it every night, but you have to ask for it). Finish with a classic—the right-on-the-money bread pudding.

823 Decatur St. ⓒ 504/525-8676. www.tujagues.com. Reservations recommended. 6-course dinner $32–$39. AE, DC, DISC, MC, V. Daily 5pm–"closing."

INEXPENSIVE

Acme Oyster House 🦪🦪 SEAFOOD/SANDWICHES   The Quarter's oldest oyster bar needed a $2-million renovation to recover from Katrina, but it looks pretty much as it always did, just spiffier (new floor, new tiling, new bathrooms, and best of all, an expanded kitchen). This joint is always loud, often crowded, and the kind of place where you're likely to run into obnoxious fellow travelers. But if you need an oyster fix or you've never tried oyster shooting (taking a raw oyster, possibly doused in sauce, and letting it slide right down your throat), come here. There's nothing quite like standing at the oyster bar and eating a dozen or so freshly shucked oysters on the half-shell. (You can have them at a table, but somehow they taste better at the bar.) If you can't quite stomach them raw, try the oyster po' boy, with beer, of course. Note that there are people who sincerely prefer Felix's across the street. The two locations are interchangeable to us, but we might be missing something.

724 Iberville St. ⓒ 504/522-5973. www.acmeoyster.com. Oysters $9–$16 per half/whole dozen, respectively; po' boys $8–$11; New Orleans specialties $8–$12; seafood $14–$18. AE, DC, DISC, MC, V. Sun–Thurs 11am–9pm; Fri–Sat 11am–10pm.

Angeli on Decatur 🦪🦪 ITALIAN/MEDITERRANEAN   This place features satisfying food with further praise for its nearly round-the-clock hours and local delivery service (every night until 2am or later)—all things hungry locals and tourists crave. It's conveniently accessible after a day's busy sightseeing or a night's busy club hopping and perfect for a light, actually rather healthy meal—a much-needed alternative to some of the extravaganzas offered by more formal restaurants in town. Portions are substantial—splitting a Greek salad produced two full plates of fresh, lovely veggies and a couple of pieces of garlic bread. Add to that a small but gooey and flavorful pizza , and you've got a tasty, affordable meal for two, at almost any hour and even in your hotel room, and a nice palate cleanser if you are a bit tired of local cuisine. It's good enough for occasional Quarter residents Brad and Angelina, after all!

1141 Decatur St. (at Gov. Nicholls St.). ✆ 504/566-0077. Main courses $6.95–$18. AE, MC, V. Sun–Thurs 11am–2am; Fri–Sat 11am–4am.

Café Beignet ✿ CAFE   At breakfast, this full-service bistro-style cafe serves Belgian waffles, an omelet soufflé, bagels and lox, or brioche French toast. Items on the lunch menu include gumbo, vegetable sandwiches, and salads. And, of course, beignets. The latter won't make us forget Café du Monde—nothing will, of course—but if you are here, make the most of it. They have a new location in the Musical Legends Park on Bourbon Street.

334B Royal St. ✆ 504/524-5530. www.cafebeignet.com. All items under $10. MC, V. Daily 8am–3pm. Other locations: 311 Bourbon St. ✆ 504/525-2611. Mon–Wed 8am–3pm; Thurs and Sun 8am–10pm; Fri–Sat 8am–midnight. 819 Decatur. ✆ 504/522 9929. Daily 8am–3pm.

Café Maspero ✿ SEAFOOD/SANDWICHES   Upon hearing complaints about the increasing presence in the Quarter of "foreign" restaurants, such as Subway, one local commented, "Good. That must mean the line will be shorter at Café Maspero." Locals do indeed line up for burgers, deli sandwiches (including a veggie muffuletta!), seafood, grilled marinated chicken, and so on, in some of the largest portions you'll ever run into. And there's an impressive list of wines, beers, and cocktails. Everything is delicious and is sold at low, low prices.

601 Decatur St. ✆ 504/523-6250. Main courses $4.25–$9. No credit cards. Sun–Thurs 11am–10pm; Fri–Sat 11am–11pm.

Clover Grill ✿ COFFEEHOUSE   We are cross with the Clover Grill. Once a place where the irreverent menu ("We're here to serve people and make them feel prettier than they are") competed with the even more outrageous staff for smart-aleck behavior, it has lost its luster. The menu has fewer jokes, and the once charmingly sassy staff is straying lately toward surly. But the burgers are still juicy and perfect and apparently are still cooked under a hubcap (they say it seals in the juices). It seems to work well enough—it's a mighty fine burger. Breakfast is still served round-the-clock, and drag queens still hang out at the tables or counters. But too many times we've come in at night requesting a shake, only to be told "no shakes." Unacceptable for a 24-hour diner. Go—but tell them they are on probation until they reclaim their original *joie de vivre*.

900 Bourbon St. ✆ 504/598-1010. www.clovergrill.com. All items under $8. AE, MC, V. Mon–Wed 8am–midnight; Thurs–Sun 24 hr. (opens Thurs 8am).

Felix's Restaurant & Oyster Bar &&& SEAFOOD/CREOLE
Like its neighbor the Acme Oyster House, Felix's is a crowded and
noisy place, full of locals and tourists taking advantage of the late
hours. It's more or less the same as the Acme. Each has its die-hard
fans, convinced their particular choice is the superior one. Have
your oysters raw, in a stew, in a soup, Rockefeller- or Bienville-style,
in spaghetti, or even in an omelet. If oysters aren't your bag, the fried
or grilled fish, chicken, steaks, spaghetti, omelets, and Creole cooking are mighty good, too. If you want something blackened, they'll
fry it up to order. They usually also have boiled crawfish in season.
In addition to this Post-K gussied up traditional location, they have
a newish Uptown location on Prytania Street (definitely open for
business) that's well worth checking out!

739 Iberville St. ℭ 504/522-4440. Half-dozen oysters $6.25; po' boys under $15;
other main courses $10–$26. AE, DISC, MC, V. Also at 4938 Prytania St. ℭ 504/
895-1330. Mon–Sat 10am–10pm; Sun 10am–9pm.

Johnny's Po' Boys && SANDWICHES For location (right
near a busy part of the Quarter) and menu simplicity (po' boys and
more po' boys), you can't ask for much more than Johnny's, which
returned to the culinary scene around December 2005. They put
anything you could possibly imagine (and some things you could-
n't) on huge hunks of French bread, including the archetypal fried
seafood (add some Tabasco, we strongly advise), deli meats, cheese
omelets, ham and eggs, and the starch-o-rama that is a french-fry
po' boy. You need to try it. *Really.* Johnny boasts that "even my fail-
ures are edible," and that says it all. And they deliver!

511 St. Louis St. ℭ 504/524-8129. Everything under $11. No credit cards. Daily
9am–3pm.

Louisiana Pizza Kitchen PIZZA The Louisiana Pizza Kitchen is
a local favorite for its creative pies and atmosphere. Pastas have a significant place on the menu, but diners come for the pizzas and Caesar salad. Individual-size pizzas, baked in a wood-fired oven, feature
a wide variety of toppings (shrimp and roasted garlic are two of the
most popular). The best thing about their pizza is that your toppings
won't get lost in an overabundance of cheese and tomato sauce.

95 French Market Place. ℭ 504/522-9500. www.louisianapizzakitchen.com. Pizzas
$8.25–$12; pastas $10–$16. AE, DC, DISC, MC, V. Sun–Thurs 11am–10pm; Fri–Sat
11am–11pm. Also at 615 S. Carrollton Ave. ℭ 504/866-5900.

Napoleon House & CREOLE/ITALIAN Folklore has it that
the name of this place derives from a bit of wishful thinking:
Around the time of Napoleon's death, a plot was hatched here to

snatch the Little Corporal from his island exile and bring him to live in New Orleans. The third floor was added expressly for the purpose of providing him with a home. Alas, it probably isn't true: The building dates from a couple of years after Napoleon's death. But let's not let the truth get in the way of a good story, or a good hangout, which this is at any time of day, but particularly late at night, when it's dark enough to hatch your own secret plans. Somewhere between tourist-geared and local-friendly, it serves large portions of adequate versions of traditional New Orleans food (po' boys, jambalaya), plus wild-card items like salads with goat cheese and even pita and hummus, plus most significantly, the only heated muffuletta in town. Hours are gradually expanding as this once again becomes a favorite local nightspot.

500 Chartres St. Ⓒ **504/524-9752.** www.napoleonhouse.com. Main courses $3.25–$7.25. AE, DISC, MC, V. Mon 11:30am–5pm; Tues–Wed 11:30am–10pm; Thurs 5–10pm; Fri–Sat 11:30am–11pm.

Petunia's ⓐ CAJUN/CREOLE Petunia's, located in an 1830s town house, dishes up enormous portions of New Orleans specialties such as shrimp Creole, Cajun pasta with shrimp and andouille, and a variety of fresh seafood. Breakfast and Sunday brunch are popular, with a broad selection of crepes that, at 14 inches, are billed as the world's largest. Options include the St. Marie, a blend of spinach, cheddar, chicken, and hollandaise; and the St. Francis, filled with shrimp, crab ratatouille, and Swiss cheese. If you have room for dessert, try the dessert crepes or the peanut butter pie.

817 St. Louis St. (between Bourbon and Dauphine sts.). Ⓒ **504/522-6440.** Main courses $7–$16 breakfast and lunch. AE, DC, DISC, MC, V. Daily 8am–6pm.

Stanley ⓐⓐ AMERICAN Proving the truth of the adage "necessity is the mother of invention," in the days following Katrina, when the Quarter was an isolated island of intrepid survivors determined to carry on regardless, and few, if any, places to eat were open (in New Orleans, that's how you know a disaster has hit), the chef-owner of Stella! began serving sandwiches and grilling burgers on the sidewalk. He ended up serving 3,000 meals in 9 days before shutting down and focusing on opening the cafe properly. The choice of name was obvious. It's right on the corner of Jackson Square, and it's a big boon to dining for tourists and locals alike. Between breakfast all day, cornmeal-crusted oyster po' boys, their drippy burgers (which we think rival Port of Call's naked monsters), and the genuine soda fountain featuring homemade ice cream, there is something for everyone nearly all day long—and well into the night.

547 St. Ann St. (corner of Jackson Sq.). ℂ **504/593-0006.** www.restaurantstanley.com. Everything under $12. AE, DISC, MC, V. Daily 7am–11pm.

2 The Faubourg Marigny

For the restaurants in this section, see the "Where to Dine in New Orleans" map on p. 80.

MODERATE

Feelings Cafe D'Aunoy 𝒜 AMERICAN/CREOLE   Friendly and funky, Feelings serves tasty, solid (if not spectacular) food. It feels like a true local find—because it is—and can be a welcome break from the scene in the Quarter or from more intense dining. Try to get a table in the pretty courtyard or on the balcony overlooking it, though the dining rooms are perfectly pleasant. Luckily, the courtyard wasn't much affected by Katrina. Let's hope the piano bar will be back soon—the ambience isn't the same without it. A typical visit produces oysters *en brochette, pâté de maison,* seafood-stuffed eggplant (shrimp, crabmeat, and crawfish tails in a casserole with spicy sausage and crisp fried eggplant), and a chocolate mousse/peanut butter pie for dessert.

2600 Chartres St. ℂ **504/945-2222.** www.feelingscafe.com. Main courses $16–$25. AE, DC, DISC, MC, V. Thurs–Sun 6–9:30pm (Sat until 10pm, bar opens at 5pm); Sun brunch 11am–2pm.

Marigny Brasserie 𝒜 ECLECTIC   Originally a neighborhood cafe, this is perhaps our first choice for a nice meal in the Frenchmen/Marigny section of town—not because the food is so outstandingly innovative, but it's interesting enough, and everything we tried was pleasing to various degrees. Strongly recommended is the Serrano fig salad—aged goat cheese wrapped in Serrano ham and tossed with mixed greens in a fig vinaigrette—and the seasonal tomato-and-Spanish-tarragon salad, one of those lovely green creations that have finally started showing up on New Orleans menus. The mushroom-crusted salmon, on a bed of fragrant sesame sticky rice and topped with lump crabmeat, was so juicy and nonfishy that it turned a former salmon avoider into a salmon believer. Rack of lamb has a sweet cherry demi-glace topping, but the seared tuna, while a fine cut of fish, needs a sauce of its own.

640 Frenchmen St. ℂ **504/945-4472.** www.marignybrasserie.com. Reservations suggested. Main courses $15–$28. AE, DC, MC, V. Sun–Thurs 5:30–10pm; Fri–Sat 5:30pm–midnight; Sun 10:30am–3pm.

INEXPENSIVE

Bywater Barbeque ⭐⭐ BARBECUE/PIZZA   This tiny, charming, popular cafe deep in a residential neighborhood is a great find. As you can guess, it features barbecue, falling-off-the-bone meat properly dry rubbed, if topped with a too-overwhelming red sauce. Ribs and pulled pork are the best of the meats, which come with sides like solid mac 'n' cheese and mayo-drenched coleslaw. And there is even more to the menu, which is oddly extensive. Weekend brunch specials include biscuits, cheese grits, and elaborate egg dishes, which are just as fab as the barbecue. There is also a lengthy pizza menu, which is where the vegetarians in the group will find relief, plus daily specials including red beans and rice on Monday. Portions are large, so split orders to make matters cheaper still, and save room for desserts like homemade chocolate cake with thick peanut butter frosting.

3162 Dauphine St. ℂ **504/944-4445.** Main courses $6.50–$18. No credit cards. Thurs–Tues 11am–9pm.

Elizabeth's ⭐⭐⭐ CREOLE   Forget paying huge sums for average and goopy breakfast food. At Elizabeth's you eat, as they say, "Real Food, Done Real Good"—and, we add, real cheap. The feature food such as Creole rice calas (sweet rice fritters), a classic breakfast dish that is nearly extinct from menus around town. They also offer food calling for health advisories, such as the praline bacon (topped with sugar and pecans—"pork candy" the shameless chef calls it; you must not miss this, but it's served only at breakfast time); or stuffed French toast (*pain perdu* piled high with cream cheese flavored with strawberries); or the breakfast po' boy, a monster sandwich the size of the Sunday *Picayune* rolled up. Note that the menu changes daily so you might want to call to see what they are offering. Meanwhile, if this wasn't enough, they are now open for dinner, featuring nightly specials like pan-seared salmon with Dijon beurre blanc sauce, Southern fried chicken livers with pepper jelly, and more humble fried shrimp and chicken.

601 Gallier St. ℂ **504/944-9272.** www.elizabeths-restaurant.com. Breakfast and lunch, everything under $10; dinner $8.50–$17. MC, V. Wed–Fri 11am–2:30pm; Sat–Sun 8am–2:30pm; Wed–Sat 6–10pm.

La Peniche Restaurant ⭐ CREOLE   A short walk into the Marigny brings you to this homey (as opposed to "homely") dive; take the walk, because rents in the Quarter are too high for any place that looks like this to be a true bargain. Back to the original menu, if not back to 24 hours (shame, that), expect fried fish, po' boys, burgers, and even quiche. Good brunch options exist as well, which is why it's packed during that time. Come for specials such as the bronzed (with Cajun spices) pork, and be sure to have some chocolate layer cake (like homemade!) and peanut butter chocolate-chip pie. If they return to late-night hours, please be careful of the sometimes-dicey neighborhood (though this is often a cop hangout, which helps).

1940 Dauphine St. ⓒ **504/943-1460.** Everything under $15. AE, MC, V. Thurs–Mon 8am–9pm.

Mona's Café & Deli ⓡⓡ MIDDLE EASTERN This local favorite finally expanded from its original Mid-City location into other parts of the city, with varying results. We like the marinated chicken with basmati rice, but they do credible versions of basic Middle Eastern fare (hummus, kabobs, and so forth). The Mid-City location is probably the best, with the Magazine location impressing us the least, but this is the most convenient for the average tourist.

504 Frenchmen St. ⓒ **504/949-4115.** Sandwiches $4–$5.95; main courses $7.95–$14. AE, DC, DISC, MC, V. Mon–Thurs 11am–10pm; Fri–Sat 11am–11pm; Sun noon–9pm. They also have locations at 3901 Banks St. and at 4126 Magazine St.

Praline Connection CREOLE/SOUL FOOD This might be heresy to some NOLA residents (although we know just as many who will back us up), but we think the Praline Connection is completely overrated and eminently missable. It's probably riding on sentiment and tradition, so if this review helps shake things up and gets it back into shape, well, then, good. This used to be the place to come for solid, reliable, and even—once upon a time—marvelous Creole and soul food. The crowds still come, not noting that what they are getting is sometimes dry and dull. Then again, everyone else has improved their food, so let's hope Praline Connection does, too. And early reports about the superior state of their fried chicken indicate that may well be so . . .

542 Frenchmen St. ⓒ **504/943-3934.** www.pralineconnection.com. Main courses $6.95–$19. AE, DC, DISC, MC, V. Mon–Sat 11am–10pm; Sun 11am–9pm.

3 Mid-City/Esplanade

For a map of the restaurants in this section, see the "Where to Stay & Dine in Mid-City" map on p. 61.

EXPENSIVE
Ralph's on the Park ⓡ BISTRO You'd be hard-pressed to find a better setting for a New Orleans restaurant than this one, featuring

an iconic view of the Spanish moss–draped giant oaks across the street in City Park, and just as likable on the inside as well, albeit a bit more L.A.-fashionable than one might expect.

The food consists mostly of reliable variations of local Creole favorites. A generously portioned steak tartare comes prettily arranged on the plate with little mounts of sea salt, mustard, and other accouterments for dressing up the meat. Their shrimp rémoulade is one of our favorites, creamy and not a bit spicy. The garlic broth bathing the escargots is drinkable—even a diner who would never have eaten a snail before was smitten. Both their blackened redfish and the roasted fish are solidly executed, while the filet mignon caused its consumer to mutter something about "buttery, so buttery," while eating it at light speed. For dessert, their playful deconstructed take on s'mores is hard to resist, but even better is the chocolate Kahlúa mousse and Creole cream cheese ice cream atop peach cobbler.

900 City Park Ave. ⓒ **504/488-1000.** www.ralphsonthepark.com. Reservations recommended. Main courses $16–$23 lunch, $24–$35 dinner. AE, MC, V. Tues–Sat 5:30–9:30pm; Fri 11:30am–2pm; Sun 11am–2pm.

MODERATE

Cafe Degas ✦✦ BISTRO/FRENCH   If you want to have a nice meal without the fuss and feathers, Degas should do the trick in terms of both food and atmosphere. The big tree in the dining room is still there, but a lovely outside tree came down in the storm. There are daily dinner and lunch specials—think quiches and real, live salads (always a happy find in this town) and straightforward but flavorful fish and meat dishes, presented in generous portions. You can go light (a salad, a plate of pâtés and cheeses) or heavy (filet of beef tenderloin with a green peppercorn–brandy sauce)—either way, you'll feel as if you ate something worthwhile. Though it's French, this is not France, and this bistro is informal enough that you can go wearing blue jeans.

3127 Esplanade Ave. ⓒ **504/945-5635.** www.cafedegas.com. Reservations recommended. Main courses $9–$13 lunch, $16–$20 dinner. AE, DC, DISC, MC, V. Wed–Sat 11am–2:30pm; Wed–Thurs 6–10pm; Fri–Sat 6–10:30pm; Sun 10:30am–3pm and 6–9pm.

Dooky Chase ✦ SOUL FOOD/CREOLE   For decades, Leah and husband Dooky Chase have served prominent African-American politicians, musicians, and businesspeople chef Leah's classic soul food as gloriously influenced by the city's French, Sicilian, and Italian traditions. This was the place people like Ray Charles (who wrote

"Early in the Morning" about it) would come to after local shows and stay up until the wee hours telling stories and eating gumbo— one of the city's best. The restaurant had 2 feet of flooding, not to mention mold issues, and rebuilding has come along very slowly, despite benefits held for the Chases both here and in other cities. (Ms. Leah is pleased she got a new stove out of the deal, though, since she's wanted one for so long. An octogenarian, she says she has to keep going long enough to cook on it!) At press time they were still struggling to open, but the wait should be over by the time you read this. The Chases lived for over a year in a FEMA trailer outside their restaurant, and they are as wonderful as their cooking. They are everything that is New Orleans, and so make a stop at the restaurant they've worked so hard for, once it comes back.

2301 Orleans Ave. ⓒ **504/821-0600.** www.dookychaserestaurant.com. Call for hours and prices.

Lola's ⓡⓡⓡ SPANISH/INTERNATIONAL "Please, oh please, don't mention Lola's in the book!" beg our local foodie friends. Why? Because this small, special place doesn't take reservations, and the nightly wait is already long as it is. But we are going to spill the beans anyway while assuring you that this is worth waiting for, thanks to incredible Spanish dishes, from various paellas to starters such as garlic shrimp tapas and a heck of a garlic soup. Try to arrive 15 to 30 minutes before opening time and wait in line. If you come later and there's a mob, don't be discouraged: Service is attentive and food comes quickly, so your wait shouldn't be too long, though we'd either not bother on the weekends or bring a book. Don't forget to bring cash—and try not to get ahead of our friends in line!

3312 Esplanade Ave. ⓒ **504/488-6946.** Main courses $8.75–$16. No credit cards or out-of-town checks. Sun–Thurs 5:30–9:30pm; Fri–Sat 5:30–10pm.

INEXPENSIVE

Liuzza's by the Track ⓡⓡ CREOLE/SANDWICHES Not to be confused with Liuzza's, and not to be overlooked either. This Liuzza's is a near-flawless example of a corner neighborhood hole in the wall. In one visit, you will either get the point or not; by the second visit, the staff will know your name. By the third visit, you might wonder why you would eat anywhere else. It's not just the fact that they serve what may be the best gumbo and red beans 'n' rice in the city, it's the monster perfect po' boys, including a drippy garlic-stuffed roast beef (with a pinch of horseradish in the mayo) and a rare barbecued-shrimp po' boy (about 3 dozen shrimp in a hollowed-out po' boy loaf, soaked in spicy butter). It's also the surprise of serious daily specials such as "grilled crab cheese" and shish kabobs. It's the salads as well, huge and full of leafy greens (the healthy aspects of which we like to ruin by having ours topped with fried crawfish and green-onion dressing); vegetarians will be thrilled with the portobello mushroom version. Try the sweet potato and andouille soup. Space is at a premium, and it is not out of the question that you could show up and simply never, ever get seated. Call ahead or plan for, say, lunch (the most popular time) at 11:45am instead of noon.

1518 N. Lopez. © **504/218-7888.** Everything under $14. DISC, MC, V. Mon–Sat 11am–7pm.

Parkway Bakery and Tavern ★★ SANDWICHES   A block or so off Bayou St. John, some enterprising folks with a good sense of history resurrected a long-boarded-up and once much-beloved po' boy shop and bakery, founded in 1922. It elicits flashbacks from old customers and deep pleasure in just about everyone. Never was that more evident than the evening the intrepid owner reopened, one of the first businesses in his area to do so. About 1,000 locals came out to sample the (then) limited menu of just one po' boy (roast beef), listen to some music, and rejoice. You won't find any innovations here, just classic po' boys (the falling-apart roast beef, and—the *sine qua non*—fried oyster have their dedicated fans, while we are believers in the hot sausage and cheese topped with roast beef debris), and many a local beloved brand name like Barq's and Zapp's. The bar is a good hang as well, lately offering live music many nights, while the bayou remains a pretty walk even if it now borders some very sad areas.

538 Hagan St. © **504/482-3047.** Everything under $13. AE, DISC, MC, V. Wed–Mon 11am–8pm (closed Tues). Call about live music.

Willie Mae's Scotch House ★★★ SOUL FOOD   This is as much a fairy tale as a restaurant review. Once upon a time, not that many people outside her humble 6th Ward neighborhood thought much about Miss Willie Mae and her chicken shack, which was also part of her home. Until 2005, when the octogenarian and her secret-recipe fried chicken were designated an "American classic" by the James Beard Association. Weeks later, home and restaurant were under eight feet of water. Weeks after that, a dedicated group of volunteers, including local and regional restaurateurs, banded together to bring back Willie Mae's. So—the most sublime fried chicken ever? It's hard to figure out how to improve upon it. There is no menu—just let your server recite the day's offerings, and wait as Miss Willie Mae's great-granddaughter, who has the secret recipes, fries you up something great. It's a reward for a beautiful effort of community, and for your stomach.

2401 St. Ann St.. © **504/822-9703**. Everything under $15. Cash only. Mon–Fri 11am–3pm.

4 Central Business District

For restaurants in this section, see the "Where to Dine in New Orleans" map on p. 80.

VERY EXPENSIVE

Emeril's *&&* CREOLE/NEW AMERICAN Emeril may be ubiquitous, but we can vouch for his first namesake restaurant. Although it may no longer be trend-setting, it certainly isn't resting on its laurels in terms of quality. What's more, there is all kinds of interesting chef action going on in the kitchen, and this may be one of the most exciting times to dine here.

Try the barbecued shrimp, which comes with a heavier sauce than the classic versions of this local dish, and is paired with charming little rosemary biscuits. Entree standouts include a precisely done Moroccan spice–crusted salmon with beluga lentils, duck schnitzel with roasted shallots, and andouille-crusted redfish. Try to save part of your generously portioned meal for leftovers, so that you have room for the notable banana cream pie; or the mini–Creole cream cheesecake; or even some delicate homemade sorbets. *One small caveat:* This is a very popular place with suit-clad businessmen at lunch (the hours of which may still be limited to Thurs and Fri when you read this) and other clear regulars who appear to get speedier service than more anonymous patrons. *Tip:* Make reservations online to avoid lengthy phone holds waiting to get through to a reservationist.

800 Tchoupitoulas St. © **504/528-9393**. www.emerils.com. Reservations highly recommended at dinner. Main courses $19–$34 lunch, $26–$39 dinner; $65 menu degustation (tasting menu) only on weekends. AE, DC, DISC, MC, V. Dinner daily 6–10pm; lunch Thurs–Fri only 11:30am–2pm.

The New Orleans Grill Room *&&* NEW AMERICAN This ultra-special-event place has had considerable chef turnover post-Katrina, but the current chef, Greg Sonnier, is a most exciting turn of events. It will be excellent fun seeing how this clever local stretches out in this locale, where many a notable chef, including John Besh, has worked. He seems to be hitting the ground running, melding all kinds of traditional local cuisine with the reaches of his own imagination. A recent menu shows appetizers such as grilled rabbit en brouchette with a lavender honey mustard sauce and seared foie gras on a pig's ear. Main courses include possibilities such as Creole cream cheese–crusted lamb with a chamomile mint tea sauce, and a salt-baked whole boneless Gulf fish. There is early-bird dining with a full interesting menu, and the possibilities at lunch make that an attractive cheaper option. If you want to dress up like serious grown-ups and take a chance on eating serious food, head here.

In the Windsor Court Hotel, 300 Gravier St. ℂ **504/522-1992**. www.windsorcourt hotel.com. Reservations recommended. Jacket required at dinner. Main courses $16–$24 lunch; $28–$39 dinner; prix-fixe lunch $24. AE, DC, DISC, MC, V. Mon–Fri 7–10:30am, noon–2:30pm, and 6–10pm; Sat–Sun 7–11am and 6–10pm.

EXPENSIVE

Café Adelaide 𝒢𝒢𝒢 CONTEMPORARY CREOLE   Former Commander's Palace (the same branch of Brennans owns both restaurants) sous chef Danny Trace has transformed this place from a very good dining option into an excellent one, one that can stand along the best in town at any time. He's playing around with classic local dishes, made with local ingredients, but with the sort of fresh and clever twists needed to keep it all out of the Creole business-as-usual rut. Try the Louisiana boucherie (pork tenderloin with black-berry honey, tasso and andouille pie or tasso braised cabbage, and *boudin* crepinette), or the Tabasco soy glazed tuna (with celery root purée). For a change, we are going to steer you toward a savory dessert, the drunken fig bleu cheese tart. At breakfast they offer the classic *pain perdu,* New Orleans's version of French toast. The drinks, especially the sweet and powerful house Swizzle Stick (which can be had on the festive cocktail sampler tree; ask for one!), make this a bar worth investigating as well. Look for specials such as three courses for $38, and four for $47.

300 Poydras St. (in the Loews Hotel). ℂ **504/595-3305**. www.cafeadelaide.com. Reservations suggested. Main courses $13–$19 lunch; $24–$36 dinner. AE, DC, DISC, MC, V. Daily 7–10:30am; Mon–Fri 11am–2:30pm; Mon–Sat 6–9:30pm. "Off-hours" menu available at bar 11am–11pm.

Cuvee 𝒢𝒢𝒢 CONTEMPORARY CREOLE   Doing its darndest to be considered the best restaurant in town, Cuvee is certainly the most innovative and interesting. There are sweetbreads in puff pas-try, and a seared tuna atop a lush avocado salad, paired with heir-loom tomato sorbet and watermelon-vodka gazpacho (what a healthy way to have a shot!). *Osso buco* comes deconstructed, with the "bone" made of potato with the marrow whipped into more potato filling the interior. Mustard-and-herb-crusted salmon comes atop crabmeat brie orzo with lemon confit. But it's the pork belly that keeps more than one local connoisseur coming back for more. Fittingly, desserts are equally witty (look for tapioca pudding with bourbon ice cream and their take on the drumstick ice-cream novelty). And then there's the wine list. You might well eat and eat and eat, and at the end, want to do it all over again.

322 Magazine St. ⓒ **504/587-9001.** www.restaurantcuvee.com. Reservations highly recommended. Main courses $20–$30 dinner. AE, DC, MC, V. Mon–Sat 6–10pm.

Restaurant August ⓐ FRENCH   So there's chef John Besh, feeding people during the dark days immediately post-Katrina, just hauling out jambalaya and anything else he can cook up in volume, and helping to bring back the venerable Willie Mae's Scotch House, proving he's as much about local indigenous cooking as he is about fancy-pants frivolity. Then he hauls off and wins the 2006 James Beard Award for Best Chef Southeast, plus scads of other gourmet praise. And here we are, having eaten here several times . . . never really being all that excited by the experience. We feel like heels, but we just don't get it. Too much use of foam and other nouvelle gimmicks, too dainty and fussy, too many flavors and ingredients crammed on a plate, or the opposite problem, work that is all construction and no flavor. Or the menu is misleading, such as the Moroccan-spiced duck, which was largely enjoyable, but not in the least bit Moroccan, or a dessert that comes out in a form distinctly different from what was described in print. We've never had a bad meal here, but we've never been other than underwhelmed.

301 Tchoupitoulas St. ⓒ **504/299-9777.** www.restaurantaugust.com. Reservations recommended. Main courses $28–$46; 5-course tasting menu $70; 3-hr.-long John Besh degustation menu with wine pairings $150 per person; whole table must participate. AE, DC, MC, V. Tues–Sat 5:30–9pm; Fri lunch 11am–1:30pm.

MODERATE

Cochon ⓐⓐ CAJUN   Anyone opening a new restaurant these days is to be lauded, so here's a round of appreciative applause for chef Donald Link of Herbsaint, and his partner Stephen Stryjewski (who is the one usually in the kitchen), who have not only braved an uncertain market, but also delivered a venture that would be delightful under any circumstances. Influenced by Link's own family background in Acadia, this features mostly small plates of Cajun-inspired dishes. If we point out that nothing is precisely Cajun, nor is there enough pork, that's not meant to be surly. We just happen to be particular about pig. And it's a compliment; we want more dishes like the garlicky cochon (roasted suckling pig) with cracklins, the pork rillette, the ribs with watermelon pickle, and the oyster-and-bacon sandwich. We also want them bigger (yes, even the "small plates") because the mouthfuls you get are so darn good. Then again, that leaves us room for orange ice box and lemon-buttermilk pie.

930 Tchoupitoulas St. (℃ **504/588-2123**. www.cochonrestaurant.com. Reservations strongly recommended on weekends. Small plates $7–$11; main courses $12–$19. AE, DISC, MC, V. Mon–Fri 11am–10pm; Sat 5:30–10pm.

Herbsaint *♠♠* BISTRO Herbsaint would be the locally made pastis found in, among other places, the popular local cocktail, the Sazerac. As a restaurant, it's an alternative to similarly inventive but much higher-priced peers in the Quarter, with thoughtful dishes planned by 2007 James Beard Best Southeast Chef Donald Link. Be sure to try the Herbsaint, tomato, and shrimp bisque—it always sends us into rhapsodies, and we aren't even soup fans—and the "small plate" of fried frogs' legs, because when else are you going to? Fresh, beautiful salads can come delectably decorated with seasonal ingredients or lush extras like burrata cheese. Carnivores might weep over the splendor of the meticulous pork belly preparations, which can be a 3-day process. The desserts are often simple, but usually standouts.

701 St. Charles Ave. (℃ **504/524-4114**. www.herbsaint.com. Reservations suggested for lunch and for 2 or more for dinner. Main courses $12–$14 lunch, $22–$27 dinner. AE, DC, DISC, MC, V. Mon–Fri 11:30am–1:30pm; Mon–Thurs 5:30–9:30pm; Fri–Sat 5:30–10pm.

Liborio's Cuban Restaurant *♠* CUBAN Nicely located in the Central Business District, this Cuban cafe attracts many local business folk at lunchtime, but despite the crowds, that might be the best time to go, when prices are very affordable (they do seem to be needlessly high at dinnertime). Plus, it's a fun space—the chartreuse sponged walls and pillowy parachute fabric upholstering the ceiling make for a festive and more aesthetically pleasing look than you might think from reading the description. Lazy ceiling fans and photos from the homeland put you in mind of Hemingway's Havana. Order the day's special or be like us, partial to Cuban specialties such as the tender, garlicky roast pork; the flatbread Cuban sandwich; and sweet fried plantains.

321 Magazine St. (℃ **504/581-9680**. Reservations suggested. Main courses $10–$18 lunch, $15–$28 dinner. AE, DC, DISC, MC, V. Mon–Sat 11am–3pm; Thurs–Sat 5:45–9pm.

Lüke 🀦🀦🀦 BISTRO Local chef John Besh's new dining locale has hit the ground running. It's hearty and authentic, but not stodgy French and German brasserie fare. There's so much to try here it's hard to narrow down a choice for you. *Flamen küche* is an Alsatian tort topped with chunks of bacon and caramelized onions. The *choucroûte maison* includes house-made sausages, pork belly, *cochon de lait* with cherry mustard and is, in short, one fine plate of pig. The big juicy cheeseburger, with caramelized onions and thick-cut bacon on an onion roll, will have you swear off fast-food imitations forever. The shrimp and grits demolishes other, dry versions around town. The handsome bistro is quite popular at lunch, no doubt in part due to the $15 express lunch special, an entree of the day plus a cup of soup. Save room for the mini profiteroles filled with warm chocolate custard.

333 St. Charles Ave. ℭ **504/378-2840.** www.lukeneworleans.com. Reservations strongly suggested at lunch. Main courses $12–$26 (mostly on lower end for lunch). AE, DC, DISC, MC, V. Daily 7am–11pm.

Palace Café 🀦🀦 CONTEMPORARY CREOLE This is where to go for low-key and non-intimidating yet still interesting dining. Housed attractively in the historic Werlein's for Music building, this popular Brennan family restaurant has the first sidewalk dining on Canal, thanks to some street renovations, which will be a treat on balmy nights. The menu focuses on evolving Creole cuisine. Be sure to order the crabmeat cheesecake appetizer, and possibly the escargots as well. As for main courses, they do fish especially well (the andouille-crusted fish is always spot on). Look for seasonal specials based on what comes from local farmers and fishermen, including house-made duck pastrami, crusted emu, or multiple duck preparations. The pork debris potpie is adorable comfort food. For dessert, they invented the by-now ubiquitous white-chocolate bread pudding, and no matter what others may claim, they have the best.

605 Canal St. ℭ **504/523-1661.** www.palacecafe.com. Reservations recommended. Main courses $12–$22 lunch, $15–$32 dinner. 3-course meal before 7pm $25. AE, DC, DISC, MC, V. Tues–Fri 11:30am–2:30pm; Tues–Sat 5:30–9pm; Sun brunch 10:30am–2:30pm.

Riche 🀦 BISTRO The first brasserie attempt by award-winning, national profile chef Todd English, this is a big, grand, all but over-the-top space with an almost tarty feel. It's a very good option for lunch, both for business and pleasure, as the portions are large, the prices (at this writing) reasonable, and the variety of menu options means a little something for everyone. In addition to fried po' boys, generously cut slices of daily quiche varieties, and a rich lobster cheddar melt sandwich, daily specials include possibilities such as a fine pulled pork sandwich. Dinner is a little more expensive, but early in the week brings fun with whole roasted suckling pigs. (Call ahead.) Finally, if pastry chef Jessica Mogardo is still there, make dessert a must-do; in a city largely stricken with boring desserts, her adventures in pineapple cake deconstruction and studies in strawberries and chocolate trio (including a thin mint popsicle) are joys.

In Harrah's hotel, 228 Poydras St. ✆ **504/533-6117.** Main courses $10–$17 lunch, $23–$34 dinner. AE, DC, DISC, MC, V. Mon–Fri 7–10:30am; Sat–Sun 11:30am–2pm; daily 6–10pm.

Tommy's ✿✿ FRENCH/ITALIAN   Those of you frustrated by the perennially long lines at Irene's in the Quarter will be delighted to know that Tommy's—the creation of Irene's eponymous co-founder—is more or less exactly the same; it has the same welcome waft of garlic that greets you from a block away and virtually the same menu. But Tommy's has one important difference: It takes reservations. Don't get us wrong, we love Irene's. But this space is less cramped in feel, if quite dark and chatty. (Forget deep conversations—the noise level is palpable.) And did we mention they take reservations? So you can actually come here and not wait 2 hours before you get to dig into fantastic chicken Rosemarino, chicken marinated in an olive oil, garlic, and rosemary sauce; and duck Tchoupitoulas, which some consider the best duck dish in New Orleans. Both dishes were made famous at Irene's, as is just about the entire menu.

746 Tchoupitoulas St. ✆ **504/581-1103.** www.tommyscuisine.com. Reservations preferred. Entrees $20–$29. AE, DISC, MC, V. Sun–Thurs 5:30–10pm; Fri–Sat 5:30–11pm.

INEXPENSIVE

Ernst Café AMERICAN   The same family has owned this old brick building since 1902. Located right next to Harrah's casino and featuring live blues music on Friday and Saturday nights, it's a big local scene, understandable given how late they stay open. Sandwiches, hamburgers, fried shrimp, salads, red beans and rice, and po' boys are on offer here.

600 S. Peters St. ✆ **504/525-8544.** www.ernstcafe.net. Main courses $10–$15. AE, DC, DISC, MC, V. Mon–Tues 3pm–"until" (usually between 2 and 6am); Wed–Sun 11am–"until."

Mother's ✿✿ SANDWICHES/CREOLE   Perhaps the proudest of all restaurants when New Orleans was named Fattest City in the U.S. was Mother's, whose overstuffed, mountain-size po' boys absolutely helped contribute to the results. It has long lines and a most typically New Orleans atmosphere (which is to say, humble, in the best way) and dining room (the "new" dining room is spiffier, if you care about such things), but who cares when faced with a Famous Ferdi Special—a giant roll filled with baked ham (the homemade house specialty), roast beef, gravy, and debris (the bits of beef that fall off when the roast is carved)? There's other food, including one of the best breakfasts in the city, but the po' boys are what New Orleans goes for, and you should, too. Be sure to allow time to stand in line, as there nearly always is one, though it can move quickly.

401 Poydras St. ℂ **504/523-9656**. www.mothersrestaurant.net. Menu items $1.75–$20. AE, MC, V. Mon–Sat 7:30am–8pm.

5 Uptown/The Garden District

For a map of restaurants in this section, see either the "Where to Dine in New Orleans" map on p. 80 or the "Where to Stay & Dine Uptown" map on p. 73.

EXPENSIVE

Brigtsen's ⟨𝒦 CAJUN/CREOLE   Nestled in a converted 19th-century house at the Riverbend, Brigtsen's is warm, intimate, and romantic. The individual dining rooms are small and cozy, each sweetly painted with murals, and the menu changes daily. Generous portions make appetizers superfluous, but their seasonal salads are so good and the BBQ shrimp with shrimp calas are hard to pass up. Brigtsen has a special touch with rabbit: One of his most mouth-watering dishes is an appetizer of rabbit tenderloin on a tasso-Parmesan grits cake with sautéed spinach and a Creole mustard sauce. You can't miss with any of the soups, especially the lovely butternut squash shrimp bisque, and there's an entree to please everyone. A broiled Gulf fish with crabmeat Parmesan crust and béarnaise sauce is a great piece of seafood. For the indecisive, a seafood platter offers samples of all sorts of fishy goodness, such as artichoke baked oyster or stuff piquillo pepper with shrimp and crabmeat con queso.

723 Dante St. ℂ **504/861-7610**. www.brigtsens.com. Reservations recommended. Main courses $22–$29. AE, DC, DISC, MC, V. Tues–Sat 5:30–10pm.

Clancy's ⟨𝒦 CREOLE   The food and neighborhood vibe alone should be worth the trip; it's a relief to get off the tourist path. The locals who cram into the smallish, oh-so-New Orleans room nightly are a loyal bunch, as New Orleans diners tend to be, but we have to say our last meal at Clancy's was only average and quite forgettable. We may have hit them on a bad night. But to ensure a better meal, follow the advice of those same locals and order the night's specials rather than sticking to the menu (though the duck dish on the menu is as good as duck gets). You could try the fried oysters with brie appetizer or smoked fried soft-shell crab topped with crabmeat (smoke flavor not overpowering, crab perfectly fried without a drop of grease to taint the dish), and veal topped with crabmeat and béarnaise sauce. Food too heavy? What the heck—make it even more so with desserts such as lemon icebox pie. One local said it was even better than his grandma's!

6100 Annunciation St. ℂ **504/895-1111**. Reservations recommended. Main courses $23–$29. AE, DC, DISC, MC, V. Mon–Sat 5:30–10:30pm; Thurs–Fri 11:30am–2pm.

Commander's Palace *★★* CREOLE   The much-beloved Commander's is perhaps *the* symbol of the New Orleans dining scene, and for good reason. The building has been a restaurant for a century, it's at the top (more or less) of the multi-branched Brennan family restaurant tree, and its chefs have gone on to their own fame and household-name status (Prudhomme and Emeril ring any bells?), plus they train and produce their own outstanding locals, so the tradition keeps going. The many months it spent shuttered— part of the roof was lost and rainwater got in, requiring a pretty much stripped-to-the-studs renovation inside and out—were a frustrating symbol of the pace of city recovery in general.

But now it's back, gleaming on the outside, and amusing on the inside with new, endearingly subtly eccentric decor. Such a relief. Service, once the gold standard for the city, as with every other establishment, remains a bit spotty in these trying staffing times, but it should never be less than eager. The current menu reflects the work chef Tory McPhail did during his months off. Favorites like the pecan-crusted Gulf fish and the tasso shrimp in pepper jelly appetizer remain, but new dishes reveal all sorts of culinary fun going on in the kitchen. A standout appetizer is the molasses and black pepper–cured pork belly. Chef Tory makes a daily gumbo of relatively unexpected ingredients that might convince even a committed Cajun cook to reconsider his own traditions. "Veal-Platte" is the amusingly named (it's a pun on a Cajun town) seared veal tenderloin covered in cracklins, while the seared duck breast (with mushrooms and shallots, a morel duck fond, and spicy honey) caused more than a few superlatives to be uttered. The dessert menu is undergoing modifications as new creations are added. We remain torn among such choices as the bread pudding soufflé, the seasonal strawberry shortcake, the signature crème brûlée, and the Creole cream cheesecake.

1403 Washington Ave. ℂ **504/899-8221.** www.commanderspalace.com. Main courses $30–$42. AE, DISC, MC, V. Mon–Fri 11:30am–1:30pm; daily 6–9:30pm; brunch Sat 11:30am–1pm and Sun 10:30am–1:30pm. Closed Christmas Day and Mardi Gras Day.

Gautreau's ✿ FRENCH   Extensive roof damage meant the usual to-the-studs renovations, but Gautreau's, a classy "old-timey" restaurant, succeeded in reopening with a new chef and a freshly redesigned menu that focuses on modern French cuisine. Here's the sort of thing you might have: the sweet mixed greens with pears, goat cheese, and a port vinaigrette—a marvelous salad in a town not known for salads (we wish it were larger), and wild mushroom and potato perogies. Pork tenderloin comes wrapped in bacon, with sides of creamed corn and other not so much French as Southern touches.

1728 Soniat St. ℂ **504/899-7397.** Main courses $22–$32. AE, MC, V. Tues–Sat 6–10pm.

Martinique Bistro ✿ FRENCH   This place is just far enough uptown to be off the regular tourist radar. Because it has only 44 seats when the courtyard is not open (100 with), you might have trouble getting a table. This is a sweet little bistro, long a local favorite, but one that hasn't quite survived the transition from its previous, gifted owner. Main-course staple shrimp with sun-dried mango and curry is still solid, as is the salmon, while the flank steak had the tenderness and robust flavor of venison, so much so a diner wondered if it might really be such. But the rest of the menu is hit-and-miss. If the weather permits, be sure to sit in the jasmine-scented courtyard.

5908 Magazine St. ℂ **504/891-8495.** Reservations recommended. Main courses $18–$30. AE, DISC, MC, V. Nov–May Fri–Sun 11am–2:30pm, Tues–Thurs 5:30–9:30pm, Fri–Sat 5:30–10pm, Sun 5:30–9pm; June–Oct Fri–Sun 11am–2:30pm, Tues–Thurs 6–9:30pm, Fri–Sat 6–10pm, Sun 6–9pm.

Table One ✿✿ BISTRO   While perhaps not the most exciting restaurant in the city, Table One is quite possibly the most beautiful; the downstairs is shiny classic brasserie including a handsome bar, while the upstairs is the classic New Orleans look, complete with gleaming chandeliers, tall windows, meticulously restored brick walls, dark polished wood, and working fireplaces. It's all fresh, new, and prettily maintained. No innovations on the menu, but the French country style pâté (with pork, duckling, and rabbit) with a spicy sweet shallot and cherry compote is hearty, the duran wheat is a strong flavor in the house-made pasta, and the filet mignon is one of the most tender in the city, a lovely cut of meat. A bleu cheese trio for dessert is one of the better options, though their cakes and parfaits are certainly fine.

2800 Magazine St. ✆ **504/872-9035.** Main courses $11–$18 lunch, $21–$29 dinner. AE, DC, DISC, MC, V. Fri–Sun 11am–3pm; Sun–Thurs 5–10pm; Fri–Sat 5–10:30pm.

Upperline ✦✦✦ ECLECTIC/CREOLE   In a small, charming house in a largely residential area, the Upperline is more low-key than high-profile places such as Emeril's. In its own way, though, it's every bit as inventive. It's a great place to try imaginative food at reasonable (by fancy-restaurant standards) prices. Standout appetizers include fried green tomatoes with shrimp rémoulade sauce (they invented this dish, which is now featured just about everywhere in town), spicy shrimp on jalapeño cornbread, duck confit, and fried sweetbreads. For entrees, there's moist roast duck with a tingly sauce (either plum or port wine), cane river country shrimp, and a fall-off-the-bone lamb shank. If you're lucky, there will be a special menu such as the all-garlic meal, in which even dessert contains garlic. For dessert, try warm honey-pecan bread pudding or chocolate-hazelnut mousse. The award-winning wine list focuses primarily on California selections.

1413 Upperline St. ✆ **504/891-9822.** www.upperline.com. Reservations suggested. Main courses $20–$32. AE, DC, MC, V. Wed–Sun 5:30–9:30pm.

MODERATE

Dante's Kitchen ✦✦ CONTEMPORARY LOUISIANA Dante's is too easily overlooked thanks to its left-of-center location and relatively low profile, but the reality is that it's just at the end of the St. Charles streetcar line. Further, its lively take on local cuisine, with a careful eye toward seasonal and local products, is worthy of greater fame. The bright and cheerful colors of the interior of its old house setting and the enthusiastic staff make it a pleasure from the start. At dinner, look for items such as redfish "on the half shell," the trio of filet mignon topped with pork debris and a Stilton sauce, and a housemade pâté plate that might include goose riellete with caper berries. Brunch is a strong alternative, especially given their splendid take on eggs Benedict, with tender rosemary crusted pork taking the place of the traditional Canadian bacon, a hint of honey adding sweetness to the hollandaise sauce, and a caramelized biscuit supporting it all.

736 Dante St. ℂ **504/861-3121.** www.danteskitchen.com. Reservations for parties of 6 or more only. Main courses $10–$16 brunch, $16–$24 dinner. AE, DISC, MC, V. Mon and Wed–Sun 5:30–10pm; Sat–Sun brunch 10:30am–2pm; closed Tues.

Dick & Jenny's ⋆⋆ ECLECTIC/CREOLE Don't let the out-of-the-way-on-a-depressing-industrial-street location (or, for that matter, a refusal to take reservations) keep you away from this reasonably priced, casual boho atmosphere restaurant. The room is small, and the wait may still be long, so you might want to time your visit for an off-hour. The menu, which remains very reasonably priced with generous portions, changes a great deal, but recent examples include an excellent summer fruit soup; solidly good spinach, mushroom, and mascarpone ravioli; blackened red fish with crawfish rice; pan-seared scallops with shrimp and sausage pie; and smoke tomato beurre. Each dish is a little busy—just one less layer on everything would help. Desserts include clever variations on classics including an ice-cream sandwich sundae with real hot fudge.

4501 Tchoupitoulas St. ℂ **504/894-9880.** Main courses $16–$24. AE, DISC, MC, V. Tues–Thurs 5:30–10pm; Fri–Sat 5:30–10:30pm.

Jacques-Imo's ⋆ ECLECTIC/CREOLE/SOUL FOOD We used to be really big fans of this local favorite, a funky, colorful neighborhood joint that the natives love. But the last few times we ate here, the food wasn't worth the wait, which can be absurdly long. So stick to the fried chicken (from a recipe from the late Austin Leslie, of Chez Helene and "Frank's Place" fame), or the catfish stuffed with crabmeat, or the solidly good shrimp Creole. Proceed with caution when it comes to the shrimp and alligator-sausage "cheesecake" (more like a quiche), which has both its fans and detractors, while lovers of chicken livers will certainly want the version here, on toast in a dark brown sauce. Try the three-layer chocolate (white, milk, and dark) mousse pie for dessert. Get there early or you'll have to wait for a table; but that may not be so bad when you're sharing a cold one under a banana tree on a warm Louisiana evening with a bunch of laid-back, like-minded souls.

8324 Oak St. ℂ **504/861-0886.** www.jacquesimoscafe.com. Reservations for 5 or more required. Main courses $14–$25. AE, DC, DISC, MC, V. Mon–Thurs 5–10pm; Fri–Sat 5–10:30pm.

Iris ⋆ CONTEMPORARY CREOLE Again, anyone who opens a new restaurant in New Orleans these days is something like a hero, and given that the chef-owner is a talented fellow, we have optimism regarding this small, pretty little place. Having said that, we also wish that the chef (who worked at Lilette before this and clearly learned well from the experience) would be just a little more bold and audacious, since he's currently sticking to some tried-and-true local contemporary formulas, not that one can really blame him. The menu changes daily, but possibilities include hamachi with grilled green garlic, sunchoke and cauliflower soup with sunflower shoots, and a pretty piece of Yukon salmon with a side of English peas and spinach. It's all very pretty, fresh food, meticulously prepared and a delicate contrast to heavier Creole fare around town. Portions are modest compared to other places, and the prices are a bit high for what you get.

8115 Jeannette St. ℂ **504/862-5848.** www.irisneworleans.com. Main courses $23–$29. AE, DISC, MC, V. Mon–Sat 6pm–"until."

La Crêpe Nanou ✪ FRENCH   La Crêpe Nanou is another not-so-secret local secret. It's always crowded. It's a romantic spot (windows angled into the ceiling let you gaze at the stars) that is simultaneously 19th century and quite modern. You can order crepes wrapped around a variety of stuffings, including crawfish. But you might want to save your crepe consumption for dessert (big and messy, full of chocolate and whipped cream) and concentrate instead on the big healthy salads and moist, flaky fish, particularly the whole grilled fish with herbs. It's big enough for two and is done to perfection. You can usually find knowledgeable locals ordering the mussels and extra bread to sop up the garlic white-wine sauce. Meat dishes come with your choice of sauce (garlic or cognac, for example).

1410 Robert St. ℂ **504/899-2670.** www.lacrepenanou.com. Main courses $12–$23. MC, V. Fri–Sun 6–11pm.

La Petite Grocery BISTRO   This Uptown restaurant, a pretty, if underlit, room with a relatively low noise level, generated big buzz when it opened, thanks to its pedigree (the owners are alums of the Anne Kearney Peristyle years); and thanks to some excellent reviews it quickly became one of the hottest culinary spots in town. But a sampling of visits came up with several quite good, one abysmal, and the rest firmly with a vote for "fine, but forgettable." The disappointment would probably be less if the hype weren't so great. The menu features nothing you won't find in similar bistro-style restaurants in town: unmemorable braised lamb shank, a pedestrian filet mignon over pommes lyonnaise, and dry pork shank. A foie gras pâté is good enough to finish, except for the bits of connective tissue disturbingly found within on two separate visits. Purées of root vegetables are often quite good—like gourmet baby food—and staff is good about special requests for sides and splits.

4238 Magazine St. ⓒ **504/891-3377.** Reservations highly recommended on weekends. Main courses $18–$24. AE, DC, MC, V. Tues–Sat 6–10:30pm.

Lilette ⓡⓡ BISTRO Lilette's chef-owner John Harris trained locally under Bayona's Susan Spicer, who sent him to work in France with Michelin-starred chefs. The result is a menu of more arty playfulness than many other local establishments, served in a space that uses the high ceiling and tile floor to good effect, though the result is a fashionable bistro space that would not look out of place in Tribeca. Sizzling shrimp bubbles as it arrives, just like the authentic Spanish tapas versions. Braised pork belly topped with a poached egg can be heavy rather than satisfyingly rich, but potato gnocchi in a sage brown butter sauce is light and fresh. While sandwiches are only at lunch, at any time of day you can get fancy (sometimes oddly hearty) and nicely composed dishes such as *boudin noir* (dark sausage) with homemade mustard, arugula with white balsamic vinaigrette, and grilled beets with goat cheese. Don't miss the curious signature dessert, little rounds of goat cheese crème fraîche delicately paired with pears poached in vanilla bean and raisin-flavored liquid, and topped with lavender honey—a marriage made on Mount Olympus.

3637 Magazine St. ⓒ **504/895-1636.** www.liletterestaurant.com. Reservations suggested. Main courses $9–$18 lunch, $19–$28 dinner. AE, DISC, MC, V. Tues–Sat 11:30am–2pm; Tues–Thurs 5:30–9:30pm; Fri–Sat 5:30–10:30pm.

Pascal's Manale ⓡ ITALIAN/STEAK/SEAFOOD Barbecued shrimp. This restaurant has built its reputation on that one dish, and you should come here if only for that. The place is crowded and noisy and verges on expensive, but it grows on you. It got flooded after Katrina, but extensive renovations restored the interior to just as it always was, down to the photos on the walls. It's still a top-notch place for raw oysters. The spicy barbecued-shrimp sauce may no longer be the best in the city (we are more partial these days to the buttery wonder served over at Mr. B's), but the shrimp within it—plump, sweet, kitten-size—are. Be sure to add sherry to the turtle soup, and be extra sure to skip the dull and even possibly icky desserts. Instead, get another order of shrimp. Just try not to think about your arteries too much; lick your fingers, enjoy, and vow to walk your socks off tomorrow.

1838 Napoleon Ave. ⓒ **504/895-4877.** Reservations recommended. Main courses $15–$32. AE, DC, DISC, MC, V. Wed–Fri 11:30am–2pm; Mon–Sat 5pm–"until."

INEXPENSIVE

Bluebird Cafe 👍👍 AMERICAN   Employees here tell the story of a man who awoke from an extended coma with these two words: Huevos rancheros. As soon as possible, he returned to the Bluebird for his favorite dish. A similar scene repeats each weekend morning when locals wake up with Bluebird on the brain. Why? Because this place consistently offers breakfast and lunch food that can restore and sustain your vital functions. Try the buckwheat pecan waffle, cheese grits, or homemade sausage and corned beef hash. You can also build your own omelet or see why the huevos rancheros enjoys its reputation (if you don't like runny eggs, ask for scrambled huevos). At midmorning on weekends, there is always a wait (up to 30 min.) out front. It's worth it.

3625 Prytania St. ✆ 504/895-7166. All items under $12. No credit cards. Wed–Fri 7am–2pm; Sat–Sun 8am–2pm.

Camellia Grill 👍👍 HAMBURGERS/SANDWICHES   Even though it's *only* been a part of the city's food culture since 1946, the Camellia Grill seems to have always been there. Consequently, when it wasn't there, for about 18 months after the floods, locals felt off-kilter, and plastered the front door with notes begging the place to return. It did, with a new owner who rehired all the same white-jacketed waiters (some there for 20 years or more) to serve you as you sit on a stool at the counter. The Camellia is famous for its omelets—heavy and fluffy at the same time and almost as big as a rolled-up newspaper. Notable omelet choices are the chili and cheese, and the potato, onion, and cheese. Don't forget the pecan waffle, a work of art. Wash it all down with one of the famous chocolate freezes and then contemplate a slice of the celebrated pie for dessert (the chocolate pecan is to die for).

626 S. Carrollton Ave. ✆ 504/309-2679. All items under $15. AE, DISC, MC, V. Sun–Thurs 8am–11pm; Fri–Sat 8am–1am.

Casamento's 👍👍 SEAFOOD   When the fatalities attributed to Katrina are tallied, the number will not be accurate, and not just because of post-storm confusion, but because there are many deaths that can, in their way, be blamed on the stress of the storm. Surely the death of Joe Casamento, whose father founded this oyster bar and who was, for 50 years, the best oyster opener in the city, can and should be counted. Joe spent his whole life above the shop, and never took a vacation. Joe suffered from emphysema, and died at age 80, the night he evacuated for Katrina, possibly in a panic over the fate of his city and the store that was his world. So eat here for him.

Not that you shouldn't do so on its own merits, because it probably is the best oyster joint in the city. The family restaurant takes oysters so seriously that it simply closes down when they're not in season. The oysters are cleanly scrubbed and well selected. You might also take the plunge and order an oyster loaf: a big, fat loaf of bread fried in butter, filled with oysters (or shrimp), and fried again to seal it. Casamento's also has terrific gumbo—perhaps the best in town.

4330 Magazine St. ⓒ **504/895-9761.** www.casamentosrestaurant.com. Main courses $4.95–$11. No credit cards. Wed–Sun 11am–2pm; Thurs–Sat 5:30–9pm. Closed June–Sept.

Franky & Johnny's ⓡ SEAFOOD   This is a favorite local hole-in-the-wall neighborhood joint with either zero atmosphere or enough for three restaurants, depending on how you view these things. And by "things" we mean plastic checked tablecloths, a ratty but friendly bar, and locals eating enormous soft-shell-crab po' boys with the crab legs hanging out of the bread and their mouths. You got your po' boys, your boiled or fried seafood platters with two kinds of salad, and goodness knows, you got your beer. Try that po' boy or the excellent red beans and rice with smoky sausage and other down-home dishes and know you are somewhere that isn't for tourists—and enjoy it all the more.

321 Arabella St. (at Tchoupitoulas St.). ⓒ **504/899-9146.** Main courses $5.95–$14. AE, DISC, MC, V. Mon–Sat 11am–9pm.

Joey K's ⓡ CREOLE/SEAFOOD   This is just a little local corner hangout, though one that savvy tourists have long been hip to. Indeed, it was a tourist who told us to order the trout Tchoupitoulas, and boy, were we happy—lovely pan-fried trout topped with grilled veggies and shrimp. Daily blackboard specials such as brisket, lamb shank, white beans with pork chops, or Creole jambalaya won't fail to please. Order it all to go, and you'll be dining like a real Uptown local.

3001 Magazine St. ⓒ **504/891-0997.** Main courses $6.95–$14. AE, DC, MC, V. Mon–Fri 11am–2:30pm and 5–8:30pm; Sat 8am–2:30pm and 5–8:30pm.

Slim Goodies Diner ⓡ DINER   We were already partial to this place, but when they busted out some heroic culinary moves, as the first restaurant in their neighborhood (if not in the city) to reopen, they won our hearts and loyalty forever. In the process, they not only became a meeting place for stressed-out hunkered-down locals, but they also demonstrated for other intrepid restaurant owners how they could do likewise. Come for classic diner food with modern diner clever names like "Low Carbonator" and burgers named after famous folks, though we aren't sure why the Robert Johnson has bacon and bleu cheese, unless it's something to do with the lengths one might go to (such as make a deal with the devil at the cross-roads) in order to have such a burger. There are large salads, omelets, and even sweet-potato pancakes and a biscuit topped with étouffée. It's a fine, fun stop while you are shopping, for an Uptown break-fast, or for a late-night snack before seeing an even later night show.

3322 Magazine St. ⓒ **504/891-3447.** www.slimgoodies.com. Everything under $10. No credit cards. Daily 6am–2pm.

6 Coffee, Tea & Sweets

Angelo Brocato's Ice Cream & Confectionary 🍦🍦🍦 ICE CREAM/SWEETS   In a constant stream of heartbreak, the sight of this sweet, genuine ice-cream parlor, which was celebrating its 100th birthday (run by the same family the entire time), under 5 feet of water, its classic sign askew, was particularly painful. By that same token, the news that the Brocato family (originally from Palermo; this establishment was a replica of ones found there) would be back was particularly joyful and inspiring. And that's even before you get to the goods. They make rich Italian ice cream (made fresh daily on the premises, and tasting not quite like gelato, which they also make, but similar), cookies, and candy in the kind of atmos-phere that is slowly being lost in this age of strip malls and super-stores. The chocolate ice cream is one of our all-time favorites, but the fresh lemon ice and pana cotta custard have brought us to our knees. The fresh cannolis are also inspired. Right on the new street-car line, it's not just nostalgia—it's still vibrant, a local tradition worthy of continuing another 100 years. And on hot days, it's vital!

214 N. Carrollton Ave. ⓒ **504/486-1465.** www.angelobrocatoicecream.com. Every-thing under $10. AE, DC, DISC, MC, V. Tues–Thurs 10am–10pm; Fri–Sat 10am–10:30pm; Sun 10am–9pm; closed Mon.

Café du Monde 🍦🍦🍦 *Moments* COFFEE   Excuse us while we wax rhapsodic. Since 1862 Café du Monde has been selling café au lait and beignets (and nothing but) on the edge of Jackson Square. And boy, was its reopening one of those moments when the city knew it would be coming back. A New Orleans landmark, it's *the* place for people-watching. Not only is it a must-stop on any trip to New Orleans, you may find yourself wandering back several times a day: for your morning beignet and coffee, your afternoon snack, and best of all, your 3am pick-me-up. What's a beignet? (Say ben-*yay*, by the way.) A square French doughnut–type object, hot and covered in powdered sugar. At three for about $1.75, they're a hell of a deal. Wash them down with chicory coffee, listen to the nearby buskers, ignore people trying to get your table, and try to figure out how many more stops you can squeeze in during your visit.

In the French Market, 800 Decatur St. ✆ **504/525-4544.** www.cafedumonde.com. 3 beignets for $1.75. No credit cards. Daily 24 hr. Closed Christmas. Additional location at Riverwalk Mall.

Creole Creamery 🐸🐸🐸 ICE CREAM Locals were already justly fond of this local ice-cream parlor, where innovative flavors are made fresh every day, but when it reopened about 3 weeks after Katrina, in a neighborhood (and city) where little else was available commercially, it earned a near fanatic loyal following. Thick, luscious ice cream with a rotating list of flavors from lavender-honey to red velvet cake, with stops at tiramisu, pepper, and more along the way. Completely refreshing, maybe even mandatory on a hot day, and with late enough hours to make it an option for a snack on the way to or from a club or bar Uptown.

4924 Prytania St. ✆ **504/894-8680.** Everything under $10. Cash only, no credit cards. Sun–Thurs noon–10pm; Fri–Sat noon–11pm.

EnVie COFFEE/BAKERY/SANDWICHES A Euro-style coffeehouse, very handsome, with a nice selection of drinks and pastries, some bagels and cream cheese, and even free Wi-Fi access. The staff is surly, but the location is excellent if you are waiting for the clubs on Frenchmen to get cranking.

1241 Decatur St. ✆ **504/524-3689.** Everything under $10. MC, V. Daily 7am–midnight.

La Boulangerie 🐸🐸🐸 BAKERY This bakery would be a jewel even if it were in a major bread city. Perhaps the only authentic baguettes in the city, the loaves are crusty on the outside, soft and flavorful on the inside. But we forget about the baguettes, perfect though they may be, because of the olive bread, an oval loaf studded with olives, and just slightly greasy (in a good way) with olive oil. Heaven. And, oh, the bleu-cheese bread they make only on weekends. Or the apple-bacon-onion loaves you have to order a day in advance. They also do marvelous croissants, chocolate-filled croissants, and other pastries, and even have savory sandwiches. Olive bread—and for that matter, many products—sells out early, so here is one (perhaps the only) reason to be an early bird in New Orleans. No coffee, though.

4526 Magazine St. (Uptown). ℂ **504/269-3777.** Loaf of bread $2–$6. No credit cards. Mon–Sat 6am–7pm; Sun 7am–1pm.

La Divinia Gelateria ℝℝ GELATO/ICE CREAM A superb new gelato place, part of the gelato and ice-cream boom that is taking over a town formerly most dedicated to snoballs for its frozen confections. This one has the best selection and the richest, most wonderful ice cream, but its interior needs work to make it a more inviting a place to dawdle. All dairy is made from Louisiana cows, plus they are a big part of the local sustainable and local food movement. Look for seasonal fruits and flavors, plus a daily rotation of options like dark chocolate with cayenne, or the honey sesame goat's milk, or sorbet made with local Abita Turbodog beer.

4519 Magazine. ℂ **504/342-2634.** Scoops $3.25–$5.45. AE, MC, V. Sun–Thurs 11am–10pm; Fri–Sat 11am–11pm.

P.J.'s Coffee & Tea Company ℝ COFFEE P.J.'s is a local institution, with a lot of locations around town. It offers a great variety of teas and coffees, and it roasts its own coffee beans. The iced coffee is made by a cold-water process that requires 12 hours of brewing. P.J.'s also serves mochas, cappuccinos, and lattes. The granita is prepared with P.J.'s Espresso Dolce iced coffee concentrate, frozen with milk and sugar, and served as a coffee "slushee"—great on hot, muggy days.

5432 Magazine St. ℂ **504/895-2190.** www.pjscoffee.com. 95¢–$4. AE, DC, MC, V. Daily 6am–8pm. P.J.'s has branches at Tulane University, ℂ **504/865-5705;** 644 Camp St., ℂ **504/529-3658;** and 7624 Maple St., ℂ **504/866-7031,** among other locations.

Royal Blend Coffee & Tea House ℝ COFFEE/SANDWICHES This place is set back off the street; to reach it, you walk through a courtyard. Order a sandwich, quiche, or salad at the counter and take it out into the courtyard. On Saturday afternoons, weather permitting, a guitarist serenades diners. (You can also eat inside, but it's not as much fun.) If you're just in the mood for coffee and pastry, they have plenty of that, too, and the pastry menu changes daily.

621 Royal St. ℂ **504/523-2716.** www.royalblendcoffee.com. Pastries 85¢–$2.95; lunch items $3.25–$8.50. AE, MC, V. Daily 8am–6pm. Royal Blend has a branch at 204 Metairie Rd. in Metairie, ℂ **504/835-7779.**

Rue de la Course ℝ COFFEE This is your basic comfy boho coffeehouse: cavernous in appearance, thanks to a very tall ceiling; manned by cool, friendly college kids; and full of locals seeking a quick pick-me-up, lingering over the paper, or poring over their journals. In addition to prepared coffee and tea, Rue de la Course sells decent sandwiches as well as a few newspapers and local magazines.

3121 Magazine St. ⓒ 504/899-0242. No credit cards. Mon–Fri 7am–midnight; Sat–Sun 7:30am–midnight. 2nd location: 1140 S. Carrollton Ave., ⓒ 504/861-4343.

Sophie's Gelato and Old Time Ice Cream Parlor 𝄐𝄐
GELATO/ICE CREAM   Oh, the humanity. There you are, shopping at one end of Magazine, and it's hot, and all you want is some of that fabulous ice cream that seems to be all over the city. But it's so far away! No worries; Sophie's is right behind you and ready to rescue you. All their gelato is made in-house, and they are happy to pop it into a malt or fountain soda, while you belly up to the low old-fashioned counter. Try the Heavenly Road—a mix of Rocky Road and Heavenly Hash. They also have nice sandwiches like chicken salad with walnuts, raisins, and apples for a quick pick-me-up.

1912 Magazine St. ⓒ 504/581-0291. Scoops $3–$6.50. AE, DC, DISC, MC, V. Daily 10am–10pm summer, 11am–9:30pm rest of the year.

Sucre 𝄐 SWEETS/ICE CREAM   This high-end confectionaire is heavy on style but a little disappointing in terms of culinary results. The gelato is solid but not nearly as interesting as La Divina's next door. But aesthetically, it beats all its closest competitors—a candy-colored, eye-popping work of modern design, where visitors are much-inclined to linger. We just wish we found that their picture-perfect pastries and candy tasted as good as they—and their setting—look.

3025 Magazine St. ⓒ 504/520-8311. www.shopsucre.com. Sun–Thurs 7am–10pm; Fri–Sat 7am–midnight.

5

Sights to See & Places to Be

A common sentiment voiced in the days immediately following Katrina was "I wish I had gotten to New Orleans again/for the first time before this happened." The implication is that New Orleans is no longer that place the speaker wished to visit. And that's sort of true—and yet absolutely not. By some act of grace, the most notable, from a visitor's perspective, and historic portions of New Orleans, the French Quarter and the Garden District (along with much of the rest of Uptown) were not flooded and escaped serious storm damage. With few exceptions, one is hard-pressed to find any major Katrina damage to a noteworthy (or even minor) attraction in these areas. Within the two most prominent neighborhoods, almost all significant sights have reopened, including several fine museums and the city's world-class aquarium and sweet zoo, though ongoing budget problems have prevented others from reopening. While it is true that a geographical majority of New Orleans remains either in uneasy flux, in ruins, or in stasis, these areas were never on the ordinary visitor's path. Virtually all of what the average tourist would want to see not only survived the disaster but also—2 plus years later—doesn't look as though anything happened to it at all. Its very existence makes it all the more precious.

Still, our favorite New Orleans activities involve walking, eating, listening to music, and dancing. If instead of sightseeing, that's all you do while you're visiting the town, we won't complain. At least you are here, and it is still here, and that may be enough for now.

But some people feel guilty if they don't take in some culture or history while they're on vacation. And all the local attractions do need the visitors in order to stay open. Besides, there will be occasions when you'll need to escape the rain or heat!

Frankly, New Orleans itself is one big sight—it's one of the most unusual-looking cities in America, and being nice and flat, it's just made for exploring on foot. Don't confine yourself to the French Quarter. Yes, it certainly is a seductive place, but to go to New Orleans and never leave the Quarter is like going to New York,

New Orleans Attractions

To METAIRIE
S. Broad Ave. **5** **6**

Jefferson
Soniat
Robert
Upperline
Valmont
Cadiz
Jena

Southern
Baptist Hospital

Napoleon Ave.
Gen. Pershing
Milan
Gen. Taylor

Louisiana Parkway
Toledano
Washington
Seminole

S. Dorgenois
S. Rocheblave
S. Johnson
S. Pneur

Earhart Blvd. (Calliope St.)
Erato

BROADMOOR
S. Claiborne Ave.
S. Derbigny
S. Roman

Marengo

Willow
Clara
Magnolia
S. Robertson
Freret

Martin Luther King Blvd.

Erato
Thalia
Clio

Constantinople
Pariston
Amelia
Foucher
Delachaise
Louisiana Ave.

La Salle
S. Liberty
Loyola
S. Saratoga
4th 3rd 2nd 1st
Dryades
Baronne
Carondelet
St. Charles

New Orleans
Arena

Union Passenger
Terminal (Amtrak)

Simon Bolivar

Pontchartrain Expwy.

UPTOWN

Harmony
8th 7th
6th
Prytania
Pl.

Jackson Ave.

Terpsichore
Euterpe
Polymnia

Clio
Thalia

Lee
Circle

1

2
GARDEN DISTRICT

Coliseum
Chestnut
Camp
Magazine
Constance
Laurel
Annunciation
Chippewa
St. Thomas
Rousseau

Washington
Josephine
St. Andrew
St. Mary
Felicity

Prytania
St. Charles Ave.

Melpomene
Magazine
Constance
Annunciation

Euterpe

3

4

BR
90

New Orleans
General Hospital

Race
Orange
Market
Richard

(i) Information
Ferry Service to
Algiers Point
• • • Riverwalk streetcar
route/stops
– • – St. Charles streetcar
route/stops
– • – Vieux Carre loop
route/stops

Audubon Park & Audubon Zoo **1**
Backstreet Cultural Museum **20**
Blaine Kern's Mardi Gras World **21**
City Park **18**
Confederate Memorial Museum **3**
Contemporary Arts Center **9**
Creole Queen **13**
Cypress Grove and
Greenwood Cemeteries **6**

Degas House **19**
Gallier Hall **10**
Harrah's Casino **14**
John James Audubon
(boat to Audubon Zoo) **15**
Lafayette No 1 Cemetery **2**
Louisiana Children's Museum **11**
Metairie Cemetery **5**
National World War II Museum **4**

New Orleans Convention Center **12**
Mew Orleans Museum of Art **18**
Ogden Museum of Southern Art **8**
Pitot House **18**
St. John's Bayou **18**
St. Louis Cemetery No. 1 **17**
St. Louis Cemetery No. 2 **16**
St. Louis Cemetery No. 3 **18**
The Superdome **7**

remaining in Greenwich Village, and believing you've seen Manhattan. Katrina has only demonstrated how fragile this place is, so take in more of it, as much as you can. Make sure you also take time to stroll the lush Garden District, marvel at the oaks in City Park, ride the streetcar (or the bus temporarily covering its route) down St. Charles Avenue and gape with jealousy at the gorgeous homes, or go visit some gators on a swamp tour. And yes, if you like, go and see the ruined neighborhoods; it's the only way to comprehend the extent of the disaster.

But if you leave the Quarter only to visit clubs and restaurants, we won't blame you a bit.

1 The French Quarter

There's a great deal to the French Quarter—history, architecture, cultural oddities—and to overlook all that in favor of T-shirt shops and the ubiquitous bars is a darn shame. Which is not to say we don't understand, and rather enjoy, the lure of the more playful angle of the area. We just don't want you to end up like some tourists who never get off Bourbon Street. (And regardless of where you go in the Quarter, please remember that you are walking by people's homes.)

A French engineer named Adrien de Pauger laid out the Quarter in 1718, and today it's a great anomaly in America. Almost all other American cities have torn down or gutted their historic centers, but thanks to a strict preservation policy, the area looks exactly as it always has and is still the center of town.

Aside from Bourbon Street, you will find the most bustling activity at **Jackson Square,** where musicians, artists, fortunetellers, jugglers, and those peculiar "living statue" performance artists gather to sell their wares or entertain for change. Their numbers were diminished somewhat, like so much else, after Katrina, but they are returning as they find their way home and the tourists come back. **Royal Street** is home to numerous pricey antiques shops, with other interesting stores on **Chartres and Decatur streets** and the cross streets between.

The closer you get to **Esplanade Avenue** and toward **Rampart Street,** the more residential the Quarter becomes, and buildings are entirely homes. Walk through these areas, and peep in through any open gate; surprises await in the form of graceful brick and flagstone-lined courtyards filled with foliage and bubbling fountains. The Quarter is particularly pedestrian-friendly. The streets are laid

Audubon Aquarium of
the Americas **9**

Backstreet Cultural Museum **22**

Beauregard-Keyes House **18**

The Cabildo **12**

The 1850 House **15**

Gallier House Museum **17**

Germaine Wells
Mardi Gras Museum **5**

Hermann-Grima House **4**

The Historic French Market **20**

Historic New Orleans Collection **7**

Musée Conti Wax Museum **3**

New Orleans Historic
Voodoo Museum **10**, **16**

New Orleans Historical
Pharmacy Museum **11**

Old Absinthe House **6**

Old Ursuline Convent **19**

The Old U.S. Mint **21**

Our Lady of Guadeloupe Chapel-
International Shrine of St. Jude **2**

The Presbytère **14**

St. Louis Cathedral **13**

St. Louis Cemetery No. 1 **1**

Williams Research Center **8**

out in an almost perfect rectangle, so it's nearly impossible to get lost. It's also so well traveled that it is nearly always safe, particularly in the central parts. Again, as you get toward the fringes (especially near Rampart) and as night falls, you should exercise caution; stay in the more bustling parts and try not to walk alone.

MAJOR ATTRACTIONS

Audubon Aquarium of the Americas ✸✸✸ *Kids*   The world-class Audubon Institute's Aquarium of the Americas was one of the saddest of so many terrible Katrina stories. The facility had superb hurricane contingency plans, not to mention engineering that one only wishes was shared by the levee system, and consequently both building and fishy residents came through the initial storm beautifully. But as the days following the evacuation stretched out, and the staff was forced to leave so that government relief efforts could use the building as a staging area, generators failed, and most of its 10,000 fish died, breaking the hearts of not only the staff who worked so hard to keep their charges healthy and alive, but of just about anyone who had ever visited this lovely place. Survivors included the popular otter pair, the penguins, the leafy and weedy sea dragons, and Midas, the 250-pound sea turtle. The facility's reopening in May 2006 was a cause for rejoicing. As it gets back up to speed, this will once again be a world-class aquarium, highly entertaining and painlessly educational, with beautifully constructed exhibits.

The aquarium is on the banks of the Mississippi River, a very easy walk from the main Quarter action. Five major exhibit areas and dozens of smaller aquariums hold a veritable ocean of aquatic life native to the region (especially the Mississippi River and Gulf of Mexico) and to North, Central, and South America. You can walk through the underwater tunnel in the Caribbean Reef exhibit and wave to finny friends swimming all around you, view a shark-filled re-creation of the Gulf of Mexico, or drop in to see the penguin exhibit. We particularly like the walk-through Waters of the Americas, where you wander in rainforests (complete with birds and piranhas) and see what goes on below the surface of swamps; one look will quash any thoughts of a dip in a bayou. Not to be missed are a fine exhibit on frogs, the impossibly cute giant sea otters, and the ongoing drama of the sea horse exhibit. The long-anticipated **Insectarium** (yep, a museum dedicated to the over 900,000 species of things that creep, crawl, and flutter) sustained a lot of damage, but it should be open sometime in 2008. The Insectarium will be in the former U.S. Customs House, at 423 Canal St. The **IMAX theater** 𝒜𝒜 shows two or three films at regular intervals. The Audubon Institute also runs the city's zoo at Audubon Park Uptown (p. 147).

1 Canal St., at the river. © **800/774-7394** or 504/581-4629. www.audoboninstitute. org. Aquarium $17 adults, $13 seniors, $10 children 2–12. IMAX $8 adults, $7 seniors, $5 children. Combination aquarium/IMAX tickets $31 adults, $22 seniors, $21 children. Aquarium Tues–Sun 10am–5pm. IMAX Tues–Sun 10am–5pm. Call for showtimes; advance tickets recommended. Closed Mardi Gras and Christmas.

The Historic French Market 𝒜𝒜 (Kids)   Legend has it that the site of the French Market was originally used by Native Americans as a bartering market. It began to grow into an official market in 1812. From around 1840 to 1870, it was part of Gallatin Street, an impossibly rough area so full of bars, drunken sailors, and criminals of

every shape and size that it made Bourbon Street look like Disneyland. Today it's a mixed bag, and not nearly as colorful as its past.
Still, both sections have been spiffed up with an extensive renovation
that was completed in late 2007. The Farmers Market makes a fun
amble as you admire everything from fresh produce and fish to more
tourist-oriented items like hot sauces and Cajun and Creole mixes.
Snacks like gator on a stick (when was the last time you had that?)
will amuse the kids. The Flea Market, a bit farther down from the
Farmers Market, is considered a must-shop place, but the reality is
that many of the goods are kind of junky: T-shirts, jewelry, hats,
purses, toys, sunglasses, and so on. Still, some good deals can be had.
On Decatur St., toward Esplanade Ave. from Jackson Sq. ℂ **504/522-2621.** www.
frenchmarket.org. Daily roughly 9am–6pm (tends to start shutting down about an
hour before closing).

St. Louis Cathedral ℛ   The St. Louis Cathedral prides itself on
being the oldest continuously active cathedral in the United States.
What usually doesn't get mentioned is that it is also one of the ugli-
est. The outside is all right, but the rather grim interior wouldn't
give even a minor European church a run for its money.

Still, its history is impressive and somewhat dramatic. The cathedral formed the center of the original settlement, and it is still the
major landmark of the French Quarter. This is the third building to
stand on this spot. A hurricane destroyed the first in 1722. On
Good Friday 1788, the bells of its replacement were kept silent for
religious reasons rather than ringing out the alarm for a fire—which
eventually went out of control and burned down more than 850
buildings, including the cathedral itself.

Rebuilt in 1794, the structure was remodeled and enlarged
between 1845 and 1851 by J. N. B. de Pouilly. The brick used in its
construction was taken from the original town cemetery and was
covered with stucco to protect the mortar from dampness. And then
there was Katrina. The first post-K Mass was held in October 2005,
and was attended by hundreds of locals. It's worth going inside to
catch one of the free docent tours; the knowledgeable guides are full
of fun facts about all of the above, plus the windows and murals and
how the building nearly collapsed once from water table sinkage. Be
sure to look at the slope of the floor: Clever architectural design
somehow keeps the building upright even as it continues to sink.
615 Pere Antoine Alley. ℂ **504/525-9585.** Fax 504/525-9583. www.stlouiscathedral.
org. Free admission. Mon–Sat 9am–4pm; Sun 9am–2pm. Free tours usually given in
the afternoon, pending docent availability.

HISTORIC BUILDINGS

Beauregard-Keyes House ♠　This "raised cottage," with its Doric columns and handsome twin staircases, was built as a residence by a wealthy New Orleans auctioneer, Joseph Le Carpentier, in 1826. Confederate Gen. P. G. T. Beauregard lived in the house with several members of his family for 18 months between 1865 and 1867, and from 1944 until 1970, it was the residence of Frances Parkinson Keyes (pronounced *Cause*), who wrote many novels about the region. Mrs. Keyes left her home to a foundation, and the house, rear buildings, and garden are open to the public. The gift shop has a wide selection of her novels.

1113 Chartres St., at Ursulines St. ℭ **504/523-7257.** Fax 504/523-7257. Admission $5 adults; $4 seniors, students, and AAA members; $2 children ages 6–13; free for children under 6. Mon–Sat 10am–3pm. Tours on the hour. Closed Sun and holidays.

The 1850 House ♠　James Gallier, Sr., and his son designed the historic Pontalba Buildings for the Baroness Micaela Almonester de Pontalba. The rows of town houses on either side of Jackson Square were the largest private buildings in the country at the time. Legend has it that the baroness, miffed that her friend Andrew Jackson wouldn't tip his hat to her, had his statue erected in the square, where to this day he continues to doff his chapeau toward her apartment on the top floor of the Upper Pontalba. It's probably not true, but we never stand in the way of a good story.

In this house, the Louisiana State Museum presents a demonstration of life in 1850, when the buildings opened for residential use. The self-guided tour uses a fact-filled sheet that explains in detail the history of the interior and the uses of the rooms, which are filled with period furnishings arranged to show how the rooms were typically used. It vividly illustrates the difference between the "upstairs" portion of the house, where the upper-middle-class family lived in comfort (and the children were largely confined to a nursery and raised by servants), and the "downstairs," where the staff toiled in considerable drudgery to make their bosses comfortable. *Note:* As we write this, the House remains closed, but the interesting gift shop is open with irregular hours.

Lower Pontalba Building, 523 St. Ann St., Jackson Sq. ℭ **800/568-6968** or 504/568-6968. Fax 504/568-4995. http://lsm.crt.state.la.us/1850ex.htm.

Old Absinthe House　The Old Absinthe House was built in 1806 and now houses the Old Absinthe House bar and two restaurants. The drink for which the building and bar were named is now outlawed in this country (it caused blindness and madness), but you can sip a legal libation in the bar and feel at one with the famous types who came before you, listed on a plaque outside: William Thackeray, Oscar Wilde, Sarah Bernhardt, and Walt Whitman. Andrew Jackson and the Lafitte brothers plotted their desperate defense of New Orleans here in 1815.

The house was a speak-easy during Prohibition, and when federal officers closed it in 1924, the interior was mysteriously stripped of its antique fixtures—including the long marble-topped bar and the old water dripper that was used to infuse water into the absinthe. Just as mysteriously, they all reappeared down the street at a corner establishment called, oddly enough, the Old Absinthe House Bar (400 Bourbon St.). The latter has closed, and a neon-bedecked daiquiri shack opened in its stead. The fixtures have since turned up in one of the restaurants on this site! The bar is covered with business cards (and drunks), so don't come here looking to recapture old-timey and classy atmosphere, but it's still a genuinely fun hangout.

240 Bourbon St., between Iberville and Bienville sts. © **504/523-3181.** www.old absinthehouse.com. Free admission. Sun–Thurs 9:30am–2am; Fri–Sat 9:30am–4am.

Old Ursuline Convent ✿✿   Forget tales of America being founded by brawny, brave, tough guys in buckskin and beards. The real pioneers—at least, in Louisiana—were well-educated French women clad in 40 pounds of black wool robes. That's right; you don't know tough until you know the Ursuline nuns, and this city would have been a very different place without them.

The Sisters of Ursula came to the mudhole that was New Orleans in 1727 after a journey that several times nearly saw them lost at sea or to pirates or disease. Once in town, they provided the first decent medical care (saving countless lives) and later founded the first local school and orphanage for girls. They also helped raise girls shipped over from France as marriage material for local men, teaching the girls everything from languages to homemaking of the most exacting sort.

The convent dates from 1752 (the sisters themselves moved uptown in 1824, where they remain to this day), and it is the oldest building in the Mississippi River valley and the only surviving building from the French colonial period in the United States.

1110 Chartres St., at Ursulines St. © **504/529-3040.** Admission prices and times not determined at press time.

The Old U.S. Mint ✿✿ (Kids)   The Old U.S. Mint, a Louisiana State Museum complex, houses exhibits on New Orleans jazz and on the city's Carnival celebrations. The first exhibit contains a comprehensive collection of pictures, musical instruments, and other artifacts connected with jazz greats—Louis Armstrong's first trumpet is here. It tells of the development of the jazz tradition and New Orleans's place in that history. Across the hall is a stunning array of Carnival mementos from New Orleans and other communities across Louisiana—from ornate Mardi Gras costumes to a street scene complete with maskers and a parade float.

Unfortunately, the Mint got hammered by Katrina. Luckily, nothing important inside got wet, but the organization still needed to move everything out, thanks to a month without climate control, to reevaluate the state of the collection. Because they needed to redesign exhibits, not to mention renovate pretty much everything, the Mint will reopen at some point in 2008.

400 Esplanade Ave., at N. Peters St. (enter on Esplanade Ave. or Barracks St.). ℂ 800/568-6968 or 504/568-6968. Fax 504/568-4995.

Our Lady of Guadeloupe Chapel—International Shrine of St. Jude ⚘

This is known as the "funeral chapel." It was erected (in 1826) conveniently near St. Louis Cemetery No. 1, specifically for funeral services, so as not to spread disease through the Quarter. We like it for three reasons: the catacomb-like devotional chapel with plaques thanking the Virgin Mary for favors granted, the gift shop full of religious medals including a number of obscure saints, and the statue of St. Expedite. He got his name, according to legend, when his crate arrived with no identification other than the word EXPEDITE stamped on the outside. Now he's the saint you pray to when you want things in a hurry. (We are not making this up.) Expedite has his cults in France and Spain and is also popular among the voodoo folks. He's just inside the door on the right.

411 N. Rampart St., at Conti St. Parish office: ℂ 504/525-1551. www.saintjude shrine.com. Daily 9am–5pm.

MUSEUMS

In addition to the destinations listed here, you might be interested in the **Germaine Wells Mardi Gras Museum** at 813 Bienville St., on the second floor of Arnaud's restaurant (ℂ 504/523-5433; fax 504/581-7908), where you'll find a private collection of Mardi Gras costumes and ball gowns dating from around 1910 to 1960. Admission is free, and the museum is open during restaurant hours.

The Cabildo ⚘⚘⚘   Constructed from 1795 to 1799 as the Spanish government seat in New Orleans, the Cabildo was the site of the signing of the Louisiana Purchase transfer. It was severely damaged by fire in 1988 and closed for 5 years for reconstruction, which included total restoration of the roof by French artisans using 600-year-old timber-framing techniques. It is now the center of the Louisiana State Museum's facilities in the French Quarter, located right on Jackson Square. A multiroom exhibition informatively, entertainingly, and exhaustively traces the history of Louisiana from exploration through Reconstruction from a multicultural perspective. It covers all aspects of life, not just the obvious discussions of slavery and the battle for statehood. Topics include antebellum music, mourning and burial customs, immigrants and how they fared here, and the changing roles of women in the South (which occupies a large space). As you wander through, each room seems more interesting than the last. Throughout are portraits of nearly all the prominent figures from Louisiana history plus other fabulous artifacts, including Napoleon's death mask.

701 Chartres St. ℂ 800/568-6968 or 504/568-6968. Fax 504/568-4995. http://lsm.crt.state.la.us/cabildo/cabildo.htm. Admission $6 adults, $5 students and seniors, free for children under 12. Tues–Sun 9am–5pm.

Gallier House Museum ⓕ James Gallier, Jr. (it's pronounced *Gaul*-ee-er, by the way; he was Irish, not French), designed and built the Gallier House Museum as his residence in 1857. Anne Rice fans will want to at least walk by—this is the house she was thinking of when she described Louis and Lestat's New Orleans residence in *Interview with the Vampire.* Gallier and his father were leading New Orleans architects—they also designed the old French Opera House, the original St. Charles Exchange Hotel, Municipality Hall (now Gallier Hall), and the Pontalba Buildings. This carefully restored town house contains an early working bathroom, a passive ventilation system, and furnishings of the period. Combination tickets with the Hermann-Grima House are available for an additional $4.

1118 and 1132 Royal St., between Governor Nicholls and Ursulines sts. ℂ 504/525-5661. www.hgghh.org. Admission $6 adults; $5 seniors, students, AAA members, and children ages 8–18; free for children under 8. Mon–Fri 10am–4pm. Tours offered at 10am, 11am, noon, 2pm, and 3pm.

Hermann-Grima House ⓕ The 1831 Hermann-Grima House is a symmetrical Federal-style building (perhaps the first in the Quarter) that's very different from its French surroundings. The knowledgeable docents who give the regular tours make this a satisfactory stop at any time, but keep an eye out for the frequent special tours. At Halloween, for example, the house is draped in typical 1800s mourning, and the docents explain mourning customs. The tour of the house, which has been meticulously restored, is one of the city's more historically accurate offerings. The house also contains one of the Quarter's last surviving stables, complete with stalls.

820 St. Louis St. ℂ **504/525-5661.** www.hgghh.org. Admission $6 adults; $5 seniors, students, AAA members, and children ages 8–18; free for children under 8. Mon–Fri 10am–4pm. Tours offered at 10am, 11am, noon, 2pm, and 3pm.

Historic New Orleans Collection–Museum/Research Center ★★ The Historic New Orleans Collection's museum of local and regional history is almost hidden away within a complex of historic French Quarter buildings. The oldest, constructed in the late 18th century, was one of the few structures to escape the disastrous fire of 1794. These buildings were owned by the collection's founders, Gen. and Mrs. L. Kemper Williams. There are excellent tours of the Louisiana history galleries, which feature choice items from the collection—expertly preserved and displayed art, maps, and original documents like the transfer papers for the Louisiana Purchase (1803). The collection is owned and managed by a private foundation, not a governmental organization, and therefore offers more historical perspective and artifacts than boosterism. The Williams Gallery, also on the site, is free to the public and presents changing exhibitions that focus on Louisiana's history and culture, including a terrific Katrina-related one. If you want to see another grandly restored French Quarter building (and a researcher's dream), visit the **Williams Research Center,** 410 Chartres St., near Conti Street (ℂ **504/598-7171**), which houses and displays the bulk of the collection's many thousands of items. Admission is free.

533 Royal St., between St. Louis and Toulouse sts. ℂ **504/523-4662.** Fax 504/598-7108. www.hnoc.org. Free admission; tours $5. Tues–Sat 9:30am–4:30pm; Sun 10:30am–4:30pm. Tours offered Tues–Sat 10 and 11am and 2 and 3pm. Closed major holidays and Mardi Gras.

Musée Conti Wax Museum ★ (Kids) You might wonder about the advisability of a wax museum in a place as hot as New Orleans, but the Musée Conti holds up fine. This place is pretty neat—and downright spooky in spots. A large section is devoted to a sketch of Louisiana legends (Andrew Jackson, Napoleon, Jean Lafitte, Marie Laveau, Huey Long, a Mardi Gras Indian, Louis Armstrong, and Pete Fountain) and historical episodes. The descriptions, especially of the historical scenes, are surprisingly informative and witty. They are currently open only for group tours by appointment.

917 Conti St. ℂ **504/525-2605.** www.get-waxed.com.

New Orleans Historical Pharmacy Museum ★ Founded in 1950, the New Orleans Historical Pharmacy Museum is just what the name implies. In 1823 the first licensed pharmacist in the United States, Louis J. Dufilho, Jr., opened an apothecary shop here. The Creole-style town house doubled as his home, and he cultivated the herbs he needed for his medicines in the interior courtyard. Inside you'll find old apothecary bottles, voodoo potions, pill tile, and suppository molds as well as the old glass cosmetics counter. Unfortunately, the old-timey atmosphere is assisted by itty-bitty information cards attached to the exhibits with minimal facts listed in ancient typefaces or spidery handwriting—too bad.

514 Chartres St., at St. Louis St. *©* **504/565-8027**. www.pharmacymuseum.org. Currently open for tours by appointment only.

New Orleans Historic Voodoo Museum   Some of the hardcore voodoo practitioners in town might scoff at the Voodoo Museum, but it is really the only opportunity for tourists to get acquainted with the history and culture of voodoo. Don't expect high-quality, comprehensive exhibits—the place is dark, dusty, and musty. There are occult objects from all over the globe plus some articles that allegedly belonged to the legendary Marie Laveau. Unless someone on staff talks you through it (which they will, if you ask), you might come away with more confusion than facts. Still, it's an adequate introduction—and who wouldn't want to bring home a voodoo doll from here? There is generally a voodoo priestess on-site, giving readings and making personal gris-gris bags.

724 Dumaine St., at Bourbon St. (historic voodoo). *©* **504/680-0128**. www.voodoo museum.com. Admission $7 adults; $5.50 students, seniors, and military; $4.50 high school students; $3.50 grade school students. Cemetery tour $19. Daily 10am–6pm.

The Presbytère ★★★   The Presbytère was planned as housing for clergy but was never used for that purpose. It's part of the Louisiana State Museum, which has turned the entire building into a smashing Mardi Gras museum, one that puts all other efforts in town to shame. (The Presbytère only lost a window or two, but due to staffing issues is currently operating with severely limited hours, though those should have expanded by the time you read this.)

Five major themes (History, Masking, Parades, Balls, and the Courir du Mardi Gras) trace the history of this high-profile but frankly little-understood (outside of New Orleans) annual event. The museum does an excellent job of summing up to outsiders the complex history of the city's major holiday, which is so much more than just rowdy college kids displaying nekkid body parts. The exhibits are stunning and the attention to detail is startling, with everything from elaborate Mardi Gras Indian costumes to Rex

Queen jewelry from the turn of the 20th century. There is almost too much to see (and if you are sincerely interested, you will want to read most of the detailed graphics), so allow a couple of hours to take it all in properly.

751 Chartres St., Jackson Sq. ✆ **800/568-6968** or 504/568-6968. Fax 504/568-4995. http://lsm.crt.state.la.us. Admission $6 adults, $5 seniors and students, free for children under 13. Fri–Sun 10am–4pm.

2 Outside the French Quarter

UPTOWN & THE GARDEN DISTRICT

If you can see just one thing outside the French Quarter, make it the Garden District. It has no significant historic buildings or important museums—it's simply beautiful. In some ways, even more so than the Quarter, this is New Orleans. Authors as diverse as Truman Capote and Anne Rice have been enchanted by its spell. Gorgeous homes stand quietly amid lush foliage, elegant but ever so slightly (or more) decayed. You can see why this is the setting for so many novels; it's hard to imagine that anything real actually happens here.

TROLLING ST. JOHN'S BAYOU & LAKE PONTCHARTRAIN ✸✸✸

St. John's Bayou is a body of water that originally extended from the outskirts of New Orleans to Lake Pontchartrain, and it's one of the most important reasons New Orleans is where it is today. Jean Baptiste Le Moyne, Sieur de Bienville, was commissioned to establish a settlement in Louisiana that would both make money and protect French holdings in the New World from British expansion. Bienville chose the spot where New Orleans now sits because he recognized the strategic importance of "back-door" access to the Gulf of Mexico provided by the bayou's linkage to the lake. Boats could enter the lake from the Gulf and then follow the bayou until they were within easy portage distance of the mouth of the Mississippi River. Area Native American tribes had used this route for years.

The early path from the city to the bayou is today's Bayou Road, an extension of Governor Nicholls Street in the French Quarter. Modern-day Gentilly Boulevard, which crosses the bayou, was another Native American trail.

As New Orleans grew and prospered, the bayou became a suburb as planters moved out along its shores. In the early 1800s, a canal was dug to connect the waterway with the city, reaching a basin at the edge of Congo Square. The bayou became a popular recreation area with fine restaurants and dance halls (as well as meeting places

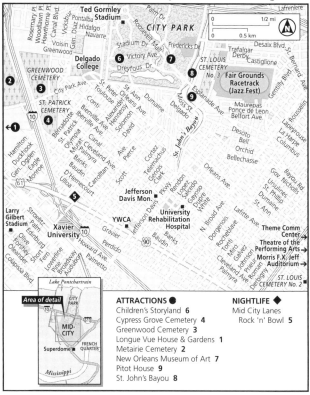

ATTRACTIONS ●

Children's Storyland **6**
Cypress Grove Cemetery **4**
Greenwood Cemetery **3**
Longue Vue House & Gardens **1**
Metairie Cemetery **2**
New Orleans Museum of Art **7**
Pitot House **9**
St. John's Bayou **8**

NIGHTLIFE ◆

Mid City Lanes
Rock 'n' Bowl **5**

for voodoo practitioners, who held secret ceremonies along its shores). Gradually, New Orleans reached beyond the French Quarter and enveloped the whole area.

The canal is gone, filled in long ago, and the bayou is a meek re-creation of itself, though it did overflow its banks during the post-Katrina flooding. It is no longer navigable (even if it were, bridges were built too low to permit the passage of boats of any size), but residents still prize their waterfront sites, and rowboats and sailboats sometimes make use of the bayou's surface. This is one of the prettiest areas of New Orleans—full of the old houses tourists love to marvel at without the hustle, bustle, and confusion of more high-profile locations. A walk along the banks and through the nearby neighborhoods is one of our favorite things to do on a nice afternoon.

GETTING THERE   The simplest way to reach St. John's Bayou from the French Quarter is to drive straight up Esplanade Avenue about 20 blocks (you can also grab the bus that says ESPLANADE at any of the bus stops along the avenue).Right before you reach the bayou, you'll pass **St. Louis Cemetery No. 3** (just past Leda St.). It's the final resting place of many prominent New Orleanians, among them Father Adrien Rouquette, who lived and worked among the Choctaw; Storyville photographer E. J. Bellocq; and Thomy Lafon, the black philanthropist who bought the old Orleans Ballroom as an orphanage for African-American children and put an end to its infamous "quadroon balls," where well-bred women of mixed color would socialize with and become the mistresses of white men. Just past the cemetery, turn left onto Moss Street, which runs along the banks of St. John's Bayou. If you want to see an example of an 18th-century West Indies–style plantation house, stop at the **Pitot House,** 1440 Moss St. (p. 144).

To continue, drive along Wisner Boulevard, on the opposite bank of St. John's Bayou from Moss Street, and you'll pass some of New Orleans's grandest modern homes—a sharp contrast to those on Moss Street. At this point, you can make a Katrina-damage tour that takes you through the once-flooded neighborhood of Gentilly, all the way to Lake Pontchartrain. Stay on Wisner to Robert E. Lee Boulevard, turn right, drive to Elysian Fields Avenue, and then turn left. That's the University of New Orleans campus on your left, which didn't have as much flooding as some of the other major campuses in the city (such as Dillard), though it did have a great deal of wind damage, and underground electrical systems took on water. Classes have resumed and the campus is coming back to life. At any point, you can take a street off to the left or the right if you wish to go through the neighborhoods in more detail, though by the time you read this, there may be less to see, depending on what sort of plans have been made for reconstruction. Regardless, please remember these are neighborhoods, not sights, and treat whatever you see, even if it's abandoned desolation, with respect.

Turn left onto the broad concrete highway, Lake Shore Drive. It runs for 5½ miles along the lake, and normally in the summer, the parkway alongside its seawall is swarming with swimmers and picnickers. On the other side are more luxurious, modern residences. Thanks to higher ground, these and other houses nearby did not flood, though they did sustain incredible wind damage. Further, the road buckled. About 2 miles down the road to the west is the fishing-oriented Bucktown neighborhood, which was totally devastated by the 17th Street Canal breech, including the marina, where expensive yachts were piled on top of each other by the power of the storm. Commercial fishing fleets (terribly hard hit by the storm) of some kind have been working out of Bucktown since the late 1800s. But as engineers need to reclaim some of the area for a temporary floodgate for the canal, fishermen, some of whom have been working this area for decades, may need to move elsewhere. The beloved Sid-Mar's restaurant is gone for good. As you return, you can drive through the Lakeview neighborhood, south of Robert E. Lee, between Canal and City Park. Here, houses look fine on the outside, but watch for the now-fading telltale water marks demonstrating that these homes sat in anywhere from 6 to 10 feet of water. At this writing, many have been gutted, with owners still trying to figure out what to do next. By the time you visit, presumably some will have been renovated or destroyed.

Lake Pontchartrain is some 40 miles long and 25 miles wide. Native Americans once lived along both sides, and it was a major waterway long before white people were seen in this hemisphere. You can drive across it over the 24-mile Greater New Orleans Causeway, the longest bridge in the world.

MUSEUMS & GALLERIES

Backstreet Cultural Museum *★* The city would be nothing without the rhythms of such rituals as brass bands, second lines, social clubs, jazz funerals, and the wholly unique Mardi Gras Indians, and this collection gathers remarkable examples and explanations for all of them in one place. It's not as slick as similar efforts at the Presbytère, but it contains even more special examples of such art as the feathered and sequined wonders that are Mardi Gras Indians' handmade suits. It's also located right in the heart of the Treme, the neighborhood that spawned so much of what is celebrated here. The owner, Sylvester, is an eccentric trip, but not only has he carefully documented this vital culture, he's also the real New Orleans, so spend some time with him.

1116 St. Claude Ave. (C) **504/522-4806.** www.backstreetmuseum.org. Admission $5. Tues–Sat 10am–5pm.

Confederate Memorial Museum *★★* Not far from the French Quarter, the Confederate Museum was established in 1891 and currently houses the second-largest collection of Confederate memorabilia in the country. It opened so soon after the end of the war that many of the donated items are in excellent condition. Among these are 125 battle flags, 50 Confederate uniforms, guns, swords, photographs, and oil paintings. You'll see personal effects of Confederate Gen. P. G. T. Beauregard and Confederate President Jefferson Davis (including his evening clothes), part of Robert E. Lee's silver camp service, and many portraits of Confederate military and civilian personalities. It's somewhat cluttered and not that well laid out—for the most part, only buffs will find much of interest here, though they can have remarkable temporary exhibitions.

929 Camp St., at St. Joseph's. ☏ **504/523-4522.** www.confederatemuseum.com. Admission $7 adults; $5 students, active military, and seniors; $2 children under 12. Weds–Sat 10am–4pm.

Contemporary Arts Center ☆☆ Redesigned in the early 1990s to much critical applause, the Contemporary Arts Center (CAC) is a main anchor of the city's young arts district (once the city's old Warehouse District, it's now home to a handful of leading local galleries). Over the past 2 decades, the center has consistently exhibited influential and groundbreaking work by regional, national, and international artists in various mediums.

900 Camp St. ☏ **504/528-3805.** Fax 504/528-3828. www.cacno.org. Gallery admission $5, $3 seniors, free for members. Performance and event tickets $7–$60. Thurs–Sun 11am–4pm.

National World War II Museum ☆☆☆ Opened on the anniversary of D-day, June 6, 2000, this is the creation of the late best-selling author (and *Saving Private Ryan* consultant) Stephen Ambrose, and it is the only museum of its kind in the country. It tells the story of all 19 U.S. amphibious operations worldwide on that fateful day of June 6, 1944. A rich collection of artifacts (including some British Spitfire airplanes) coupled with top-of-the-line educational materials (including an oral-history station) makes this one of the highlights of New Orleans.

A panorama allows visitors to see just what it was like on those notorious beaches. There is also a copy of Eisenhower's contingency speech, in which he planned to apologize to the country for the failure of D-day—thankfully, it was a speech that was never needed nor delivered. Volunteers who served on D-day are often around, ready to tell their own history in vivid and riveting detail.

945 Magazine St., in the Historic Warehouse District. ☏ **504/527-6012.** www.dday museum.org. Admission $14 adults, $8 seniors, $6 active or retired military with ID and children ages 5–17, free for military in uniform and children under 5. Tues–Sun 9am–5pm. Closed holidays.

New Orleans Museum of Art ⓐⓐ   Often called NOMA, this museum is located in an idyllic section of City Park. The front portion of the museum is the original large, imposing neoclassical building ("sufficiently modified to give a subtropical appearance," said the architect Samuel Marx); the rear portion is a striking contrast of curves and contemporary styles.

The museum opened in 1911 after a gift to the City Park Commission from Isaac Delgado, a sugar broker and Jamaican immigrant. Today it houses a 40,000-piece collection including pre-Columbian and Native American ethnographic art; 16th- through 20th-century European paintings, drawings, sculptures, and prints; Early American art; Asian art; a gallery entirely devoted to Fabrege; and one of the six largest decorative glass collections in the United States. A great addition to the city's artistic offerings came when the museum opened the **Besthoff Sculpture Garden** ⓐⓐⓐ, 5 acres of gardens, grass, and walkways that spotlight 50 modern sculptures by artists such as Henry Moore, Gaston Lachaise, Elizabeth Frink, George Segal, and others, including a version of the famous pop art LOVE sculpture. The garden, which lost only one piece to the storm (and the artist had it repaired by the beginning of 2006!) has quickly become a New Orleans cultural highlight and is open Wednesday to Sunday from 10am to 5pm, with free admission.

1 Collins Diboll Circle, at City Park and Esplanade. ⓒ **504/658-4100.** www.noma. org. Admission $8 adults, $7 seniors (over 64) and students, $4 children 3–17, free to Louisiana residents. Wed–Sun 10am–4:30pm. Closed most major holidays.

The Ogden Museum of Southern Art ⓐⓐⓐ   The premier collection of Southern art in the United States. Though the building is dazzling, it is built around an atrium that takes up a great deal of space that could be devoted to still more displays. It does make for a dramatic interior, but given such a marvelous collection, one is greedy for more art rather than more architecture. But the facility is wonderful, the artists are impressive, and the graphics are well designed, informative, and often humorous. Just the permanent exhibit of self-taught/outsider art alone makes this worth a visit. Special exhibits are thoughtfully constructed, often containing enriching details—for example a blues soundtrack for a display of Delta musicians, a video documentary on the late Benny Andrews. Though the hours (at press time) are still limited, they have resumed their delightful Ogden After Hours, which includes a live band (anything from 1930s country to old Delta blues guys to the New Orleans Klezmer All-Stars) playing in the atrium, adding a soundtrack to your visit.

925 Camp St. ⓒ **504/539-9600.** www.ogdenmuseum.org. Admission $10 adults, $8 seniors and students, $5 children 5–17. Thurs 6–8pm; Fri–Sun 11am–4pm.

MORE INTERESTING NEW ORLEANS BUILDINGS

Degas House 🌣 Legendary French Impressionist Edgar Degas felt very tender toward New Orleans; his mother and grandmother were born here, and he spent several months in 1872 and 1873 visiting his brother at this house. It was a trip that resulted in a number of paintings, and this is the only residence or studio associated with Degas anywhere in the world that is open to the public. One of his paintings showed the garden of the house behind his brother's. His brother liked that view, too; he later ran off with the wife of the judge who lived there. His wife and children later took back her maiden name, Musson. The Musson home, as it is formally known, was erected in 1854 and has since been sliced in two and redone in an Italianate manner. Both buildings have been restored and are open to the public via a tour. A very nice (though humble) B&B is also run on the premises.

2306 Esplanade Ave., north of the Quarter, before you reach N. Broad Ave. ⓒ **504/821-5009.** www.degashouse.com. $10 adults, $8 seniors. Daily 10am–5pm by advance appointment only.

Gallier Hall This impressive Greek Revival building was the inspiration of James Gallier, Sr. Erected between 1845 and 1853, it served as City Hall for just over a century and has been the site of many important events in the city's history—especially during the Reconstruction and Huey Long eras. Several important figures in Louisiana history lay in state in Gallier Hall, including Jefferson Davis and General Beauregard. More than 5,000 mourners came to Gallier Hall on July 14, 2001, to pay their respects to the flamboyant R&B legend Ernie K-Doe, who was laid out in a white costume and a silver crown and scepter before being delivered to his final resting place in the company of a big, brassy jazz procession.

545 St. Charles Ave. Not usually open to the public.

Pitot House 🌣 The Pitot House is a typical West Indies–style plantation home, restored and furnished with early-19th-century Louisiana and American antiques. Dating from 1799, it originally stood where the nearby modern Catholic school is. In 1810 it became the home of James Pitot, the first mayor of incorporated New Orleans (he served 1804–05). Tours here are usually given by a most knowledgeable docent and are surprisingly interesting and informative.

1440 Moss St., near Esplanade Ave. ℭ **504/482-0312**. Fax 504/482-0363. www. pitothouse.org. Admission $5 adults, $4 seniors and students, free for children under 8, parties of 10 or more $3 each. Wed–Fri 10am–3pm or by appointment.

The Superdome ℛ Completed in 1975 (at a cost of around $180 million), the Superdome is a landmark civic structure that the world will never look at the same way again. When it was proposed as a shelter during Katrina, that suggestion was intended as the last resort for those who simply had no other evacuation choice. As such, adequate plans were not in place, and when tens of thousands of refugees came or were brought there, within 24 hours it turned into hell on earth. Along with the Convention Center, it became a symbol of suffering, neglect, and despair, as people were trapped without sufficient food, water, medical care, or, it seemed, hope.

As it happened, the New Orleans Saints reopened the Superdome in 2006 with much hoopla for its first home game, against the Atlanta Falcons on Monday Night Football. The halftime show was anchored by a special blend of Green Day and U2, singing their charity cover of an old punk song. Over and over, regulars and even those who had taken refuge here remarked on the gleaming success of the $118-million renovation that wiped out any physical trace of the misery the Dome hosted during the dark Katrina days. As if that wasn't enough, the Saints won! And they went on to a winning season and playoff berths, for once! We won't comment on hopes for their future season, as we don't want to jinx it, but do join us locals in a chant of "WHO DAT?!"

Inside, no posts obstruct the spectator's view of sporting events, be they football, baseball, or basketball, while movable partitions and seats allow the building to be configured for almost any event. Most people think of the Superdome as a sports center only (the Super Bowl has been held here numerous times, and the Sugar Bowl is back), but this flying saucer of a building has played host to conventions, balls, and big theatrical and musical productions.

1500 block of Poydras St., near Rampart St. ℭ **504/587-3663**. www.superdome.com.

FLOATING ACROSS THE RIVER TO ALGIERS POINT

Algiers, annexed by New Orleans in 1870, stretches across the Mississippi River from New Orleans. and it is easily accessible via the free ferry that runs from the base of Canal Street. *Take note:* This ferry is one of New Orleans's best-kept secrets—it's a great way to get out onto the river and see the skyline. With such easy access (a ferry leaves every 15–20 min.), who knows why the point hasn't been better assimilated into the larger city, but it hasn't. Though it's only about ¼ mile across the river from downtown and the French Quarter, it still has the feel of an undisturbed turn-of-the-20th-century suburb.

The last ferry returns at around 11:15pm, but be sure to check the schedule before you set out, just in case. While you're over there, you might want to stop in at:

Blaine Kern's Mardi Gras World *ⓇⓇ* *Kids*   Few cities can boast a thriving float-making industry. New Orleans can, and no float maker thrives more than Blaine Kern, who makes more than three-quarters of the floats used by the various krewes every Carnival season. Blaine Kern's Mardi Gras World offers tours of its collection of float sculptures and its studios, where you can see floats being made year-round. Yes, they were back at work on the 2006 Mardi Gras, despite losing many already-completed floats, shortly after Katrina. (Nothing can stop the party!) Visitors see sculptors at work, doing everything from making small "sketches" of the figures to creating and painting the enormous sculptures that adorn Mardi Gras floats each year. You can even try on some heavily bejeweled and dazzling costumes (definitely bring your camera!). Although they could do more with this tour, the entire package does add up to a most enjoyable experience, and it is rather nifty to see the floats up close. All tours include King Cake and coffee.

223 Newton St., Algiers Point. ⓒ **800/362-8213** or 504/361-7821. www.mardigras world.com. Admission $17 adults, $13 seniors (over 65), $10 children 4–11, free for children under 4. Daily 9:30am–4:30pm. Last tour at 4:30pm. Closed Mardi Gras, Easter, Thanksgiving, and Christmas. Cross the river on the Canal St. Ferry and take the free shuttle from the dock (it meets every ferry).

3 Parks & Gardens

One of the many unsettling details following weeks of Katrina flooding was how normally verdant New Orleans had turned to shades of gray and brown. The vegetation had drowned. Regular rainfall is restoring New Orleans's lushness, but parks and gardens all took a beating from high winds, from battered plants to fallen trees. There is something particularly painful about the loss of the latter, especially centuries-old oaks. With enough funds and TLC, all but the most badly damaged buildings can be repaired, but a massive old oak cannot be replaced in our lifetime. Look for most of the following to be perhaps a bit less substantial, foliage-wise, than they might have been in previous years, though with some nurturing, they should all come back.

PARKS

Audubon Park *★★ Kids*   Across from Loyola and Tulane universities, Audubon Park and the adjacent Audubon Zoo (see "A Day at the Zoo," below) sprawl over 340 acres, extending from St. Charles Avenue all the way to the Mississippi River. This tract once belonged to city founder Jean-Baptiste Le Moyne and later was part of the Etienne de Boré plantation, where sugar was granulated for the first time in 1794. Although John James Audubon, the country's best-known ornithologist, lived only briefly in New Orleans (in a cottage on Dauphine St. in the French Quarter), the city has honored him by naming both the park and the zoo after him. There is no historical evidence to suggest that Audubon was much of a golfer; nevertheless, a golf course now fills the middle of the park that bears his name.

The huge trees with black bark are live oaks; some go back to plantation days, and more than 200 additional ones were recently planted here, though any number of young and old oaks did not survive Hurricane Katrina. Still, a gratifyingly large number of trees are left, which is good, because with the exception of the trees, it's not the most visually interesting park in the world—it's just pretty and a nice place to be. The park includes the Ogden Entrance Pavilion and Garden (at St. Charles Ave.) and a smattering of gazebos, shelters, fountains, and statuary.

Without question, the most utilized feature of the park is the 1¾-mile paved, traffic-free road that loops around the lagoon and golf course. Along the track are 18 exercise stations; tennis courts and horseback-riding facilities can be found elsewhere in the park. Check out the pavilion on the riverbank for one of the most pleasant views of the Mississippi you'll find. The Audubon Zoo is toward the back of the park, across Magazine Street.

6500 Magazine St., between Broadway and Exposition Blvd. ℂ 504/581-4629. www.auduboninstitute.org. **Note:** The park opens daily at 6am and officially closes at 10pm.

City Park *★★★*   Once part of the Louis Allard plantation, City Park has been here a long time and has seen it all—including that favorite pastime among 18th-century New Orleans gentry: dueling. At the entrance, you'll see a statue of General P. G. T. Beauregard, whose order to fire on Fort Sumter opened the Civil War and who New Orleanians fondly refer to as "the Great Creole." The extensive, once-beautifully landscaped grounds were, unlike Audubon Park, Katrina-ized, enduring serious flooding. Given what it went through, it looks pretty good, but full recovery will take some time. It holds botanical gardens and a conservatory, four golf courses, picnic areas, lagoons for boating and fishing, tennis courts, a bandstand, two miniature trains, and **Children's Storyland,** an amusement area, including fairy-tale figures upon which one can climb and carouse, and an antique carousel, though at press time it was closed for repairs with no reopening date scheduled (see "Especially for Kids," later in this chapter). At Christmastime, the mighty oaks (too many of which fell during the storm), already dripping with Spanish moss, are strung with lights—quite a magical sight—and during Halloween there is a fabulous haunted house. You'll also find the **New Orleans Museum of Art** at Collins Diboll Circle, on Lelong Avenue, in a building that is itself a work of art (see "Museums & Galleries," earlier in this chapter).

1 Palm Dr. ℂ 504/482-4888. www.neworleanscitypark.com. Daily 6am–7pm.

GARDENS
Longue Vue House & Gardens 🖈🖈   The Longue Vue House is a unique expression of Greek Revival architecture set on an 8-acre estate. It's like stumbling across a British country-house estate.

Constructed from 1939 to 1942, Longue Vue House & Gardens is listed on the National Register of Historic Places and is accredited by the American Association of Museums. The mansion was designed to foster a close rapport between indoors and outdoors, with vistas of formal terraces and pastoral woods. The charming gardens, some inspired by the Generalife, the former summerhouse of the sultans in Granada, Spain, naturally got pounded by the storm and flooding, requiring extensive restoration. Replanting is ongoing (salt content in the soil has made some of this process drag on), but it's already looking pretty good. Look also for fountains and a colonnaded loggia. It goes without saying that this is a must for garden enthusiasts, but you might be surprised what a nice time you could have regardless. We are completely smitten with the delightful Discovery Garden, fully back up and running. Once again, kids can play (and maybe even learn) from various clever and amusing exhibits.

7 Bamboo Rd., New Orleans, near Metairie. ℂ 504/488-5488. www.longuevue.com. Admission $10 adults, $9 seniors, $5 children and students. Wed–Sat 10am–5pm; Sun 1–5pm. Hourly tours start at 10am. Closed Jan 1, Mardi Gras, Easter Sunday, July 4th, Labor Day, Thanksgiving, and Dec 24–25.

A DAY AT THE ZOO
Audubon Zoo 🖈🖈🖈 *Kids*   It's been more than 20 years since the Audubon Zoo underwent a total renovation that turned it from one of the worst zoos in the country into one of the best. The achievement

is still worth noting, and the result is a place of justifiable civic pride that delights even non-zoo fans. What's more, nearly perfectly planned and executed hurricane preparation meant the zoo virtually sailed through the catastrophe, with almost zero animal loss.

Here, in a setting of subtropical plants, waterfalls, and lagoons, some 1,800 animals (including rare and endangered species) live in natural habitats rather than cages. Don't miss the replica of a Louisiana swamp (complete with a rare white gator) or the "Butterflies in Flight" exhibit, where more than 1,000 butterflies live among lush, colorful vegetation. A memorable way to visit the zoo is to arrive on the stern-wheeler **John James Audubon** (see "Organized Tours," below) and depart on the St. Charles Avenue streetcar. You can reach the streetcar by walking through Audubon Park or by taking the free shuttle bus.

6500 Magazine St. ✆ **504/581-4629.** www.auduboninstitute.org. Admission $12 adults, $9 seniors (65 and over), $7 children 2–12. Tues–Sun 10am–5pm. Last ticket sold 1 hr. before closing. Closed Mardi Gras Day, Thanksgiving Day, and Dec 25.

4 New Orleans Cemeteries ★★★

Along with Spanish moss and lacy iron balconies, the cities of the dead are part of the indelible landscape of New Orleans. Their ghostly and inscrutable presence enthralls visitors, who are used to traditional methods of burial—in the ground or in mausoleums.

Why are bodies here buried aboveground? Well, it rains in New Orleans—a lot—and then it floods. Soon after New Orleans was settled, it became apparent that Uncle Etienne had an unpleasant habit of bobbing back to the surface (doubtless no longer looking his best). Add to that cholera and yellow fever epidemics, which helped increase not only the number of bodies but also the infection possibility, and given that the cemetery of the time was inside the Vieux Carré, it's all pretty disgusting to think about.

So in 1789 the city opened St. Louis No. 1, right outside the city walls on what is now Rampart Street. The "condo crypt" look—the dead are placed in vaults that look like miniature buildings—was inspired to a certain extent by the famous Père Lachaise cemetery in Paris. Crypts were laid out haphazardly in St. Louis No. 1, which quickly filled up even as the city outgrew the Vieux Carré and expanded around the cemetery. Other cemeteries soon followed and eventually were incorporated into the city proper. They have designated lanes, making for a more orderly appearance. The rows of tombs look like nothing so much as a city—a city where the dead inhabitants peer over the shoulders of the living.

Tips **Safety First**

You will be warned against going to the cemeteries alone and urged to go with a scheduled tour group (see "Organized Tours," below). Thanks to their location and layout—some are in dicey neighborhoods, and the crypts obscure threats to your safety—some cemeteries can be quite risky, making visitors prime pickings for muggers and so forth. Other cemeteries, those with better security and in better neighborhoods, not to mention with layouts that permit driving, are probably safe. Ironically, two of the most hazardous, St. Louis No. 1 and Lafayette No. 1, are often so full of tour groups (though somewhat less so these days) that you could actually go there without one and be fairly safe. On the other hand, a good tour is fun and informative, so why not take the precaution?

If you're going to make a day of the cemeteries, you should also think about renting a car. You won't be driving through horrendous downtown traffic, you can visit tombs at your own pace, and you'll feel safer.

For many years, New Orleans cemeteries were in shambles. Crypts lay open, exposing their pitiful contents—if they weren't robbed of them—bricks lay everywhere, marble tablets were shattered, and visitors might even trip over stray bones. Thanks to local civic efforts, several of the worst eyesores have been cleaned up, though some remain in deplorable shape. Though it may seem silly, concerns were high for the fate of the cemeteries during the disaster days, because they are such an important part of the New Orleans landscape. But "the system worked," as one local expert said; the tombs sailed through with no problems and are marked only with the same high-water marks on their sides borne by any other structure in the flooded areas.

THREE CEMETERIES YOU SHOULD SEE WITH A TOUR

St. Louis No. 1   This is the oldest extant cemetery (1789) and the most iconic. Here lie Marie Laveau, Bernard Marigny, and assorted other New Orleans characters. Louis the vampire from Anne Rice's *Vampire Chronicles* even has his (empty) tomb here. Also, the acid-dropping scene from *Easy Rider* was shot here.

Basin St. between Conti and St. Louis sts.

St. Louis No. 2   Established in 1823, the city's next-oldest cemetery is unfortunately in such a terrible neighborhood (next to the so-
called Storyville Projects) that regular cemetery tours don't usually
bother with it. If there is a tour running when you are in town, go—
it's worth it. Marie Laveau II, some Storyville characters, and others
lie within its 3 blocks.

Note: As of this writing, there is no regular tour of St. Louis No.
2, which is absolutely unsafe. Do not go there, even in a large group,
without an official tour.

N. Claiborne Ave. between Iberville and St. Louis sts.

Lafayette No. 1   Right across the street from Commander's Palace
restaurant, this is the lush Uptown cemetery. Once in horrible condition, it's been beautifully restored. Anne Rice's Mayfair witches
have their family tomb here.

1427 Sixth St.

SOME CEMETERIES YOU COULD SEE ON YOUR OWN

If you decide to visit the cemeteries below on your own, please exercise caution. Take a cab to and from or consider renting a car for the
day. Most of these cemeteries (such as St. Louis No. 3 and Metairie)
have offices that can sometimes provide maps; if they run out, they
will give you directions to any grave location you like. All have sort-
of-regular hours—figure from 9am to 4pm as a safe bet.

Cypress Grove and Greenwood Cemeteries   Located across
the street from each other, both were founded in the mid-1800s by
the Firemen's Charitable and Benevolent Association. Each has
some highly original tombs; keep your eyes open for the ones made
entirely of iron. These two cemeteries are an easy streetcar ride up
Canal Street from the Quarter.

120 City Park Ave. and 5242 Canal Blvd. By car, take Esplanade north to City Park
Ave., turn left until it becomes Metairie Ave.

Metairie Cemetery   Don't be fooled by the slightly more modern look—some of the most amazing tombs in New Orleans are
here. Not to be missed is the pyramid-and-Sphinx Brunswig mau-
soleum and the "ruined castle" Egan family tomb, not to mention
the former resting place of Storyville madam Josie Arlington. Other
famous residents include Confederate General P. G. T. Beauregard
and jazz greats Louis Prima and Al Hirt.

5100 Pontchartrain Blvd. ℂ **504/486-6331.** By car, take Esplanade north to City
Park Ave., turn left until it becomes Metairie Ave.

St. Louis No. 3   Conveniently located next to the Fair Grounds racetrack (home of the Jazz Fest), St. Louis No. 3 was built on top of a former graveyard for lepers. Storyville photographer E. J. Bellocq lies here. The Esplanade Avenue bus will bring you here.
3421 Esplanade Ave.

5 Organized Tours

IN THE FRENCH QUARTER

Historic New Orleans Tours 𝕂𝕂𝕂 (✆ 504/947-2120; www.tourneworleans.com) is the place to go for authenticity rather than sensationalism. Here, the tour guides are carefully chosen for their combination of knowledge and entertaining manner, and we cannot recommend the guides or the tours highly enough. The daily French Quarter tours are the best straightforward, nonspecialized walking tours of this neighborhood. They also offer a Voodoo tour, a Haunted tour, and a Garden District tour. Costs for all tours are $15 adults, $13 students and seniors with ID, $7 children ages 6 to 12, and free for children under 6.

The Bienville Foundation 𝕂𝕂𝕂, run by Roberts Batson (✆ 504/945-6789; info@decafest.org; www.decafest.org), offers a live-on-stage Scandal Tour entitled "Amazing Place, This New Orleans," and a highly popular and recommended Gay Heritage Tour. The tours last roughly 2½ hours and generally cost $20 per person. Times and departure locations also change seasonally, so call or e-mail to find out what's happening when.

Kenneth Holdrich, a professor of American literature at the University of New Orleans, runs **Heritage Literary Tours** 𝕂𝕂𝕂, 732 Frenchmen St. (✆ 504/949-9805). Aside from his considerable academic credentials, he knew both Tennessee Williams and the mother of John Kennedy Toole. In addition to a general tour about the considerable literary legacy of the French Quarter, some tours, arranged in advance, can be designed around a specific author, like the Tennessee Williams tour. The narratives are full of facts both literary and historical, are loaded with anecdotes, and are often downright humorous. Group tours ($20 per person for adults) can be "scheduled for your convenience."

BEYOND THE FRENCH QUARTER

Author Robert Florence (who has written two excellent books about New Orleans cemeteries) loves his work, and his **Historic New**

Orleans Tours ᕕᕕᕕ (✆ **504/947-2120**) are full of meticulously researched facts and more than a few good stories. A very thorough tour of the Garden District and Lafayette Cemetery (a section of town not many of the other companies go into) leaves daily at 11am and 1:45pm from the Garden District Book Shop (in the Rink, corner of Washington Ave. and Prytania St.). Rates are $15 for adults, $13 for students and seniors, $7 for children 7 to 12, and free for children under 7.

Tours by Isabelle ᕕᕕ (✆ **504/391-3544**; www.toursbyisabelle. com) offers eight different tours for small groups in air-conditioned passenger vans. Most of their business is currently coming from the Post-Katrina City Tour ($58) (which is the only way they still show the city apart from what is listed below and in walking tours). It is 70 miles long and takes 3 hours and 20 minutes. It still shows French Quarter, City Park, and other places that date from the beginning of the city's history, but otherwise is highly geared toward post-Katrina damage and sights, and is comprehensive. You will see four levee breaches and go to Chalmette and St. Bernard to see the Murphy oil spill (plus other neighborhoods that get overlooked). This may seem exploitative, but most of the drivers are from these affected areas, and this gives them work. Prices and departure times vary. Make reservations as far in advance as possible.

Gray Line ᕕᕕ, 2 Canal St., Suite 1300 (✆ **800/535-7786** or 504/569-1401; www.graylineneworleans.com), like all businesses around town, took a hard hit, between severely reduced staff (most of whom, including the head of the local company, lost their homes), and, of course, being a business that involves sightseeing. Consequently, they took the controversial move of adding Katrina disaster tours to their menu. Initially, locals thought the tours a bad idea, but upon reflection, the majority agreed: These sights need to be seen, so that this disaster, and its victims, are not forgotten. And, as we have said, the only way to really understand the scope of this catastrophe is to see it for yourself. Certainly, the company has gone to great lengths to operate these tours with respect. Guides are locals with their own storm stories to tell, tourists are not allowed to exit the vans while in the damaged neighborhoods, a portion of the ticket price goes to Katrina relief (and passengers can choose which organization, out of a selection, their money will go to), and petitions to various government agencies are sent around for voluntary signatures.

SWAMP TOURS

Swamp tours can be a hoot, particularly if you get a guide who calls alligators to your boat for a little snack of chicken (please keep your hands inside the boat—they tend to look a lot like chicken to a gator). On all of the following tours, you're likely to see alligators, bald eagles, waterfowl, egrets, owls, herons, ospreys, feral hogs, otters, beavers, frogs, turtles, raccoons, deer, and nutria (maybe even a black bear or a mink)—and a morning spent floating on the bayou can be mighty pleasant. Most tours last approximately 2 hours.

Dr. Wagner's Honey Island Swamp Tours 𝕽𝕽 (℃ 985/641-1769 or 504/242-5877; www.honeyislandswamp.com) takes you by boat into the interior of Honey Island Swamp to view wildlife with native professional naturalist guides. **Westwego Swamp Adventures** 𝕽 (℃ 800/633-0503; www.westwegoswampadventures.com), located on Bayou Segnette in the town of Westwego, offers an "authentic Cajun Heritage" tour (no fake Cajuns, but we bet some heavy put-on accents!). It includes transportation from most downtown hotels for an additional fee.

Pearl River Eco-Tours 𝕽𝕽, 55050 Hwy. 90, Slidell, LA 70461 (℃ 866/59-SWAMP or 504/581-3395; www.pearlriverecotours.com), is built on Southern hospitality. You may have seen them on Bobby Flay's Food Network show. The boat captain, Neil, has been doing tours of Honey Island Swamp for over 10 years, and his wife answers the phones. They are always friendly, and the swamp is beautiful, even during the months the gators are in hibernation.

MYSTICAL & MYSTERIOUS TOURS

While most of the ghost tours are a bunch of hooey hokum, we are pleased that there is one we can send you to with a clear conscience: **Historic New Orleans Tours** 𝕽𝕽𝕽 (℃ 504/947-2120) offers a Cemetery and Voodoo Tour, the only one that is fact- and not sensation-based, though it is no less entertaining for it. The trip goes through St. Louis Cemetery No. 1, Congo Square, and an active voodoo temple. It leaves Monday through Saturday at 10am and 1pm, Sunday at 10am only, from the courtyard at 334-B Royal St. Rates are $15 for adults, $13 for students and seniors, and free for children under 12. They are also offering a nighttime haunted tour, perhaps the only one in town where well-researched guides will offer genuine thrills and chills.

BOAT TOURS

For those interested in doing the Mark Twain thing, a number of operators offer riverboat cruises; some cruises have specific destinations like the zoo or Chalmette, while others just cruise the river and harbor without stopping. Docks are at the foot of Toulouse and Canal streets, and there's ample parking. Call for reservations, which are required for all these tours, and to confirm prices and schedules.

Among the boats are the steamboat *Natchez* and the stern-wheeler *John James Audubon,* 2 Canal St., Suite 1300 (✆ **800/233-BOAT** or 504/586-8777; www.steamboatnatchez.com), a fun way to reach the Audubon Zoo; and the paddle-wheeler *Creole Queen,* Riverwalk Dock (✆ **800/445-4109** or 504/529-4567; www.neworleanspaddle wheels.com), which departs from the Poydras Street Wharf.

6 Especially for Kids

The following destinations are also particularly well suited for younger children.

Children's Storyland ⭐⭐ *Kids*   The under-8 set will be delighted with this playground, where well-known children's stories and rhymes have inspired the charming decor. It offers plenty to slide down and climb on, and generally gets juvenile ya-yas out.

Kids and adults will enjoy the carousel, two Ferris wheels (one big, one small), bumper cars, some miniature trains, a ladybug-shaped roller coaster, and other rides at the **Carousel Gardens,** also in City Park. Delighting local families since 1906, the carousel is one of only 100 all-wood merry-go-rounds in the country, and the only one in the state. *Note:* At press time the carousel itself was closed for renovation.

City Park at Victory Ave. ✆ **504/483-9381.** Admission $3. Carousel Gardens amusement park "open seasonally" Fri 10am–2:30pm, Sat–Sun 11am–5pm; Storyland Sat–Sun 10am–5pm.

Louisiana Children's Museum ⭐⭐⭐ *Kids*   This popular two-story interactive museum is really a playground in disguise that will keep kids occupied for a good couple of hours. Along with changing exhibits, the museum offers an art shop with regularly scheduled projects, a mini-grocery store, a chance to be a "star anchor" at a simulated television studio, and lots of activities exploring music, fitness, water, and life itself.

420 Julia St., at Tchoupitoulas St. ✆ **504/523-1357.** Fax 504/529-3666. www.lcm. org. Admission $7. Mon–Sat 9:30am–4:30pm; Sun noon–4:30pm.

7 Gambling

After years of political and legal wrangling—much of which is still an ongoing source of fun in the daily paper—**Harrah's Casino** opened. "Oh, goody," we said, along with other even more sarcastic things, as we experienced severe disorientation stepping inside for the first time. Then again, post-Katrina, the Harrah's company was financially generous to all their hurricane-affected employees and has been similarly generous with Katrina relief benefits. So what the hey; come here and spend your money, if you like. Acting as the staging area for the police after the storm, it only needed a bit of brushing up to restore it. It's exactly like a Vegas casino (100,000 sq. ft. of nearly 3,000 slot machines and 120 tables plus a buffet and twice-nightly live "Mardi Gras parade" shows), which is mighty shocking to the system and also a bit peculiar because like many a Vegas casino, it is Mardi Gras/New Orleans–themed—but exactly like a Vegas casino interpretation of same, which means it's almost exactly *not* like the real thing. It can be found on Canal Street at the river (© **504/533-6000;** www.harrah.com).

8 The Top Nearby Plantations

Both of the following are an easy partial-day trip from the city (they are less than an hour's drive away), and make a nice contrast in terms of architectural style and presentational approach.

Laura: A Creole Plantation ✹✹✹   If you see only one planta-tion, make it this one. Laura is the very model of a modern planta-tion—that is, when you figure that today's crop is tourism, not sugar cane or indigo. And it's all thanks to the vision of developer and gen-eral manager Norman Marmillion, who was determined to make this property rise above the average antebellum mansion. The hoop-skirted tours found elsewhere are banished in favor of a compre-hensive view of daily life on an 18th- and 19th-century plantation, a cultural history of Louisiana's Creole population, and a dramatic, entertaining, in-depth look at one extended Creole family.

This is a classic Creole house, simple on the outside but with real magic within. Unlike many other plantation homes, much is known about this house and the family that lived here, thanks to extensive records, particularly the detailed memoirs of Laura Locoul (for whom the plantation is named). Sadly, a huge fire hit the plantation on August 8, 2004. Employees worked hard and saved many artifacts, and a significant portion of the original house survived. Tours continued the very next morning, and renovation ultimately turned a disaster into opportunity. During the restoration, they returned the house to the 1805 period, with new accurate details. Basic tours of what remains of the main building and the property start every 20 minutes and last about 55 minutes and are organized around true (albeit spiced-up) stories from the history of the home and its residents. (*Of special note:* The stories that eventually became the beloved B'rer Rabbit were first collected here by a folklorist in the 1870s.)

2247 La. 18, Vacherie, LA 70090. ℂ **888/799-7690** or 225/265-7690. www.laura plantation.com. Admission $15 adults, $5 children 6–17, free for children under 6. Daily 10am–4pm. Last tour begins at 4pm. Closed Jan 1, Mardi Gras, Easter, Thanksgiving, and Christmas.

Oak Alley Plantation 🎞🎞🎞   This is precisely what comes to mind when most people think "plantation." A splendid white house, its porch lined with giant columns, approached by a magnificent drive lined with stately oak trees—yep, it's all here. Consequently, this is the most famous (and probably most photographed) plantation house in Louisiana. (Parts of *Interview with the Vampire* and *Primary Colors* were shot here.) It's also the slickest operation, with a large parking lot, an expensive lunch buffet (bring your own picnic), hoop-skirted guides, and golf carts traversing the black-topped lanes around the property.

The house was built in 1839 by Jacques Telesphore Roman III and was named Bon Séjour—but if you walk out to the levee and look back at the ¼-mile avenue of 300-year-old live oaks, you'll see why steamboat passengers quickly dubbed it "Oak Alley." Roman was so enamored of the trees that he planned his house to have exactly as many columns—28 in all. Oak Alley lay disintegrating until 1914, when Mr. and Mrs. Jefferson Hardin of New Orleans bought it. Then, in 1925, it passed to Mr. and Mrs. Andrew Stewart, whose loving restoration is responsible for its National Historic Landmark designation.

Little is known about the families who lived here; consequently, tours focus on more general plantation facts. Over the last few years, renovations have given the rooms and furnishings a face-lift, returning the house to its 1830s roots, and though the furnishings are not original, they are strict to the time period and mostly correspond to the Romans' actual inventory.

Overnight accommodations are available in five really nice century-old Creole cottages (complete with sitting rooms, porches, and air-conditioning). Rates are $125 to $165 and include breakfast but not a tour. The overpriced restaurant is open for breakfast and lunch daily from 8:30am to 3pm.

3645 La. 18 (60 miles from New Orleans), Vacherie, LA 70090. ℂ **800/44-ALLEY** or 225/265-2151. www.oakalleyplantation.com. Admission $10 adults, $5 students 13–18, $3 children 6–12, free for children under 6. Daily 10am–4pm. Closed New Year's Day, Thanksgiving, and Christmas.

9 A Side Trip to Cajun County

The official name of this area is Acadiana, and it consists of a rough triangle of Louisiana made up of 22 parishes (counties), from St. Landry Parish at the top of the triangle to the Gulf of Mexico at its base. Lafayette is Acadiana's "capital," and it's dotted with such towns as St. Martinville, New Iberia, Abbeville, and Eunice. You won't find its boundaries on any map, nor the name "Acadiana" stamped across it. But those 22 parishes are Cajun Country, and its history and culture are unique in America.

Contact the excellent **Lafayette Parish Convention and Visitors Commission,** 1400 NW Evangeline Thruway (P.O. Box 52066), Lafayette, LA 70505 (ℂ **800/346-1958** in the U.S., 800/543-5340 in Canada, or 337/232-3737; fax 337/232-0161; www.lafayettetravel. com). The office is open weekdays from 8:30am to 5pm and weekends from 9am to 5pm.

EUNICE 𝆑𝆑𝆑

Founded in 1894 by C. C. Duson, who named the town for his wife, Eunice is a prairie town, not as picturesque as, say, Opelousas or Washington. But some of the most significant Cajun cultural happenings come out of this friendly town, including the Saturday-morning jam sessions at the Savoy Music Center, the Liberty Theater's live radio broadcasts, and the exhibits and crafts demonstrations at the Prairie Acadian Cultural Center, all of which will greatly enrich your understanding of Cajun traditions and modern life.

Liberty Theater 𝆑𝆑𝆑 *(Moments)*   This classic 1927 theater has been lovingly restored and turned into a showcase for Cajun music. There's live music most nights, but Saturday attracts the big crowds for the *Rendezvous des Cajuns* radio show. From 6 to 8pm, Cajun historian and folklorist Barry Ancelet hosts a live program—simulcast on local radio—that features Cajun and zydeco bands. It

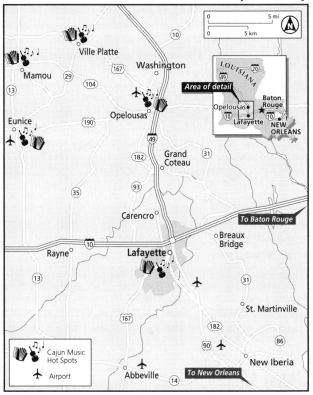

includes anything from up-and-comers to some of the biggest names as well as folk tales and jokes. Oh, and it's all in French. Locals and tourists alike pack the seats and aisles, with dancing on the sloped floor by the stage. Don't understand what's being said? As Barry points out, turn to your neighbors—they will be happy to translate. This is the right way (actually, *the* way) to begin your Saturday night of music in Cajun Country.

Second St. and Park Ave. ℰ 337/457-7389. www.eunice-la.com. Admission $5 adults, $3 children, free for children under 6.

Prairie Acadian Cultural Center ✸✸✸ *Finds*   A terrific small museum, the Acadian Cultural Center is devoted to Cajun life and culture. Exhibits explain everything from the history of the Cajuns to how they worked, played, and got married. The graphics are lively and very readable and are well combined with the objects on display (most were acquired from local families who have owned them for generations). The center has a collection of videos about Cajun life and will show any and all of them in the small theater (just ask). Anything by Les Blanc is a good choice, but you might also check out *Anything I Can Catch,* a documentary about the nearly lost art of hand-fishing. (You *need* to see someone catch a giant catfish with his bare hands!)

250 West Park. © **337/457-8490.** www.lsue.edu/acadgate/lafitte.htm. Free admission; donations accepted. Tues–Fri 8am–5pm; Sat 8am–6pm. Closed Christmas.

Savoy Music Center 🎻🎻🎻 *(Moments*   On weekdays this is a working music store with instruments, accessories, and a small but essential selection of Cajun and zydeco CDs and tapes. In the back is the workshop where musician Marc Savoy lovingly crafts his Acadian accordions—not just fine musical instruments but works of art—amid cabinets bearing his observations and aphorisms. On most Saturday mornings, though, this nondescript faded-green building on the outskirts of Eunice is the spiritual center of Cajun music. Keeping alive a tradition that dates from way before electricity, Marc and his wife, Ann (or one of their sons, who are now thriving musicians in their own right) host a jam session where you can hear some of the region's finest music and watch the tunes being passed down from generation to generation. Here, the older musicians are given their due respect, with octogenarians often leading the sessions while players as young as those in their preteens glean all they can—if they can keep up. Meanwhile, guests munch on hunks of *boudin* sausage and sip beer while listening or socializing. All comers are welcome. But don't come empty-handed—a pound of *boudin* or a six-pack of something is appropriate. And if you play guitar, fiddle, accordion, or triangle, bring one along and join in. Don't try to show off. Simply follow along with the locals, or you're sure to get a cold shoulder.

Hwy. 190 E. (3 miles east of Eunice). © **337/457-9563.** www.savoymusiccenter.com. Tues–Fri 9am–5pm; Sat 9am–noon.

LAFAYETTE 🎻🎻

Stop by the **Lafayette Parish Convention and Visitors Commission Center,** 1400 NW Evangeline Thruway (© **800/346-1958** in the U.S., 800/543-5340 in Canada, or 337/232-3808; www.lafayette travel.com). Turn off I-10 at exit 103A, go south for about a mile, and you'll find the office in the center of the median. It's open week-days from 8:30am to 5pm and weekends from 9am to 5pm. Near the intersection of Willow Street and the thruway, the attractive offices are in Cajun-style homes set on landscaped grounds that hold a pond and benches. It is a restful spot to sit and plan your Cajun Country excursion.

We also highly recommend the **Festival International de Louisiane** ♠, a 6-day music and art festival that many find to be a good alternative to New Orleans's increasingly crowded Jazz Fest. There's an interesting lineup each year, with an emphasis on music from other French-speaking lands. The festival takes place in the center of town with streets blocked off. In contrast to Jazz Fest, it's low-key and a manageable size. Best of all, it's free! The festival is held at the end of April; for dates, call or write the Festival Interna-tional de Louisiane, 735 Jefferson St., Lafayette, LA 70501 (© **337/ 232-8086;** www.festivalinternational.com).

SEEING THE SIGHTS

You shouldn't leave this area without exploring its bayous and swamps. Gliding through misty bayous dotted with gnarled cypress trees that drip Spanish moss, seeing native water creatures and birds in their natural habitat, and learning how Cajuns harvest their beloved crawfish is an experience not to be missed.

To arrange a voyage, contact **McGee's Landing Atchafalaya Basin Swamp Tours** (1337 Henderson Levee Rd., Henderson; © **337/228-2384;** www.mcgeeslanding.com; $18 adults, $15 sen-iors, $12 children ages 4–12, free for children under 3). Tours last 90 minutes and go to Henderson Lake in the Atchafalaya Basin. You can also talk to someone at the helpful and friendly Breaux Bridge Tourism Board (© **337/332-8500**) for further suggestions.

Vermilionville ♠♠   This reconstruction of a Cajun-Creole set-tlement from the 1765-to-1890 era sits on the banks of the brood-ing Bayou Vermilion, adjacent to the airport on U.S. 90. While it may sound like a "Cajunland" theme park, it's actually quite a valid operation. Hundreds of skilled artisans labored to restore original Cajun homes and to reconstruct others that were typical of such a village. Homes of every level in society are represented, from the humblest to the most well-to-do. (It *must* be authentic: One Cajun we know refuses to go, not because he dislikes the place or finds it offensive but because "I already *live* in Vermilionville!")

300 Fisher Rd., off Surrey St. ℂ **866/99-BAYOU** or 337/233-4077. www.vermilionville. org. Admission $8 adults, $6.50 seniors, $5 students, free for children under 6. Tues–Sun 10am–4pm. Closed New Year's Eve, New Year's Day, Martin Luther King Day, Mardi Gras, Thanksgiving, and Dec 24–25. Take I-10 to exit 103A. Take Evangeline Thruway south to Surrey St. and then follow signs.

ACCOMMODATIONS

Aaah! T'Frere's Bed & Breakfast 𝒜𝒜𝒜   Everything about this place cracks us up, from the name (it's so they're first in any alphabetical listing) to the evening "T'Juleps" to the owners' gorgeous son who cooked us breakfast but swore he was really a supermodel (did you hear us argue?) to the cheerful owners themselves, Pat and Maugie Pastor—the latter would be adorable even if she didn't preside over breakfast in red silk pajamas every day. Oh, wait, did we mention the goofily named breakfasts? They are daily extravaganzas, easily the best around, like the "Ooh-La-La, Mardi Gras" breakfast—eggs in white sauce on ham-topped biscuits, cheese and garlic grits, tomato grille, sweet potatoes, and chocolate muffins. The rooms (and grounds) are gorgeous, though the ones in the Garconniere in the back are a bit more Country Plain than Victorian Fancy. We particularly like Mary's Room, with its priceless antique wood canopy bed and working fireplace. Look, they've been in business for years, they know how to do this right; just stay here, okay?

1905 Verot School Rd., Lafayette, LA 70508. ℂ **800/984-9347.** Fax 337/984-9347. www.tfreres.com. 8 units, all with private bathroom. $95–$120 double; extra person $30. Rates include full breakfast. AE, DC, DISC, MC, V. **Amenities:** Welcome drinks and Cajun canapés (hors d'oeuvres). *In room:* A/C, TV, Wi-Fi, dataport, coffeemaker, terry-cloth robes.

DINING

Prejean's 𝒜𝒜 CAJUN   An unpretentious family restaurant, this likeable place has live Cajun music every night. Their glory days may or may not be behind them, but the hearty meals at Prejean's still make this worth a drop-in. Their smoked duck and andouille gumbo (sans pheasant) is a Fest favorite, and justly so, as are the crawfish enchiladas, which made one taster swear off the usual sort forever. Look for fried crawfish *boudin* balls and the seafood-stuffed mushrooms (think a sort of mini crab cake stuffed into a 'shroom) for appetizers, and shrimp stuffed with tasso and jack cheese, and then wrapped in bacon, or a more traditional, more staid blackened fish on top of crawfish étouffée for an entree. Matters are cheaper and lighter at lunch when the menu includes a BBQ shrimp po' boy and less expensive versions of the dinner menu.

3480 I-49 N. (C) **337/896-3247.** Fax 337/896-3278. www.prejeans.com. Reservations recommended for 15 or more. Children's menu $3.50–$8.95; main courses $16–$27. AE, DC, DISC, MC, V. Sun–Thurs 7am–10pm; Fri–Sat 7am–11pm. Take I-10 to exit 103B and then I-49 north to exit 2/Gloria Switch.

Randol's Restaurant and Cajun Dance Hall ✿ CAJUN   In addition to better-than-average Cajun food, Randol's offers a good-size, popular dance floor where dancers are likely to be locals enjoying their own *fais-do-do*. In fact, they eagerly volunteer when owner Frank Randol needs dancers for his traveling Cajun food-and-dance show. A house specialty is the seafood platter, which includes a cup of seafood gumbo, fried shrimp, fried oysters, fried catfish, stuffed crab, crawfish étouffée, French bread, and coleslaw.

2320 Kaliste Saloom Rd. (C) **800/YO-CAJUN** or 337/981-7080. www.randols.com. Reservations accepted only for parties of 8 or more. Main courses $7.95–$27. MC, V. Sun–Thurs 5–9:30pm; Fri–Sat 5–10:30pm. Closed major holidays. From New Orleans, take I-10 west to exit 103A. Follow Evangeline Thruway to Pinhook Rd., turn right, and follow Pinhook to Kaliste Saloom Rd. (on the right). Randol's will be on your right.

VILLE PLATTE ✿

If you've fallen in love with Cajun music and want to take some home with you, you have a good reason to detour to the town of Ville Platte.

Floyd's Record Shop ✿✿   Long before Cajun and zydeco were known outside the region, Floyd Soileau was recording and releasing the music on three labels: Swallow for Cajun, Maison de Soul for zydeco, and Jin (named after his charming wife) for swamp pop, the regional offshoot of 1950s and early 1960s pop and soul styles. Eventually, he built a whole operation of recording, pressing (his plant was pressing vinyl well into the CD age), and selling records, by mail order and at this store. For fans of the music, this is a must-stop locale with a fine selection of Floyd's releases by such great artists as D. L. Menard (the Cajun Hank Williams) and Clifton Chenier (the King of Zydeco), as well as other releases that may be hard to find anywhere else.

434 E. Main St. (C) **800/738-8668** or 337/363-2185. Fax 337/363-5622. www.floydsrecords.com. DISC, MC, V. Mon–Sat 8:30am–4:30pm.

DINING
The Pig Stand ✿✿ PIG   As you might guess, The Pig Stand serves pig—oh, and such pig! It's a little dump of a local hangout (and we

mean that in the best way possible) that also serves divine barbecued chicken and other Southern specialties for cheap prices. New owners are adding New Orleans po' boy, soft-shell crab, and other dishes from the big city to their menu. It's a real treat, so don't miss it. And it's just down the street from Floyd's in case you worked up an appetite buying music.

318 E. Main St. ✆ 337/363-2883. Main courses $12 and under. AE, DISC, MC, V. Tues–Thurs 7am–9pm; Fri–Sat 7am–10pm; Sun 7am–2pm.

6

Shopping

Shopping in New Orleans is a highly evolved leisure activity, with a shop for every strategy and a fix for every shopaholic—and every budget. Don't assume those endless T-shirt shops on Bourbon Street or even the costly antiques stores on Royal Street are all that New Orleans has to offer. The range of shopping here is as good as it gets—many a clever person has come to New Orleans just to open up a quaint boutique filled with strange items gathered from all parts of the globe or produced by local, somewhat twisted, folk artists.

General hours for the stores in New Orleans are from 10am to 5pm, but call ahead to make sure. In these post-Katrina days, operating hours can change abruptly, and many shops that have rather limited hours listed below may have been able to expand their hours since we went to press, while, conversely, some may have had to reduce hours further.

1 Major Hunting Grounds

CANAL PLACE At the foot of Canal Street (365 Canal St.), where the street reaches the Mississippi River, this shopping center holds more than 50 shops, many of them branches of some of this country's most elegant retailers: Brooks Brothers, Saks Fifth Avenue, Gucci, Williams-Sonoma, and Coach. Open Monday to Saturday from 10am to 6pm, Sunday from noon to 6pm (www.theshopsat canalplace.com).

THE FRENCH MARKET Shops within the market begin on Decatur Street across from Jackson Square; offerings include candy, cookware, fashion, crafts, toys, New Orleans memorabilia, and jewelry. It's open from 10am to 6pm (and the Café du Monde, next to the Farmers Market, is open 24 hr.). Quite honestly, you'll find a lot of junk here, but there are some very good buys mixed in (www. frenchmarket.org).

JACKSON BREWERY Just across from Jackson Square at 600–620 Decatur St., the old brewery building has been transformed

...ble of shops, cafes, delicatessens, restaurants, and entertain-
...t. Keep in mind that many shops in the Brewery close at 5:30 or
6pm, before the Brewery itself. Open daily from 10am to 6pm.

JULIA STREET   From Camp Street down to the river on Julia
Street, you'll find some of the city's best contemporary-art galleries
(many are listed below, under "Art Galleries"). Some of the works
are a bit pricey, but there are good deals to be had if you're collecting and fine art to be seen if you're not.

MAGAZINE STREET   This is the Garden District's premier shopping street. More than 140 shops (some of which are listed below)
line the street in 19th-century brick storefronts and quaint cottage-
like buildings. Among the offerings are antiques, art galleries, bou-
tiques, crafts, and dolls. The most promising section goes, roughly,
from the 3500 to 4200 blocks (from about Aline St. to Milan St.,
with the odd block or so of nothing). Other good groupings can be
found in the 1800 to 2100, 2800 to 3300, and 5400 to 5700 blocks.
Be sure to pick up a copy of *Visit Magazine Street: For a Shopper's
Dream,* a free guide and map to most (if not all) of the stores on the
6 miles of Magazine Street, which is available all along the street.

RIVERBEND   To reach this district (in the Carrollton area), ride
the St. Charles Avenue streetcar (or the shuttle bus temporarily running in its place) to stop no. 44, then walk down Maple Street 1
block to Dublin Park, the site of an old public market that was once
lined with open stalls. Nowadays a variety of renovated shops
inhabit the old general store, a produce warehouse made of barge
board, and the town surveyor's raised-cottage home.

RIVERWALK MARKETPLACE   A mall is a mall is a mall, unless
it has picture windows offering a Mississippi River panorama. Even
though you almost certainly have a mall at home, this one, at 1 Poydras St., is worth visiting. Besides, if you packed wrong and need
T-shirts instead of sweaters or vice versa, this is the closest Gap to
the Quarter. Note that the best river views are in the upper section
of the mall closest to the convention center. Open daily from 10am
to 6pm. Validated parking with any purchase of $10 or more.

2 Shopping A to Z
ANTIQUES
Aesthetics & Antiques ✰✰   The shop calls itself a "Baby
Boomer's Gumbo," which seems to translate as all the stuff that's too
good, quirky, or collectible to let go at a yard sale. Prices are already

reasonable but they will bargain if you buy enough. On a recent visit, we bought old sheet music, a piece of Sputnik encased in Lucite, and a collie figurine from the 1940s. Throw in some china, boxes of vintage postcards, some better prices on the increasingly costly vintage Mardi Gras beads, vintage jewelry, and you begin to get the idea. 3122 Magazine St. ℭ **504/895-7011.** Mon–Tues and Thurs–Sat 11am–6pm; Sun 1–5:30pm. Closed Wed.

Audubon Antiques ✦ Audubon has everything from collectible curios to authentic antique treasures at reasonable prices. There are two floors of goods, so be prepared to lose yourself. 2025 Magazine St. ℭ **504/581-5704.** Mon–Sat 10:30am–5pm. Call before visiting because sometimes the owner steps out!

Harris Antiques ✦✦✦ Harris features 18th- and 19th-century European fine art and antiques, jewelry, grandfather clocks, French mantle clocks, bronzes, and marbles. The company is a long-standing family-run business; it has helped many younger collectors make some of their initial purchases. 233 Royal St. ℭ **504/523-1605.** www.harris antiques.com. Mon–Sat 10am–5:30pm.

Ida Manheim Antiques At this gallery you'll find an enormous collection of Continental, English, and Oriental furnishings along with porcelains, jade, silver, and fine paintings, and sometimes attitude to match. The store is also the agent for Boehm Birds. 409 Royal St. ℭ **888/627-5969** or 504/620-4114. www.idamanheimantiques.com. Mon–Sat 9am–5pm.

Jack Sutton Antiques ✦ There are a number of Suttons around New Orleans, mostly on Royal. This one, our favorite, specializes in jewelry and objects. The selection of estate jewelry ("estate" meaning older than yesterday but less than 100 years) is often better than that at other antiques stores—the author's engagement ring came from here—but due to the ebb and flow of the estate business, particularly post-Katrina, you can never be sure what may be offered. 315 Royal St. ℭ **888/996-0555** or 504/522-0555. Mon–Sat 10am–5:30pm.

Keil's Antiques ✦✦✦ Keil's was established in 1899 and is currently run by the fourth generation of the founding family. The shop has a considerable collection of 18th- and 19th-century French and English furniture, chandeliers, jewelry, and decorative items. This is our choice for antiques browsing, because somewhere on these three crowded floors (and more in a warehouse), there is something for every budget, from a $2,000 chest of drawers to six-figure items. 325 Royal St. ℭ **504/522-4552.** www.keilsantiques.com. Mon–Sat 9am–5pm.

Lucullus ✸✸✸ An unusual shop, Lucullus has a wonderful collection of culinary antiques as well as 17th-, 18th-, and 19th-century furnishings to "complement the grand pursuits of cooking, dining, and imbibing," not just silverware and china (if you can call a French platter, ca. 1820, something so simple as "china"), but coffee grinders, dining room furniture, fixtures such as mirrors and lights, and even absinthe glasses and spoons. The owner has added Art Deco flatware and table decorations. 610 Chartres St. ✆ **504/528-9620.** Mon–Sat 9am–5pm.

Miss Edna's Antiques ✸ Miss Edna's carries eclectic antiques—furniture, specialty items, curios—and paintings, with a focus on 19th-century works. Miss Edna recently moved a few feet up Magazine, doubling her inventory and expanding her art collection. 2035 Magazine St. ✆ **504/524-1897.** Mon–Sat 10am–5pm. Closed Tues during summer.

Rothschild's Antiques ✸ Rothschild's is a fourth-generation furniture merchandiser. Some of the most interesting things you'll find here are antique, estate, and custom-made jewelry. There's a fine selection of antique silver, marble mantels, porcelains, and English and French furnishings including chandeliers. 321 Royal St. ✆ **504/523-5816.** Mon–Sat 9:30am–5pm; Sun and any day by appointment.

Sigle's Antiques & Metalcraft ✸ If you've fallen in love with the lacy ironwork that drips from French Quarter balconies, this is the place to pick out some pieces to take home. In addition, Sigle's has converted some of the ironwork into useful household items such as plant holders. 935 Royal St. ✆ **504/522-7647.** Mon–Sat 10am–noon; Sun 1–4:30pm.

Whisnant Galleries ✸ The quantity and variety of merchandise in this shop is mind-boggling. You'll find all sorts of unusual and unique antique collectibles including items from Ethiopia, Russia, Greece, South America, Morocco, and other parts of North Africa and the Middle East. 222 Chartres St. ✆ **504/524-9766.** Mon–Sat 9:30am–5:30pm; Sun 10am–5pm.

ART GALLERIES

With one major exception, galleries in New Orleans follow the landscape of antiques shops: **Royal and Magazine streets.**

Ariodante A contemporary-craft gallery, Ariodante features handcrafted furniture, glass, ceramics, jewelry, and decorative accessories by nationally acclaimed artists. Rotating shows offer a detailed look at works by various artists. 535 Julia St. ✆ **504/524-3233.** Daily 11am–5pm.

Arthur Roger Gallery Project ✪✪ Arthur Roger sets the pace for the city's fine-art galleries. Since opening in New Orleans more than 20 years ago, Roger has played a major role in developing the art community and in tying it to the art world in New York. The gallery represents many artists including Francis Pavy (who did the 1997 and 2007 Jazz Fest posters), Ida Kohlmeyer, Douglas Bourgeois, Paul Lucas, Clyde Connell, Willie Birch, Gene Koss, and George Dureau. 730 Tchoupitoulas. ✆ **504/524-9393**. www.arthurroger gallery.com. Tues–Sat 11am–6pm.

Bergen Putman Gallery The city's largest selection of posters and limited-edition graphics on such subjects as Mardi Gras, jazz, and the city itself and by such artists as Erté, Icart, Nagel, Maimon, and Tarkay is available here. Bergen also features a large collection of works by sought-after African-American artists. The service by Margarita and her staff is friendly and extremely personable. 730 Royal St. ✆ **800/621-6179** or 504/523-7882. www.bergenputmangallery.com. Daily 9am–9pm.

Berta's and Mina's Antiquities ✪✪ In years past, this was just another place that bought and sold antiques and secondhand furniture and art. That all ended on the day in 1993 that Nilo Lanzas (Berta's husband and Mina's dad) began painting. Now you can barely see the furniture in the shop for all the new art. Dubbed "folk art" or "outsider art," Lanzas's works are colorful scenes from life in New Orleans or his native Latin America, stories out of the Bible, or images sprung from his imagination. Mina has brought in her work as well, and her joyful celebrations of local life and landscapes are attracting their own following. 4138 Magazine St. ✆ **504/895-6201**. Mon–Sat 10am–6pm; Sun 11am–6pm.

Bryant Galleries This gallery represents renowned artists Ed Dwight, Fritzner Lamour, and Leonardo Nierman as well as other American, European, and Haitian artists. The varied work on display here may include jazz bronzes, glasswork, and graphics. The staff is very friendly and helpful. 316 Royal St. ✆ **800/844-1994** or 504/ 525-5584. www.bryantgalleries.com. Sun–Wed 10am–5pm; Thurs–Sat 10am–8pm.

Cole Pratt Gallery, Ltd. ✪ This gallery showcases the work of Southern artists whose creations include abstract and realist paintings, sculptures, and ceramics. The art is of the highest quality and the prices are surprisingly reasonable. 3800 Magazine St. ✆ **504/891-6789**. www.coleprattgallery.com. Tues–Sat 10am–5pm.

The Davis Galleries ✹✹✹ One of two world-class galleries in New Orleans (the other being A Gallery for Fine Photography; see below), this may be the best place in the world for Central and West African traditional art. The owner makes regular trips to Africa for collecting. Works on display might include sculpture, costuming, basketry, textiles, weapons, and/or jewelry. 904 Louisiana Ave. ✆ 504/895-5206. www.davisafricanart.com. By appointment only. Call to see if regular hours have returned.

Diane Genre Oriental Art and Antiques ✹✹ If all of the 18th- and 19th-century European antiques in the stores along Royal are starting to look the same, it's time to step into Diane Genre's shop. By comparison, the atmosphere in here seems as delicate as one of the ancient East Asian porcelains on display. Hold your breath and get an eyeful of furniture, 18th-century Japanese wood-block prints, and a world-class collection of Chinese and Japanese textiles. There are also scrolls, screens, engravings, and lacquers. 431 Royal St. ✆ 504/595-8945. Fax 504/899-8651. www.dianegenreorientalart.com. By appointment only. Call to see if regular hours have returned.

Galerie Royale ✹✹ This gallery's collection is built around the works of William Tolliver, an African-American artist from Mississippi whose untimely death at the age of 48 in 2000 received national coverage. Tolliver came to painting relatively late in his life and without formal training. Despite this, he quickly became an internationally recognized contemporary Impressionist painter. At Galerie Royale you can find a selection of Tolliver's museum-quality pieces as well as work by other artists including Salvador Dalí, Bonny Stanglmaier, and Verna Hart. 3648 Magazine St. ✆ 504/894-1588. www.galerieroyale.com. Fri–Sat 11am–11pm, or by appointment.

A Gallery for Fine Photography ✹✹✹ It would be a mistake to skip this incredibly well-stocked photography gallery (one of two world-class galleries in New Orleans—the other is The Davis Galleries; see above). Even if you aren't in the market, it's worth looking around. It really is like a museum of photography, with just about every period and style represented and frequent shows of contemporary artists. When they aren't swamped, the staff is more than happy to show you some of the many photos in the files. The gallery emphasizes New Orleans and Southern history and contemporary culture (you can buy Ernest Bellocq's legendary Storyville photos) as well as black culture and music. There is something in just about every price range as well as a terrific collection of photography books if that better fits your budget. 241 Chartres St. ℂ **504/568-1313.** www.agallery.com. Thurs–Mon 10am–5pm.

Kurt E. Schon, Ltd. *✿✿* Here you'll find the country's largest inventory of 19th-century European paintings. Works include French and British Impressionist and post-Impressionist paintings as well as art from the Royal Academy and the French Salon. 510 St. Louis St. ℂ **504/524-5462.** www.kurteschonltd.com. Mon–Fri 10am–5pm; Sat 10am–3pm.

LeMieux Galleries *✿* LeMieux represents contemporary artists and fine craftspeople from Louisiana and the Gulf Coast. They include Leslie Staub, Charles Barbier, Pat Bernard, Mary Lee Eggart, Leslie Elliottsmith, JoAnn Greenberg, David Lambert, Deedra Ludwig, Shirley Rabe Masinter, Evelyn Menge, Paul Ninas, Billy Solitario, and Kate Trepagnier. 332 Julia St. ℂ **504/522-5988.** Fax 504/522-5682. www.lemieuxgalleries.com. Mon 11am–5pm; Tues–Sat 10am–6pm.

New Orleans Glassworks and Printmaking Studio *✿✿✿* Here, within 25,000 square feet of studio space, are a 550-pound tank of hot molten glass and a pre–Civil War press. At Glassworks, the sister school to the Louvre Museum of Decorative Arts, established glasswork artists and master printmakers display their work in the on-site gallery and teach classes in glass blowing, kiln-fired glass, hand-engraved printmaking, papermaking, and bookbinding. Beginning in October, visitors may design their holiday ornaments. 727 Magazine St. ℂ **504/529-7277.** www.neworleansglassworks.org. Mon–Fri 11am–5pm.

Peligro *✿✿✿* A bit out-of-the-way from the usual Quarter shopping routes, but worth checking out, Peligro is one of the best folk-art galleries in the city, with an emphasis on primitive and outsider art (but also work from Latin American countries). The owners have a terrific eye for up-and-coming artists. At times they have smaller items that make marvelous, original gifts. 305 Decatur St. ℂ **504/581-1706.** Mon–Sat 10:30am–6pm; Sun noon–6pm.

Shadyside Pottery *✿* If you want to see a master potter at work, Shadyside Pottery is an excellent place to stop. Charlie Bohn, who apprenticed in Japan, can be seen at his wheel pretty much all the time. He specializes in the Japanese tradition of raku, a type of pottery that has a "cracked" look. Open most days, though if it's important that you see him, you might call ahead to make sure he hasn't taken a rare day off. 3823 Magazine St. © 504/897-1710. www. shadysidepottery.com. Mon–Sat 10am–5pm.

BATH & BEAUTY PRODUCTS & DAY SPAS

Hove 𝕽𝕽𝕽   Founded in 1931, Hove is the oldest perfumery in the city. It features all-natural scents (except the musk, which is synthetic), and the selection is almost overwhelming. Strips with various options, for both men and women, are laid out to help you. They have some original creations ("Kiss in the Dark") and some very Southern smells, such as vetiver and tea olive. This is the place to establish your signature scent, and a good choice for unique presents for people back home. Lit buffs will be amused by the letter from author Tom Robbins, confirming that the shop in his *Jitterbug Perfume* was more or less based on Hove's appearance. 824 Royal St. © 504/525-7827. www.hoveparfumeur.com. Mon–Sat 10am–5pm.

Ritz-Carlton Spa 𝕽𝕽𝕽   The finest spa in just about any town, the newly refurbished Ritz spa is tranquil, majestic, classy, lush—and costly. But who cares? With this kind of atmosphere, not to mention the new Prada treatment line, it's all about the pampering. In addition to a wide range of exotic scrubs and rubs, plus wraps, water treatments, and more, they have a luxe sauna and relaxation areas, and a full-service salon for beauty treatments. 921 Canal St. © 504/524-1331. www.ritzcarlton.com. Daily 9am–8pm.

BOOKS

Literary enthusiasts will find many destinations in New Orleans. **Maple Street Book Shop,** 7523 Maple St. (© 504/866-4916), is an Uptown mecca for bookworms, and the **Maple Street Children's Book Shop** is next door at 7529 Maple St. (© 504/861-2105).

Beckham's Bookshop 𝕽   Beckham's has two entire floors of old editions, rare secondhand books, and thousands of classical LPs that will tie up your whole afternoon or morning if you don't tear yourself away. The owners also operate **Librairie Bookshop,** 823 Chartres St. (© 504/525-4837), which has a sizable collection of secondhand books. 228 Decatur St. © 504/522-9875. Daily 10am–5pm.

Crescent City Books 𝕽   This shop features two floors of dusty treasures (the emphasis is on history, social history, literary criticism, philosophy, and art) and a staff that ranges from nonchalant to quite sweet and helpful. 204 Chartres St. © 800/546-4013 or 504/524-4997. www.crescentcitybooks.com. Mon–Sat 10am–7pm; Sun 11am–6pm.

FAB, Faubourg Marigny Art & Books 🎭 This well-stocked gay and lesbian bookstore also carries some local titles. It has a used section, CDs, posters, cards, and gifts (all with a more or less gay or lesbian slant) and holds regular readings and signings. The staff makes this a fine resource center—you can call them for local gay and lesbian info. They have recently added a collection of gay- and lesbian-themed figurative art on display and available for sale. 600 Frenchmen St. ℂ **504/947-3700.** Daily noon–10pm.

Faulkner House Books 🎭🎭🎭 This shop is on a lot of walking tours of the French Quarter because it's where Nobel prize–winner William Faulkner lived while he was writing his early works *Mosquitoes* and *Soldiers' Pay.* Those who step inside instead of just snapping a photo and walking on will find something remarkable: possibly the best selection per square foot of any bookstore in the whole wide world, with every bit of shelf space occupied by a book that's both highly collectible and of literary value. The shop holds a large collection of Faulkner first editions and rare and first-edition classics by many other authors, and it has a particularly comprehensive collection of New Orleans–related work. 624 Pirates Alley. ℂ **504/524-2940.** www.faulknerhousebooks.net. Daily 10am–6pm.

Garden District Book Shop 🎭🎭🎭 Owner Britton Trice has stocked his shop with just about every regional book you can think of; if you want a New Orleans or Louisiana-specific book, no matter what the exact focus (interiors, exteriors, food, Creoles, you name it), you should be able to find it here. This is also where Anne Rice does book signings whenever she has a new release. They usually have autographed copies of her books plus fancy special editions of Rice titles that they publish themselves and a large selection of signed books by local (such as Poppy Z. Brite) and nonlocal authors (from Clive Barker to James Lee Burke). 2727 Prytania St. (in the Rink). ℂ **504/ 895-2266.** Fax 504/895-0111. www.gardendistrictbookshop.com. Mon–Sat 10am– 6pm; Sun 10am–4pm.

Octavia Books 🎭 We do love our independent bookstores, and although this may be a bit far uptown, a sweet, tiny patio, complete with waterfall, is the customer's reward—what better way to linger over a purchase from stock that is chosen with obvious literary care? Book signings and other literary events are common. 513 Octavia St. (at Laurel St.). ℂ **504/899-7323.** www.octaviabooks.com. Mon–Sat 10am–6pm; Sun noon–5pm.

CANDIES & PRALINES

Aunt Sally's Praline Shop *✿*   At Aunt Sally's you can watch skilled workers perform the 150-year-old process of cooking the original Creole pecan pralines right before your eyes. The large store also has a broad selection of regional cookbooks, books on the history of New Orleans and its environs, Creole and Cajun foods, folk and souvenir dolls, and local memorabilia. In addition, Aunt Sally's has a collection of zydeco, Cajun, R&B, and jazz CDs and cassettes. They'll ship any purchase. In the French Market, 810 Decatur St. ☎ **800/642-7257** or 504/944-6090. www.auntsallys.com. Mon–9am–5am; Tues 9am–6pm; Wed–Fri 9am–8pm; Sat 8am–9pm; Sun 8am–6pm.

Laura's Candies *✿*   Laura's is said to be the city's oldest candy store, established in 1913. It has fabulous pralines, but it also has rich, delectable golf ball–size truffles—our personal favorite indulgence, although they've gotten a bit pricey as of late. 331 Chartres St. ☎ **504/525-3880**. www.laurascandies.com. Daily 10am–6pm.

Leah's Candy Kitchen *✿✿*   After you've tried all of the city's Creole candy shops, you might very well come to the conclusion that Leah's tops the list. Everything here, from the candy fillings to the chocolate-covered pecan brittle, is made from scratch by second- and third-generation members of Leah Johnson's praline-cookin' family, who have been confecting confections since 1944. 714 St. Louis St. ☎ **888/523-5324** or 504/523-5662. www.leahspralines.com. Mon–Sat noon–6pm.

COSTUMES & MASKS

Costumery is big business in New Orleans, and not just in the days before Lent. In this city you never know *when* you're going to want or need a costume. A number of shops in New Orleans specialize in props for Mardi Gras, Halloween, and other occasions. ***Here's a tip:*** New Orleanians often sell their costumes back to these shops after Ash Wednesday, and you can sometimes pick up an outfit that's only been worn once at a small fraction of its original cost.

Little Shop of Fantasy   In the Little Shop of Fantasy, owners Laura and Anne Guccione sell the work of a number of local artists and more than 20 mask makers. Mike creates the feathered masks, Jill does the velvet hats and costumes, and Laura and Anne produce homemade toiletries. Some of the masks and hats are just fun and fanciful, but there are many fashionable ones as well. 517 St. Louis. ☎ **504/945-2435**. www.neworleansmasks.com. "Most days 11am–6pm."

Uptown Costume & Dance Company ✿ The walls of this small store are covered with spooky monster masks, goofy arrow-through-the-head-type tricks, hats, wigs, makeup, and all other manner of playfulness. It draws a steady, yearlong stream of loyal customers: kids going to parties, dancers, clowns, actors, and so forth. Conventioneers come here for rental disguises. At Mardi Gras, though, things really get cooking. 4326 Magazine St. ✆ **504/895-7969.** Tues–Fri noon–6pm; Sat 10am–6pm.

FASHION & VINTAGE CLOTHING

Fleur de Paris and Fleur de Paris Millinery ✿✿✿ Remember when a woman was simply not dressed unless she wore a hat? Help bring back those times by patronizing this shop, which makes hand-blocked, stylishly trimmed hats. Expensive, but works of art often are. They will also stay open late and even bring in champagne for special parties! Additionally, you can find 25 years worth of experience in their ever-changing collection of vintage gowns. The 1920s and 1930s elegance on display constantly brings us to our knees with covetousness. 712 Royal St. ✆ **504/525-1899.** Daily 10am–6pm.

House of Lounge ✿✿ If you want to be a couch potato, you might as well be a well-dressed one. Or do you want to treat your humble bedroom more like a boudoir? House of Lounge offers all sorts of silky robes and impressive "hostess gowns," plus sexy lingerie (and admittedly, there isn't much difference between the categories). 2044 Magazine St. ✆ **504/671-8300.** www.houseoflounge.com. Tues–Sat noon–6pm.

Trashy Diva ✿✿ Despite the name, there is nothing trashy about the vintage clothes found here. The heyday of women's garments—in the sense of designs that know how to flatter curves—is present in these floaty and velvety numbers that will please everyone from the hat-and-gloves-wearing crowds to the inner flappers to the Goth teens. There is often a sales rack in the back that's full of incredible bargains. 2048 Magazine St. ✆ **888/818-DIVA** or 504/299-8777. www.trashy diva.com. Mon–Sat noon–6pm; Sun 1–5pm.

UAL ✿✿✿ Once one of the secrets of the well-informed—and really well-dressed—local fashionistas, it was a cause for both rejoicing and mourning when United Apparel Liquidators moved from their obscure Metairie location to a central one right in the middle of the Quarter. The shop gets discontinued or leftover items from designers of all levels and sells them at ridiculous markdowns—a $1,500 garment going for $350. As if that wasn't enough, they often have hourly sales (20% off all accessories, for example). The problem is that average sizes go fast, and there often isn't more than one of anything. 518 Chartres. © 504/301-4437. Mon–Wed 10am–6pm; Thurs–Sat 10am–8pm; Sun 11am–6pm.

Violet's 𝕲𝕲   This is our greatest temptation among French Quarter shops, given how we feel about romantic, Edwardian, and '20s-inspired clothes in lush velvets and satins. There are some dazzling creations here with appropriate accessories (jewelry, hats, scarves) as well. 808 Chartres St. No phone at press time. Sun–Thurs–11am–7pm; Fri–Sat 10am–8pm.

Yvonne LaFleur—New Orleans 𝕲   Yvonne LaFleur, a confessed incurable romantic, is the creator of beautifully feminine original designs. Her custom millinery, silk dresses, evening gowns, lingerie, and sportswear are surprisingly affordable, and all are enhanced by her signature perfume. Her store is in the Riverbend district. 8131 Hampson St. © 504/866-9666. www.yvonnelafleur.com. Mon–Wed and Fri–Sat 10am–6pm; Thurs 10am–8pm.

GIFTS

Aux Belles Choses 𝕲𝕲   This shop feels as though it could be located at a lonely crossroads in rural France. Perhaps it's the endless variety of country French home, kitchen, and garden items. If you like creamy French soaps you'll probably leave with a handful—this place has many that are hard to find on this side of the Atlantic. The shop has everything from beautiful linens to old English pudding pots—terrific wedding and other special-occasion gifts. 3912 Magazine St. © 504/891-1009. www.abcneworleans.com. Wed–Sat 10am–5pm.

Belladonna Retail Therapy 𝕲𝕲   If you've booked a treatment at the day spa, allow yourself extra time to browse through the shop. Between the jewelry lines, including simple silver work etched with wee inscriptions of quotes from Shakespeare and others; the selection of gorgeous housewares; the cute clothes; and the clever gift items, there is a lot to coo over. 2900 Magazine St. © 504/891-4393. www. belladonnadayspa.com. Mon–Tues and Fri–Sat 9am–6pm; Wed–Thurs 9am–8pm.

Scriptura 𝕲𝕲   If you can't bear to scratch down notes with a pencil on a steno pad from the drugstore, you're a prime candidate for a romp through Scriptura. This store has everything related to the elegant art of scribbling. You can get designer stationery, glass fountain pens, sealing wax, and all types of journals. They have also opened a new location at 3301 Veterans, Suite 137. 5423 Magazine St. Ⓒ **504/897-1555**. www.scriptura.com. Mon–Sat 11am–5pm.

Shop of the Two Sisters ✮   This shop has upscale "girly" items such as throw pillows, lamps, sconces, accessories, unique accent pieces (with an emphasis on florals and fruits), and upholstery. Here you'll find consumerism at its most beautiful, but be prepared to pay for it. 1800 Magazine St. Ⓒ **504/525-2747**. www.shopofthetwosisters.com. Mon–Sat 10am–5pm.

Simon of New Orleans ✮✮   Folk artist Simon, whose brightly painted signs are seen throughout New Orleans in homes and businesses, will paint-to-order your own personal sign and ship it to you. This gallery and shop is shared with Simon's wife, Maria, who has particularly good taste in primitive furniture, antiques, and hodgepodgery. 2126 Magazine St. Ⓒ **504/561-0088**. Mon by appt; Tues–Sat 10am–5pm.

MUSIC

Louisiana Music Factory ✮✮✮   This popular and terrific store carries a large selection of regional music—including Cajun, zydeco, R&B, jazz, blues, and gospel—plus books, posters, and T-shirts. It also has frequent live music and beer bashes—shop while you bop! It's the place to get yourself informed about New Orleans music. 210 Decatur St. Ⓒ **504/586-1094**. www.louisianamusicfactory.com. Mon–Sat 10am–7pm; Sun noon–6pm.

7

New Orleans After Dark

New Orleans is one of the most beautiful cities in the United States, possibly the world, but we won't mind if you never see the sights—provided, however, that the omission is because you are spending the daylight hours recovering from the equally extraordinary nightlife.

This is a city of music and rhythm. It is impossible to imagine New Orleans without a soundtrack of jazz, Cajun, and zydeco. Music streams from every doorway, and sometimes it seems people are dancing down the street. Sometimes they really are. (After all, this is the town that sends you to your grave with music and then dances back from the cemetery.) You walk along Bourbon Street, for example, and with every step you hear music of all varieties. Maybe none of it is world-class, but that doesn't matter too much. It's just that it's there and in such variety. Plus, it's darn infectious.

This is also the city of decadence and good times rolling. Not to mention really loose liquor laws and drinks in "go" cups (plastic containers you can take with you—many bars and clubs even have walk-up windows for easy refills). And all this increases at night. We aren't just talking about the open-air frat party that is Bourbon Street some (okay, most) evenings. In fact, we prefer not to talk about that at all.

Most important is that virtually every night, dozens of clubs all over town offer music that can range from average to extraordinary but is never less than danceable. In most places, cover prices vary from night to night and performer to performer, but rarely will you have to pay more than $10—and then only for more high-falutin' places such as the House of Blues. When the clubs get too full, no matter: The crowd spills into the street, talking, drinking, and still dancing right there on the sidewalk. Sometimes the action outside is even more fun than inside.

Club hopping is easy, though with some exceptions some of the better choices will require leaving the Quarter by cab or some other vehicle. Don't worry—most are a cheap taxi ride away, and many are within an additional, even cheaper cab ride, if not walking distance, of each other. We strongly urge you to leave the Quarter at night to visit some of the town's better joints.

However, if you aren't up to that, don't fret. Some of the best jazz and brass-band clubs are right in the Quarter. And only steps away is the excellent scene in the Frenchmen section of the Faubourg Marigny, where at least six clubs and bars are going at once within 3 blocks of each other. However you decide to do it, don't miss it. New Orleans at night is not New Orleans during the day, and not to take advantage of it is to miss out. You could stay in your hotel room with the covers pulled over your head, but if that's what you want, you came to the wrong city: Just tell yourself you'll sleep when you get home.

For up-to-date information on what's happening around town, look for current editions of *Gambit, Offbeat,* and *WhereY'at,* all distributed free in most hotels and all record stores. You can also check out *Offbeat* on the Internet (**www.nola.com**; once you get to the NOLA home page, go to the music and entertainment section). Other sources include the *Times-Picayune*'s daily entertainment calendar and Friday's **"Lagniappe"** section of the newspaper. Additionally, **WWOZ** (90.7 FM) broadcasts the local music schedule several times throughout the day.

1 Jazz & Blues Clubs

THE FRENCH QUARTER & THE FAUBOURG MARIGNY

Blue Nile ⓕⓕ   It's taken a long while for the dedicated owner of Blue Nile to get it back in order after post-storm damage and insurance tussles, but his victory is complete with a well-scrubbed new facility. Grit like that, plus loyalty to the city, should be rewarded, which is easy, since the Nile is smack in the center of the thriving Frenchmen club scene, and so is easily added to your list of stops. The two-story club has better than average sightlines, except for near the bar where archways can obstruct views. There should be excellent pizza (it's owned by the same people who do Rocco's in the Quarter) for late-night munchies upstairs, and at least three shows a week by a wide variety of locals plus late-night DJ's. 532 Frenchmen St. ⓒ 504/948-BLUE. www.bluenilelive.com. Cover varies.

Donna's ⓕⓕⓕ   A corner bar at the very northern edge of the Quarter, Donna's has become one of the top spots for great local

New Orleans Nightlife

Apple Barrel **11**
Blue Nile **13**
Cafe Brasil **12**
Circle Bar **2**
The Columns **1**
Cowpokes **16**
d.b.a. **10**

Feelings Cafe **18**
The Howlin' Wolf **3**
Mother-in-Law Lounge **7**
Mulate's **4**
Pals Lounge **6**
Polo Lounge **5**
Ray's Boom Boom Room **14**

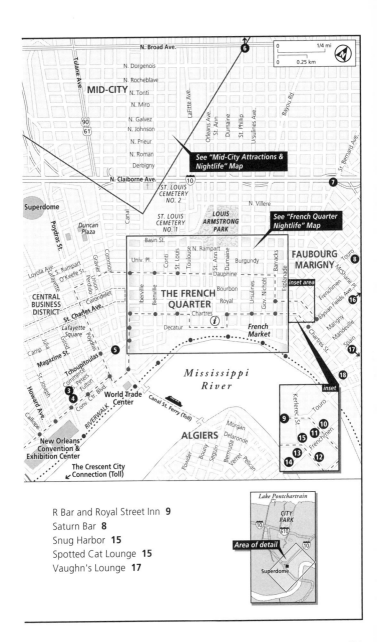

R Bar and Royal Street Inn **9**
Saturn Bar **8**
Snug Harbor **15**
Spotted Cat Lounge **15**
Vaughn's Lounge **17**

music, including the revival of the brass-band experience and a variety of jazz and blues traditions. But the main asset may be Donna herself, often monitoring the door to make sure you don't bring in drinks from outside and making sure you do order something inside. She's been one of the true boosters of new generations of New Orleans music (she's managed both the hip-hop-edged brass band Soul Rebels and the new-funk ensemble Galactic) and has helped promote awareness of veteran brass bands like Treme and Olympia. As with most real New Orleans hangouts, atmosphere is minimal, but spirits (liquid and otherwise) are high. The cover charge for performances is usually no more than the cost of a good mixed drink. *Note:* Donna's is in a transitional neighborhood, so be careful upon entering and leaving. 800 N. Rampart St. © 504/596-6914. www.donnasbarandgrill.com. Closed Tues–Wed. Cover varies.

The Famous Door   Open since 1934, The Famous Door is the oldest music club on Bourbon Street. Many local jazz, pop, and rock musicians have passed through here. One of them, Harry Connick, Jr., played his first gigs here at the age of 13. 339 Bourbon St. © 504/598-4334. No cover; no drink minimum.

Fritzel's European Jazz Pub 🎷   You might walk right past this small establishment, but that would be a big mistake because the 1831 building brings some of the city's best musicians to play on its tiny stage. In addition to the regular weekend program of late-night jazz (Fri–Sat from 10:30pm, Sun from 10pm), there are frequent jam sessions in the wee hours during the week when performers end their stints elsewhere and gather to play "musicians' music." The full bar also stocks a variety of schnapps (served ice-cold) and German beers. 733 Bourbon St. © 504/561-0432. No cover; 1-drink minimum per set.

Maison Bourbon 🎷🎷   Despite its location and the sign saying the building is "dedicated to the preservation of jazz," Maison Bourbon is not a tourist trap. The music is very authentic, and often superb, jazz. From about midafternoon until the wee hours, Dixieland and traditional jazz hold forth, often at loud and lively volume. Players include Wallace Davenport, Steve Slocum, and Tommy Yetta. Patrons must be at least 21 years old. 641 Bourbon St. © 504/522-8818. 1-drink minimum per person.

Palm Court Jazz Café 🎷🎷   This is one of the most stylish jazz haunts in the Quarter. It's an elegant setting in which to catch top-notch jazz groups Wednesday through Sunday. The music varies nightly but is generally traditional or classic jazz. If you collect jazz

French Quarter Nightlife

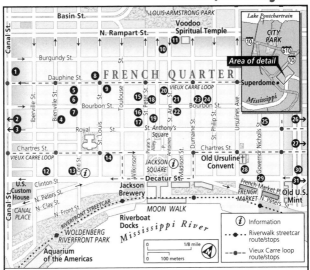

The Abbey **28**

Apple Barrel **31**

Beque's at the
Royal Sonesta **7**

The Bombay Club **5**

The Bourbon Pub-
Parade Disco **21**

Cafe Brasil **27**

Cafe Lafitte in Exile **23**

Carousel Bar & Lounge **3**

Checkpoint Charlie's **30**

The Corner Pocket **8**

Dickie Brennan's Steakhouse **2**

Donna's **11**

The Famous Door **6**

Feelings Cafe **31**

French 75 **4**

Fritzel's European Jazz Pub **18**

Golden Lantern **25**

Good Friends Bar & Queen's
Head Pub **20**

House of Blues **12**

Kerry Irish Pub **13**

Lafitte's Blacksmith Shop **24**

LeRoundup **9**

Library Lounge at the
Ritz-Carlton **1**

Mason Bourbon **15**

Napoleon House Bar & Café **14**

Orleans Grapevine Wine
Bar & Bistro **19**

Oz **22**

Palm Court Jazz Café **29**

Pat O'Brien's **17**

Preservation Hall **16**

R Bar and Royal Street Inn **26**

Rawhide **10**

Snug Harbor **31**

records, peek at the records for sale in a back alcove. *Tip:* You might want to make reservations—it's that kind of place. 1204 Decatur St. ℭ 504/525-0200. www.palmcourtjazzcafe.com. Cover $5 per person at tables; no cover at bar.

Preservation Hall 𝕬𝕬𝕬 The gray, bombed-out building that looks as if it were erected just shortly after the dawn of time (or at least the dawn of New Orleans) doesn't seem like much, but it's a mecca for traditional-jazz fans. This is an essential spot for anyone coming to New Orleans. No amplification, no air-conditioning—it doesn't get any more authentic than this. It's not quite as dirt-cheap as it used to be, but it still is one of your must-do stops on your trip.

With no seats, terrible sightlines, and constant crowds, you won't be able to see much, but you won't care because you will be having a too fun and cheerfully sweaty time. Patrons start lining up at 6:15pm—the doors open at 8pm, so the trick to avoid the line is to get here either just as the doors open or later in the evening. The band plays until midnight, and the first audience usually empties out around 10pm.

A sign on the wall gives prices for requests—figure on $10 for "Saints Go Marchin' In," $5 for everything else. Or just offer something. Thanks to the casual atmosphere, not to mention the cheap cover, Preservation Hall is one of the few nightspots where it's appropriate to take kids. Early in the evening you'll notice a number of local families doing just that. Call ahead for current open hours. 726 St. Peter St. ℭ **888/946-JAZZ** or 504/522-2841. www.preservation hall.com. Cover $8.

Snug Harbor 𝕬𝕬 If your idea of jazz extends beyond Dixieland and if you prefer a concert-type setting over a messy nightclub, get your hands on Snug Harbor's monthly schedule. On the fringes of the French Quarter (1 block beyond Esplanade Ave.), Snug Harbor is the city's premier showcase for contemporary jazz, with a few blues and R&B combos thrown in for good measure. This is the surest place to find Ellis Marsalis (patriarch of the Marsalis dynasty) and Charmaine Neville (of the Neville family).

Not only does Snug offer good music, but the two-level seating provides generally good viewing of the bandstand. (Beware the pillars upstairs, especially if you don't get seats along the rail and have to sit a way back, though.) You should buy tickets in advance, but be warned: Waiting for a show usually means hanging in the crowded, low-ceilinged bar, where personal space is at a minimum—not recommended for claustrophobes. 626 Frenchmen St. (C) **504/949-0696.** www.snugjazz.com. Cover $12–$20, depending on performer. Doors open at 7pm, sets start at 8 and 10pm.

ELSEWHERE AROUND THE CITY

Vaughan's Lounge Tucked deep in the Bywater section of New Orleans, Vaughan's Lounge is way down-home—as in, it's in a residential neighborhood and feels almost as though you're in someone's house. The long bar takes up so much room that people almost fall over the band at the end of the room. In the back room, you might find people playing Ping-Pong. Thursday—Kermit Ruffins's night—is the night to go to Vaughan's. Go early and get some of the barbecue Kermit is often cooking up before a show—he likes to barbecue as much as he likes to play, and he tends to bring his grill along with him wherever he is playing. Or you might catch a Mardi Gras Indian practice. Thanks to the many post-Katrina volunteers around the Bywater area, Vaughan's has become a major scene even beyond its original NOLA role. Be sure to call ahead to see if there will be live music on—and be sure to take a taxi. 4229 Dauphine St. (C) **504/947-5562.** Cover varies, usually $8–$10.

2 Cajun & Zydeco Joints

Mid City Lanes Rock 'n' Bowl ★★★ Anything we just said about tourist traps and inauthentic experiences does not apply here. It does not get any more authentic than a club set in the middle of a bowling alley, which is itself set in the middle of a strip mall. Actually, as a bowling alley, Mid City bowling is nothing to write home about unless you like lanes that slope. But as a club, it's one of the finest and best experiences in New Orleans. Certainly it's the best place for zydeco, particularly on the nights devoted to Zydeco Wars, when the audience votes on whether, say, Geno Delafose or C. J. Chenier is the King of Zydeco. It also features top New Orleans rock and R&B groups and some touring acts. On good nights (though we do wonder if Mid City has any that aren't), the dance floor is crowded beyond belief, the noise level is ridiculous, the humidity level is 300%, and you won't want to leave. You might even bowl a few frames. While the owner is quite committed to keeping his business open and in this location, the ground floors of the aforementioned strip mall flooded badly (though the Rock 'n' Bowl itself escaped without damage), and while the hope is that whatever the future of the compound is does not affect the club, you should probably call in advance to make sure the status quo remains. 4133 S. Carrollton Ave. ⓒ **504/482-3133**. www.rockandbowl.com. Tues–Sun 5pm until "the party closes down." Bowling $15 per hour; show admission $5–$10.

Mulate's ⓕ   This is a branch of the original (out in Cajun Country) and a not-unlikely place to find authentic, and decent, Cajun bands. The stage and dance area are relatively spacious, and the food isn't bad. During Jazz Fest 2006, when Beausoleil played, none other than Bob Dylan dropped by to listen! 201 Julia St., at Convention Center Blvd. ⓒ **800/854-9149** or 504/522-1492. www.mulates.com. No cover.

3 Rhythm, Rock & the Rest of the Music Scene

Most clubs in New Orleans feature an eclectic lineup that reflects the town's music scene; the ReBirth Brass Band, for example, attracts as many rock fans as it does brass-band fans. Consequently, the bulk of the club scene escapes categorization (and, of course, booking policies are often subject to change)—even the local papers refer to club lineups as "mixed bags." Check listings (in *Offbeat* and *Gambit* magazines, for example) night by night. Some places are generally good fun on their own regardless of who is playing; any night at the **Maple Leaf** is going to be a good one, while wandering from spot to spot in the Frenchmen section is a well-spent evening. Really, in New Orleans, you can't go too wrong going just about anywhere simply to hang out. And in the process, you might get exposed to a new, wonderful genre of music or an incredible band.

THE FRENCH QUARTER & THE FAUBOURG MARIGNY

Cafe Brasil ⓕ   Day (when it is a great place to get a cup of coffee and to hear gossip) or night (when it delivers danceable music), Cafe Brasil anchors the lively and popular Frenchmen section of the Faubourg Marigny. It features Latin or Caribbean music, R&B, or jazz usually on weekend nights, and chances are whatever is playing will be infectious. Anticipate a hip and trendy, though still casual, crowd and be prepared to act cool. The decent-size dance floor fills up quickly, and the crowd spills into the street to see and be seen. 2100 Chartres St. No phone at press time. Cover varies.

Checkpoint Charlie's   Somewhere between a biker bar and a college hangout, the dark Checkpoint Charlie's only *seems* intimidating—an effect that's helped by the hard-rock sounds usually blaring from the stage. It's easy to overlook straight rock with all the other

New Orleans sounds around, but this would be the place to start trying to find it. R&B and blues also sneak into the mix as well as the occasional acoustic open-mic night. A full bar, food, and pool tables help soften the ambience for the easily intimidated, and it's open 24 hours, making it a less-touristy place for a quick drink during the day. Plus, there's a coin laundry, so a dusty traveler can clean up while enjoying the music. 501 Esplanade Ave. ⓒ 504/281-4847. No cover.

d.b.a. ⚞⚞   It's been around long enough that its prefab yuppie patina has worn off, aging it into another excellent New Orleans bar. Better still, their live bookings are increasing in profile, with a wide variety of excellent local acts, including magnificent crooner John Boutte as a frequent performer. It helps that when they say an act goes on at 7pm, they usually do. Early shows are often free, but get to the later shows early if you want to see the band, because the stage is set fairly low and the talkers at the bar can be loud. The list of 160 beers, wines, and other drinks is most impressive. 618 Frenchmen St. ⓒ 504/942-3731. www.drinkgoodstuff.com/no. Cover varies.

House of Blues ⚞   New Orleans was a natural place for this franchise to set up shop, but its presence in the French Quarter seems rather unnatural. With all the great, funky, authentic music clubs in town, why build one with ersatz "authenticity" that wouldn't be out of place in Disneyland? And while it's noble that they've patronized many deserving Southern "primitive" artists to line the walls with colorful works, there's a certain Hearst Castle grab-bag element to that, too, which diminishes the value and cultural context of the individual works. That isn't to say the facility is without its good points. The music room has adequate sightlines and good sound, and the chain's financial muscle assures first-rate bookings, from local legends such as the Neville Brothers to such ace out-of-towners as Los Lobos. But patronizing this club rather than the real thing, like Tipitina's (which lost considerable business after the HOB opened), is akin to eating at McDonald's rather than Mother's. Having said all of that, a smaller room, the **House of Blues Parish,** features both local and national acts, and on any given day, probably offers more (for a cheaper price) than the big room. 225 Decatur St. ⓒ 504/529-2583. www.hob.com. Cover varies.

Ray's Boom Boom Room ⚞⚞   A splendid new addition to the already terrific Frenchmen club scene, this long two-story room, sparkling new and the epitome of New Orleans style, is partly owned by local music fave and staunch supporter Kermit Ruffins. Music covers the gamut, with acts on both the small stage near the street-facing window and on the larger stage at the back. Well on its way to becoming *the* club of Frenchmen, not to mention a nice place for an early or late-night bite. Go help them become just that, okay? 508 Frenchmen St. No phone at press time. Daily 11am–"until." Cover varies.

The Spotted Cat Cocktail Lounge 𝕮𝕮𝕮   Right now, this is our favorite live-music venue in New Orleans, but that's because of our particular New Orleans aesthetic bent: We are partial to cramped rooms where the band plays without much (if any) amplification, and what they play is usually fresh takes on classic and big-band jazz. You'll have to hang around a bit to grab those few seats by the window, and in the meantime endure some space-crowding from the enthusiastic jitterbuggers, but once you've settled down, you may not want to leave for a long while. Traditional and Gypsy jazz is regularly featured in both early and late shows. On Fridays, you'll find us hanging around the doorway, listening to the New Orleans Jazz Vipers, not to mention other nights for Va-va-voom and more. 623 Frenchmen St. ℂ 504/943-3887. No cover.

ELSEWHERE AROUND THE CITY

Throughout this book, we keep nagging you to leave the Quarter. This advice is most important at night. It's not that there aren't some worthwhile, memorable clubs in the Quarter or at the fringes. It's just that there are so many terrific (and, in some cases, outright better) ones elsewhere. And not only do they feature some of the best music in town (if not, on some nights, in the country), they aren't designed as tourist destinations, so your experience will be that much more legitimate.

Carrollton Station 𝕮𝕮   Way uptown in the Riverbend area, Carrollton Station is a gourmet beer house that, thanks to some renovations to the room and the stage, is emerging as a prime folk, acoustic, and local rock venue in town. A long, narrow space means that folks at the back won't get to see much of what's up onstage, but hey, that puts them closer to the bar, so everyone wins. The crowd is a good mix of college students, music aficionados, and fans of whatever act is appearing on a given night. 8140 Willow St. ℂ 504/865-9190. www.carrolltonstation.com. Cover varies on weekends. No cover weekdays.

The Howlin' Wolf 𝕮   Pre-Katrina this was arguably the premier club in town in terms of the quality and fame of its bookings, and it is especially so since an October 2005 move down the block and across the street has put it into an even better space. With 10,000 square feet (quite a bit more than they used to have), including more bathrooms, a wide but shallow room (which means great sightlines from about anywhere; sightlines are a problem in most New Orleans clubs), a bar that came from Al Capone's hotel in Chicago, and bookings that range from top local acts to national touring rock bands, it's probably the best place right now to see a show. In addition to regular bookings, they are currently doing a lot of comedy nights. Howlin' Wolf does draw some top touring rock acts, though it is not at all limited to rock—El Vez, the Mexican Elvis, is as likely to play as a country band or the latest in indie and alternative rock (performers in the past included Frank Black, the Jon Spencer Blues Explosion, and Iris DeMent). 907 S. Peters St., in the Warehouse District. ☏ **504/522-WOLF.** www.howlin-wolf.com. Cover varies.

Maple Leaf Bar ⟲⟲⟲   This is what a New Orleans club is all about, and its reputation was only furthered when it became the very first live music venue to reopen, just weeks after Katrina, with an emotional, generator-powered performance by Walter "Wolfman" Washington. It's medium-size but feels smaller when a crowd is packed in, and by 11pm on most nights, it is, with personal space at times becoming something you can only wistfully remember. But that's no problem. The stage is against the window facing the street, so more often than not, the crowd spills onto the sidewalk and into the street to dance and drink (and escape the heat and sweat, which are prodigious despite a high ceiling). With a party atmosphere like this, outside is almost more fun than in. But inside is mighty fine. A good bar and a rather pretty patio out back (the other place to escape the crush) make the Maple Leaf worth hanging out at even if you don't care about the music on a particular night. But if the ReBirth Brass Band is playing, do not miss it; go and dance until you drop. 8316 Oak St. ☏ **504/866-9359.** Cover varies.

Tipitina's ⟲⟲⟲   Dedicated to the late piano master Professor Longhair and featured in the movie *The Big Easy,* Tip's was long *the* New Orleans club. But due to circumstances both external (increased competition from House of Blues and others as well as the club's capacity being cut in half by city authorities) and internal (some gripes about pre-Katrina booking quality) its star has faded some. It remains a reliable place for top local bands, though, and if you can catch Troy Andrews or especially Dr. John on one of his excursions back to his city, it's a must.

The place is nothing fancy—just four walls, a wraparound balcony, and a stage, all of it overseen by a giant drawing of 'Fess his own self. Oh, and a couple of bars, of course, including one that serves the people milling outside the club, which as at other top locales is as much a part of the atmosphere as what's inside. Bookings range from top indigenous acts (a brass-bands blowout and a jazz piano night are the perennial highlights of Jazz Fest week) to touring alt-rock and roots acts, both U.S.-based and international. 501 Napoleon Ave. ℂ 504/895-8477 or 504/897-3943 for concert line. www.tipitinas.com. Cover varies.

4 The Bar Scene

You won't have any trouble finding a place to drink in New Orleans. Heck, thanks to "go" (or *geaux*) cups, you won't have to spend a minute without a drink in your hand. (It's legal to have liquor outside as long as it's in a plastic cup. Actually, given the number of people who take advantage of this law, it almost seems illegal *not* to have such a cup in your hand.) Note that many of the clubs listed above are terrific spots to hoist a few (or a dozen), while some of the bars below also provide music—but that is strictly background for their real design. Piano bars, in particular, have begun to pop up; they're everywhere; in addition to the ones listed below, you can find a piano bar in almost every large hotel, and plenty of others off by themselves.

Many bars stay open all the time or have varying hours depending upon the night or the season. If you have your heart set on a particular place, it's always best to call and make sure what their hours will be for that day. Unless noted, none of the places listed below has a cover charge.

THE FRENCH QUARTER & THE FAUBOURG MARIGNY

In addition to the places below, you might consider the clubby bar at **Dickie Brennan's Steakhouse,** 716 Iberville St. (p. 88; ℂ 504/522-2467), a place where manly men go to drink strong drinks, smoke smelly cigars (they have a vast selection for sale), and chat up girlie girls. Or you could enjoy the low-key sophistication found at **Beque's at the Royal Sonesta,** 300 Bourbon St. (ℂ 504/586-0300), where a jazz trio is usually playing.

The Abbey   Despite the name, this place is more basement rumpus room (walls covered with stickers and old album covers) than Gothic church (well, there are some motley stained-glass windows).

But it's been a bar since the 1930s, the jukebox plays The Cramps and Iggy Pop and the Stooges' "I Wanna Be Your Dog," and the clientele is very David Lynchian (maybe still left over from the place's heyday 20 years ago!). Still, you might find this a scary dump rather than a cool dump. 1123 Decatur St. ✆ **504/523-7177.** Open 24 hr.

Apple Barrel A small, dusty, wooden-floored watering hole complete with jukebox and darts (of course). You can find refuge here from the hectic Frenchmen scene (catch your breath and have a beer)—or gear up to join in, as they usually have live music (tending toward local blues acts like Coco Robicheaux) most nights. 609 Frenchmen St. ✆ **504/949-9399.**

The Bombay Club This posh piano bar features jazz Friday and Saturday evenings, with hopes for an expanded calendar at some point. It's also a restaurant (the food is not great) and a martini bar—the drink has been a specialty here for years, so don't accuse the club of trying to ride the current martini trend. In fact, the Bombay's martinis are hailed by some as the best in town. 830 Conti St. ✆ **800/699-7711** or 504/586-0972. www.thebombayclub.com.

Carousel Bar & Lounge ✪✪ Piano music is featured here Wednesday through Saturday, but the real attraction is the bar itself—it really is a carousel, and it really does revolve ("and has since 1949!" said a justly proud employee). The music goes on until 2am (or simply "until" these days). But don't think of this as a cheesy place: It's really a great spot to step back in time and have a cocktail—not a beer, of course, but a grown-up drink. A top choice for those not interested in Bourbon frat-party fun or even the young and the frenzied on Frenchmen Street. And if the bartender isn't busy or indifferent, they make a fine Sazerac. In the Monteleone Hotel, 214 Royal St. ✆ **504/523-3341.**

Feelings Cafe ✪ Here's a funky, low-key neighborhood restaurant and hangout set around a classic New Orleans courtyard, which is where most folks drink—unless they are hanging out with the piano player, a currently every-other-Friday performer, with the occasional guest hitting the keys on other nights. It's authentic in the right ways but is also more cheerful than some of the darker, hole-in-the-wall spots that deserve that adjective. 2600 Chartres St. ✆ **504/945-2222.** www.feelingscafe.com.

French 75 Bar ✪✪ A beautiful bar space in one of the Quarter's most venerable restaurants, it feels like drinking in New Orleans should, in terms of classy presentation and atmosphere. Any dedicated cocktailian should come by to test the bartenders on their knowledge or to experiment with curious beverages. In Arnaud's restaurant, 813 Bienville St. ℂ **504/523-5433.**

Kerry Irish Pub ℱ This traditional Irish pub has a variety of beers and other spirits but is most proud of its properly poured pints of Guinness and hard cider. The pub is a good bet for live Irish and "alternative" folk music; it's also a place to throw darts and shoot pool. In case you want one last nightcap on your way back through the Quarter, you should know that Kerry specializes in very-late-night drinking. 331 Decatur St. ℂ **504/527-5954.** www.kerryirishpub.com.

Lafitte's Blacksmith Shop ℱℱℱ It's some steps away from the main action on Bourbon, but you'll know Lafitte's when you see it. Dating from the 1770s, it's the oldest building in the Quarter and it looks it (though we all could have done without that really bad exterior remodel job that made fake what had been authentic exposed brick and plaster). Legend has it that the privateer brothers Pierre and Jean Lafitte used the smithy as a "blind" for their lucrative trade in contraband (and, some say, slaves they'd captured on the high seas). Like all legends, that's probably not true. In other towns, this would be a tourist trap—definitely worth swinging by even if you don't drink. 941 Bourbon St. ℂ **504/593-9761.**

The Library Lounge at the Ritz-Carlton ℱℱℱ This gorgeous and comfortable (albeit crowded on weekend nights) bar would be recommended as a sophisticated yet unintimidating place to drink just for its own visual aesthetic. But put fourth-generation bartender Chris McMillian in the mix, and you have pretty much *the* bar for serious drinkers. And by "serious drinkers" we mean people who revere the art of the cocktail. As McMillian makes the best mint julep in the country for you, he'll recite its history (in the form of an ode to the julep written in the 1890s by a Kentuckian newspaperman) as he muddles and mixes and pours. At the **Ritz-Carlton** (p. 45), 921 Canal St. ℂ **504/524-1331.**

Napoleon House Bar & Café ℱℱℱ Set in a landmark building, the Napoleon House is one of the best barrooms in the country, a must-do and just the place to go to have a quiet drink (as opposed to the very loud drinks found elsewhere in the Quarter) and maybe hatch some schemes. Like Lafitte's (see above), it's dark, dark, dark, with walls you really wish could talk. Also like Lafitte's, it seems too perfect to be real—surely this must be constructed just for the tourists. It's not. Be sure to try the Pimm's Cup. 500 Chartres St. ℂ **504/524-9752.** www.napoleonhouse.com.

Orleans Grapevine Wine Bar & Bistro 🐸🐸 Now that *Sideways* has shown us all what a great big metaphor for life wine can be, come sample the possibilities off the staggering list at this quiet little refuge. Take note of their special menu of seasonal tasties and consider making a meal of it, too. 720 Orleans Ave. 🕐 504/523-1930.

Pat O'Brien's Pat O'Brien's is world-famous for the gigantic, rum-based drink with the big-wind name. The formula (according to legend) was stumbled upon by bar owners Charlie Cantrell and George Oechsner while they were experimenting with Caribbean rum during World War II. The drink is served in signature 29-ounce hurricane lamp–style glasses. The bar now offers a 3-gallon Magnum Hurricane that stands taller than many small children. It's served with a handful of straws and takes a group to finish (we profoundly hope)—all of whom must drink standing up. Naturally, the offerings and reputation attract the tourists and college yahoos in droves. Which is not to say that Pat's isn't worth a stop—it's a reliable, rowdy, friendly introduction to New Orleans. Just don't expect to be the only person who thinks so. Fortunately, it's large enough to accommodate nearly everyone—in three different bars, including a large lounge that usually offers entertainment (an emcee and alternating piano players)—with the highlight, on nonrainy days at least, being the attractive tropical patio.

There's no minimum and no cover, but if you buy a drink and it comes in a glass, you'll be paying for the glass until you turn it in at the register for a $3 refund. 718 St. Peter St. 🕐 **504/525-4823**. www.pat obriens.com.

R Bar and Royal Street Inn 🐸🐸🐸 The R (short for Royal St.) Bar is a quintessential neighborhood bar in a neighborhood full of artists, wannabe artists, punk-rock intellectuals, urban gentrifiers, and well-rounded hipsters. It's a talkers' bar and a haven for strutting, overconfident pool players. On Mardi Gras day this is also the headquarters for the locals described above—it's their designated meeting place and watering hole on Fat Tuesday. The R Bar has a large selection of imported beers and one of the best alternative and art-rock jukeboxes in the city. Thanks to all this (or perhaps in spite of some of it), it's just a cool little local bar. 1431 Royal St. 🕐 **504/948-7499**. www.royalstreetinn.com.

ELSEWHERE AROUND THE CITY

Circle Bar 🐸🐸 This tiny bar is among the most bohemian-hip in town, courtesy of the slightly twisted folks behind Snake & Jake's. Ambience is the key; it's got the ever-popular "elegant decay" look, from peeling wallpaper to a neon glow from an old K&B drugstore sign on the ceiling. The jukebox keeps the quirky romantic mood going, thanks to bewitching, mood-enhancing selections from the Velvet Underground, Dusty Springfield, and Curtis Mayfield. The clientele is laid-back. Live music includes mostly local acts. 1032 St. Charles Ave., in the CBD at Lee Circle. ℭ **504/588-2616.**

The Columns 𝕽𝕽   Here's a local favorite for drinks on the white-columned porch under spreading oak trees. Why? Well, aside from the Old South setting, beers at happy hour are a measly $2, and mixed drinks are not much more. Watching a downpour from the safety of that classic veranda is rather on the awesome side. Inside, you will think you've stumbled onto the set of *Pretty Baby*—because, in fact, you have. The interiors were shot here. 3811 St. Charles Ave., Uptown. ℭ **504/899-9308.** www.thecolumns.com.

Kingpin 𝕽𝕽   For those who want that *Barfly* experience without the smelly drunks and in the company of other like-minded folks of a certain (20-something) age, come to Kingpin. Nominally Elvis-themed (though expect bashes on key dates in the timeline of Himself), this absurdly small space is increasingly popular among hipster/rocker/Dave Navarro types, when they can find it, that is. (*Hint:* It's near the Upperline restaurant.) 1307 Lyons St., Uptown. ℭ **504/891-2373.**

Mother-in-Law Lounge 𝕽𝕽   Ernie K-Doe may be gone, but this shrine to his glorious self and funky lounges everywhere lives on, thanks to wife, Antoinette, the keeper of the K-Doe legend and the bar's owner. Named after his biggest hit, a rousing 1961 number-one pop/R&B novelty, this is a true neighborhood dive bar. You may want to be careful in the neighborhood, but once you're there, be sure to play one of K-Doe's songs on the jukebox and drink a toast to the man who billed himself as "Emperor of the Universe." Call first—hours are erratic (and often early). 1500 N. Claiborne Ave., northeast of the Quarter. ℭ **504/947-1078.** www.kdoe.com.

Pals Lounge 𝕽𝕽   Well-heeled backers (including Rio Hackford, son of director Taylor) have turned Pals Lounge into a retro hipster bar, and are offering an alternative watering hole for the increasingly gentrified St. John's Bayou neighborhood. As compensation to the working-class clientele who lost their old hangout, it sells Pabst Blue Ribbon for a buck a can. Now you have vintage barflies mingling with the neighborhood bohos who come with their dogs or riding their bikes. 949 N. Rendon St., Bayou St. John. ℭ **504/488-PALS.**

The Polo Lounge ★★   The Windsor Court is probably the city's finest hotel (p. 64), and The Polo Lounge is the place to go if you're feeling particularly stylish. Sazeracs and cigars are popular here. Don't expect to find any kids; if you like to seal your deals with a drink, this is likely to be your first choice. In the Windsor Court hotel, 300 Gravier St., in the CBD. ✆ **504/523-6000.**

Saturn Bar ★   The Saturn Bar is among the hipster set's most beloved dives, but it's hard to decide if the love is genuine or comes from a postmodern, ironic appreciation of the grubby, art-project (we can only hope) interior. The irascible owner, already in failing health, died shortly after Katrina, but his family has vowed to carry on, even adding live bands a couple times a week. Given the vibe, said bands are usually fairly wacky. The neighborhood demands that caution be exercised—get someone to walk you to and from your car, especially if you are a woman alone. 3067 St. Claude Ave., in the Bywater. ✆ **504/949-7532.**

Snake & Jake's Xmas Club Lounge ★★   Though admittedly off the beaten path, this tiny, friendly dive is the perfect place for those looking for an authentic neighborhood bar. Co-owned by local musician Dave Clements, decorated (sort of) with Christmas lights, and featuring a great jukebox heavy on soul and R&B, this is the kind of place where everybody not only knows your name, they know your dog's name, 'cause you can bring the dog, too. There is almost no light at all, so make friends and prepare to be surprised. 7612 Oak St., Uptown. ✆ **504/861-2802.** www.snakeandjakes.com.

5 Gay Nightlife

For more information, you can check *Ambush*, 828-A Bourbon St. (✆ **504/522-8047**; www.ambushmag.com), a great source for the gay community in New Orleans and for visitors. The magazine's website has a lot of handy-dandy links to other sites of gay interest, including info on local gay bars (www.gaybars.com/states/louisian.htm).

BARS

In addition to those listed below, you might also try the **Golden Lantern,** 1239 Royal St. (✆ **504/529-2860**), a nice neighborhood spot where the bartender knows the patrons by name. If Levi's and leather is your scene, then **Rawhide,** 740 Burgundy St. (✆ **504/525-8106**; www.rawhide2010.com), is your best bet; during Mardi

Gras, it hosts a great gay costume contest that's not to be missed. The rest of the year, it's a hustler bar.

The Bourbon Pub–Parade Disco This is more or less the most centrally located of the gay bars, with many of the other popular gay bars nearby. The downstairs pub offers a video bar (often featuring surprisingly cutting-edge, innovative stuff) and is the calmer of the two; it's open 24 hours daily and usually gets most crowded in the hour just before the Parade Disco opens. (*Note:* A $5 cover charge gets you all the draft beer you can drink 5–9pm.) The Parade Disco is upstairs and features a high-tech dance floor complete with lasers and smoke. 801 Bourbon St. ℂ **504/529-2107.** www.bourbonpub.com.

Café Lafitte in Exile This is one of the oldest gay bars in the United States, having been around since 1953. There's a bar downstairs, and upstairs you'll find a pool table and a balcony that overlooks Bourbon Street. The whole shebang is open 24 hours daily. This is a cruise bar, but it doesn't attract a teeny-bopper or twinkie crowd. One of the most popular weekly events is the Sunday evening "Trash Disco," when, you guessed it, they play trashy disco music from the '70s and everyone has a lot of fun. 901 Bourbon St. ℂ **504/522-8397.** www.lafittes.com.

The Corner Pocket While the boast that they have the hottest male strippers in town may be perhaps too generous, you can decide for yourself by checking out this bar Thursday through Sunday nights after 10pm. Locals who aren't a bit ashamed of themselves claim that the cutest boys can be found on Friday nights, and sigh that the management has the strippers wear the sort of garments that prevent peeking (not that that prevents anyone from trying). The bar itself is none too special (and despite the name, the only draw for the pool table is that players might not be especially clothed). The average age of the clientele is around 70. 940 St. Louis St. ℂ **504/568-9829.** www.cornerpocket.net.

CowPokes Looking for a gay country bar? Never let it be said that Frommer's lets you down. This is a particularly nice gay country bar, though it resides in a transitional neighborhood, so do let a cab bring you out for some of the weekly activities, including free line-dance lessons on Tuesday and karaoke and lube wrestling on Wednesday. 2240 St. Claude. ℂ **504/947-0505.**

Good Friends Bar & Queens Head Pub This bar and pub is very friendly to visitors and often wins the Gay Achievement Award for Best Neighborhood Gay Bar. They describe themselves as "always snappy casual!" The local clientele is happy to offer suggestions about where you might find the type of entertainment you're looking for. Downstairs is a mahogany bar and a pool table. Upstairs is the quiet Queens Head Pub, which was recently decorated in the style of a Victorian English pub. The bar is open 24 hours. 740 Dauphine St. ℭ 504/566-7191. www.goodfriendsbar.com.

LeRoundup   LeRoundup attracts the most diverse crowd around. You'll find transsexuals lining up at the bar with drag queens and well-groomed men in khakis and Levi's. Expect encounters with working boys. It's open 24 hours. 819 St. Louis St. ℭ 504/561-8340.

DANCE CLUBS

Oz   Oz is the place to see and be seen, with a primarily young crowd (like its across-the-street neighbor, The Bourbon Pub–Parade Disco; see above). It was ranked the city's best dance club by *Gambit* magazine, and *Details* magazine named it one of the top 50 clubs in the country. The music is great, there's an incredible laser-light show, and from time to time there are go-go boys atop the bar. Oz hosts frequent theme nights, so call ahead if you're going and want to dress accordingly. 800 Bourbon St. ℭ 504/593-9491. www.ozneworleans. com. Cover varies; straights pay extra.

Index

See also Accommodations and Restaurant indexes below.

GENERAL INDEX

Abbey, The 190–191
Accommodations, 38–78. *See also*
    Accommodations Index
    Central Business District, 62–71
    chain hotels, 65
    Faubourg Marigny, 57–59
    The French Quarter, 42–57
    Lafayette, 162
    during Mardi Gras, 16
    Mid-City/Esplanade, 59–62
    Uptown/Garden District, 72
Aesthetics & Antiques, 166–167
Airport, 21
    arriving at the, 26
Air travel, 21
Algiers Point, 31, 145–146
Allstate Sugar Bowl Classic, 6
Ambush Magazine, 23, 195
American Express, 35
Antiques, 166–168
Apple Barrel, 191
Ariodante, 168
Art for Arts' Sake, 11
Art galleries, 168–172
Arthur Roger Gallery Project, 169
ATMs (automated-teller
    machines), 4–5
Audubon Antiques, 167
Audubon Aquarium of the Americas,
    129–130
Audubon Park, 147
Audubon Zoo, 148–149

Babysitters, 35
Backstreet Cultural Museum, 141
Bars, 190–195
    gay, 195–197
Beauregard-Keyes House, 132
Beque's at the Royal Sonesta, 190
Bergen Putman Gallery, 169
Berta's and Mina's Antiquities, 169

Besthoff Sculpture Garden, 143
Biking, 35
Blaine Kern's Mardi Gras World, 146
Blue Nile, 179
Boat tours, 155
The Bombay Club, 191
Bookstores, 172–173
The Bourbon Pub-Parade Disco, 196
Bryant Galleries, 169
Buses, 32–33
Bywater, 28

Cabildo, The 134–135
Café Lafitte in Exile, 196
Cajun Country, 158–164
Cajun Mardi Gras, 17–18
Canal Place, 165
Canal Street streetcar, 33
Candies and pralines, 174
Carousel Bar & Lounge, 191
Carousel Gardens, 155
Car rentals, 22
Carrollton Station, 188
Car travel, 21–22, 34
Celebration in the Oaks, 13
Cemeteries, 149–152
Central Business District (CBD), 26, 30
    accommodations, 62–71
    restaurants, 106–112
Children's Storyland, 155
Christmas New Orleans-Style, 12–13
Circle Bar, 193–194
City Park, 147–148
Climate, 5–6
Cole Pratt Gallery, 169
The Columns, 194
Confederate Memorial Museum,
    141–142
Contemporary Arts Center, 142
The Corner Pocket, 196
Costumes and masks, 16, 174–175
CowPokes, 196
Cypress Grove and Greenwood
    Cemeteries, 151

D.b.a., 187
Degas House, 144
Diane Genre Oriental Art and
    Antiques, 170
Dickie Brennan's Steakhouse, 190
Disabilities, travelers with, 22
Discount passes, 32
Donna's, 179, 182

E The 1850 House, 132
Emergencies, 35
Essence Music Festival, 10
Eunice, 18, 158–160

Families with children, sights and
    attractions, 155
The Famous Door, 182
Fashion (clothing), 175–176
Faubourg Marigny, 28
    accommodations, 57–59
    nightlife, 179, 182, 184–193
    restaurants, 100–102
Faubourg Treme, 28, 30
Feelings Cafe, 191
Festival International de Louisiane
    (Eunice), 161
Festivals Acadiens, 11
Festival Tours International, 21
Floyd's Record Shop (Ville Platte), 163
French 75 Bar, 191–192
The French Market, 165
The French Quarter, 27
    accommodations, 42–57
    nightlife, 179, 182, 184–193
    restaurants, 82–100
    safety, 31–32
    sights and attractions, 128
    tours, 152
French Quarter Festival, 8
Fritzel's European Jazz Pub, 182

Galerie Royale, 170
A Gallery for Fine Photography,
    170–171
Gallier Hall, 144
Gallier House Museum, 135
Gambling, 156
Gay and lesbian travelers, 23
    nightlife, 195–197

Germaine Wells Mardi Gras Museum,
    134
Gifts and souvenirs, 176–177
Go Fourth on the River, 9
Golden Lantern, 195
Good Friends Bar & Queens Head
    Pub, 196–197
Great French Market Tomato
    Festival, 9
Greek Festival, 9
Greenwood Cemetery, 151
Gumbo Festival, 11

Halloween, 11–12
Harris Antiques, 167
Hermann-Grima House, 135–136
The Historic French Market, 130–131
Historic New Orleans Collection-
    Museum/Research Center, 136
Hospitals, 35
Hotels. *See* Accommodations
House of Blues, 187
House of Blues Parish, 187
Hove, 172
The Howlin' Wolf, 188–189

Ida Manheim Antiques, 167
Insectarium, 130
International Arts Festival, 9
The Irish Channel, 31

Jackson Brewery, 165
Jackson Square, 128
Jack Sutton Antiques, 167
Jazz and blues clubs, 179–185
Jazz Fest (New Orleans Jazz & Heri-
    tage Festival), 8–9, 18–21
Julia Street, 166

Keil's Antiques, 167
Kerry Irish Pub, 192
Kingpin, 194
Krewe of Orpheus, 15
Kurt E. Schon, 171

Lafayette, 160–163
    Mardi Gras, 17
Lafayette Cemetery No. 1, 151

Lafitte's Blacksmith Shop, 192
Laura: A Creole Plantation (Vacherie), 156–157
LeMieux Galleries, 171
LeRoundup, 197
Liberty Theater (Eunice), 158–159
The Library Lounge at the Ritz-Carlton, 192
Liquor laws, 36
Little Shop of Fantasy, 174
Longue Vue House & Gardens, 148
Louis Armstrong New Orleans International Airport (MSY), 21
Louisiana Children's Museum, 155
Louisiana Music Factory, 177
Lucullus, 168
Lundi Gras, 6–7, 14–15

Magazine Street, 166
Maison Bourbon, 182
Mamou, 18
Maple Leaf Bar, 189
Mardi Gras, 7, 13–18
    Cajun, 17–18
    day of, 15–16
    planning a visit during, 16
    season, 14
Mardi Gras Indians, 15
Metairie Cemetery, 151
Mid-City/Esplanade Ridge, 28
    accommodations, 59–62
    attractions and nightlife, 139–140
    restaurants, 102–106
Mid City Lanes Rock 'n' Bowl, 185–186
Miss Edna's Antiques, 168
Money matters, 4–5
Mother-in-Law Lounge, 194
Mulate's, 186
Musée Conti Wax Museum, 136

Napoleon House Bar & Café, 192
National World War II Museum, 142
Neighborhoods, 27–28, 30–31
New Orleans Film Festival, 11
New Orleans Glassworks and Print-making Studio, 171
New Orleans Historical Pharmacy Museum, 136–137
New Orleans Historic Voodoo Museum, 137

New Orleans Jazz & Heritage Festival (Jazz Fest), 8–9, 18–21
New Orleans Metropolitan Convention and Visitors Bureau, 4, 6, 17, 26
New Orleans Museum of Art, 143
New Orleans Wine & Food Experience, 9
Newspapers and magazines, 36
New Year's Eve, 13
Nightlife, 178–197
    bars, 190–197
    Cajun and zydeco joints, 185–186
    rhythm, rock and the rest of the music scene, 186–190

Oak Alley Plantation (Vacherie), 157
Ogden Museum of Southern Art, 143–144
Old Absinthe House, 132–133
Old Ursuline Convent, 133
The Old U.S. Mint, 133–134
Orleans Grapevine Wine Bar & Bistro, 193
Our Lady of Guadeloupe Chapel-International Shrine of St. Jude, 134
Oz, 197

Package deals, Jazz Fest, 21
Palm Court Jazz Café, 182, 184
Pals Lounge, 194
Parking
    during Jazz Fest, 20–21
    during Mardi Gras, 16
Parks and gardens, 146–148
Pat O'Brien's, 193
Peligro, 171
Pharmacies, 36
Pitot House, 140, 144–145
Plantations, 156–158
Police, 36
The Polo Lounge, 195
Ponderosa Stomp, 20
Pontchartrain, Lake, 138, 141
Post offices, 36
Prairie Acadian Cultural Center (Eunice), 159–160
The Presbytère, 137–138
Preservation Hall, 184

Radio, 36–37
Rainfall, average, 6
Rawhide, 195–196
Rayne Frog Festival, 10–11
Ray's Boom Boom Room, 187–188
R Bar and Royal Street Inn, 193
Restaurants, 79–124. *See also* Restaurants Index
    Central Business District, 106–112
    coffee, tea and sweets, 121–124
    Faubourg Marigny, 100–102
    the French Quarter, 82–100
    during Mardi Gras, 16
    Mid-City/Esplanade, 102–106
    Uptown/Garden District, 112–121
Ritz-Carlton Spa, 172
Riverbend, 166
Riverwalk Marketplace, 166
Rothschild's Antiques, 168

Safety, 31–32
    during Mardi Gras, 17
St. Charles Avenue streetcar, 33
St. John's Bayou, 138, 140
St. Joseph's Day Parade, 7
St. Louis Cathedral, 131
St. Louis Cemetery No. 1, 150
St. Louis Cemetery No. 2, 151
St. Louis Cemetery No. 3, 140, 152
St. Patrick's Day Parades, 7
Satchmo Summerfest, 10
Saturn Bar, 195
Savoy Music Center (Eunice), 160
Seasons, 5–6
Senior travel, 23
Shadyside Pottery, 171–172
Shopping, 165–177
Sigle's Antiques & Metalcraft, 168
Snake & Jake's Xmas Club Lounge, 195
Snug Harbor, 184–185
Southern Decadence, 10
Spring Fiesta, 8
Streetcars, 33
The Superdome, 145
Super Sunday, 7–8
Swamp Festival, 12
Swamp tours, 154, 161

Tales of the Cocktail, 10
Taxes, 37
Taxis, 34–35
    airport, 26
Temperatures, average, 6
Tennessee Williams New Orleans Literary Festival, 8
The Davis Galleries, 170
The Spotted Cat Cocktail Lounge, 188
Time zone, 37
Tipitina's, 189–190
Tours, organized, 152–155
Train travel, 22
Transit information, 37
Transportation, 32–35
Traveling to New Orleans, 21–22

Uptown Costume & Dance Company, 175
Uptown/Garden District, 30–31
    accommodations, 72
    restaurants, 112–121
    safety, 32
    sights and attractions, 138

Vaughan's Lounge, 185
Vermilionville (Lafayette), 161–162
Ville Platte, 163–164
Visitor information, 4, 26–27
Visitor Information Center, 27
VisiTour pass, 32
Voodoo Music Experience, 12

Warehouse District, 30
Weather, 5–6
    updates, 37
Whisnant Galleries, 168
Williams Research Center, 136
Words & Music: A Literary Fest in New Orleans, 12

ACCOMMODATIONS
The 1896 O'Malley House, 61–62
Aaah! T'Frere's Bed & Breakfast (Lafayette), 162
Ashton's Bed & Breakfast, 60
Astor Crowne Plaza: The Alexa, 66–67

B&W Courtyards Bed & Breakfast, 57
Bienville House, 52
Block-Keller House, 60–61
Bourbon Orleans Hotel-A Wyndham Historic Hotel, 53
Bourgoyne Guest House, 53–54
Chateau LeMoyne-Holiday Inn French Quarter, 47–48
Chateau Sonesta Hotel New Orleans, 48
Chimes B&B, 74–75
The Columns, 75
Comfort Suites, 65
Cotton Exchange, 65
Country Inn and Suites by Carlson, 65
Courtyard by Marriott, 65
Dauphine Orleans Hotel, 48–49
The Depot at Madame Julia's, 71
Drury Inn & Suites, 70
Embassy Suites, 65
The Frenchmen, 58
The Garlands Historic Creole Cottages, 49
The Grand Victorian Bed & Breakfast, 72
Hampton Inn and Suites, 65
Hampton Inn Garden District, 76
Harrah's, 62
Hilton New Orleans Riverside Hotel, 63
Hilton St. Charles, 67
Holiday Inn Express, 65
Homewood Suites, 65
Hotel InterContinental, 63–64
Hotel Maison de Ville, 42–44
Hotel Monteleone, 49–50
Hôtel Provincial, 54
Hotel St. Marie, 54
Hotel Villa Convento, 55
The House on Bayou Road, 59–60
International House, 67
JW Marriott Hotel New Orleans, 64
Lafitte Guest House, 50
Lamothe House, 55
La Quinta Inn and Suites, 65
Le Cirque, 68
Le Pavillion Hotel, 71
Le Richelieu Hotel, 55–56
Loews New Orleans Hotel, 68
Loft 523, 64
Magnolia Mansion, 72
Maison Dupuy, 50–51
Maison Orleans, 44

Maison Perrier Bed & Breakfast, 74
Marriott, 65
The McKendrick-Breaux House, 74
Melrose Mansion, 45
New Orleans Guest House, 57
Omni Royal Orleans, 51
Park View Guest House, 76–77
The Pelham, 68–69
Place d'Armes Hotel, 56
Prince Conti Hotel, 56
Prytania Park Hotel, 77
Quality Inn, 65
Ramada Plaza Hotel-The Inn on Bourbon, 45
Renaissance Arts Hotel, 69
Residence Inn by Marriott, 65
Ritz-Carlton, New Orleans, 45–46
Royal Sonesta, 46–47
Royal Street Inn & R Bar, 58–59
St. Charles Guesthouse, 77–78
St. James Hotel, 69
St. Louis, 52
Sheraton, 65
Soniat House, 47
SpringHill Suites by Marriott, 65
Westin New Orleans at Canal Place, 52
The Whitney-A Wyndham Historic Hotel, 70
Windsor Court, 64–66
W New Orleans, 66

RESTAURANTS

Acme Oyster House, 96
Angeli on Decatur, 96–97
Angelo Brocato's Ice Cream & Confectionary, 121
Antoine's, 82, 84
Arnaud's, 84–85
Bacco, 85
Bayona, 85–86
Bluebird Cafe, 119
Bourbon House Seafood, 86
Brennan's, 86–87
Brigtsen's, 112
Broussard's, 87
Bywater Barbeque, 101
Café Adelaide, 107
Café Beignet, 97
Cafe Degas, 103
Café du Monde, 121–122

Café Giovanni, 87
Café Maspero, 97
Camellia Grill, 119
Casamento's, 119–120
Clancy's, 112–113
Clover Grill, 97
Cochon, 108–109
Commander's Palace, 113–114
Court of Two Sisters, 88
Creole Creamery, 122
Cuvee, 107–108
Dante's Kitchen, 115–116
Dick & Jenny's, 116
Dickie Brennan's Steakhouse, 88
Dominique's, 88–89
Dooky Chase, 103–104
Elizabeth's, 101
Emeril's, 106
EnVie, 122
Ernst Café, 111
Feelings Cafe D'Aunoy, 100
Felix's Restaurant & Oyster Bar, 98
Franky & Johnny's, 120
Galatoire's, 89
Gautreau's, 114
Herbsaint, 109
Irene's Cuisine, 92–93
Iris, 116–117
Jacques-Imo's, 116
Joey K's, 120
Johnny's Po' Boys, 98
K-Paul's Louisiana Kitchen, 90
La Boulangerie, 122–123
La Crêpe Nanou, 117
La Divinia Gelateria, 123
La Peniche Restaurant, 101–102
La Petite Grocery, 117–118
Liborio's Cuban Restaurant, 109
Lilette, 118
Liuzza's by the Track, 104–105
Lola's, 104
Louisiana Pizza Kitchen, 98
Lüke, 110
Marigny Brasserie, 100

Martinique Bistro, 114
Mona's Café & Deli, 102
Mother's, 111–112
Mr. B's Bistro, 93
Muriel's, 90
Napoleon House, 98–99
The New Orleans Grill Room,
  106–107
Nola, 90–91
Palace Café, 110
Parkway Bakery and Tavern, 105
Pascal's Manale, 118
The Pelican Club, 91
Peristyle, 91–92
Petunia's, 99
The Pig Stand (Ville Platte), 163–164
P.J.'s Coffee & Tea Company, 123
Port of Call, 93–94
Praline Connection, 102
Prejean's (Lafayette), 162–163
Ralph & Kacoo's, 94
Ralph's on the Park, 102–103
Randol's Restaurant and Cajun Dance
  Hall (Lafayette), 163
Red Fish Grill, 94–95
Rémoulade, 95
Restaurant August, 108
Rib Room, 92
Riche, 110–111
Royal Blend Coffee & Tea House, 123
Rue de la Course, 123–124
Sekisui Samurai, 95
Slim Goodies Diner, 120–121
Sophie's Gelato and Old Time Ice
  Cream Parlor, 124
Stanley, 99–100
Stella!, 92
Sucre, 124
Table One, 114–115
Tommy's, 111
Tujague's, 95–96
Upperline, 115
Willie Mae's Scotch House, 105

FROMMER'S® COMPLETE TRAVEL GUIDES

Alaska
Amalfi Coast
American Southwest
Amsterdam
Argentina
Arizona
Atlanta
Australia
Austria
Bahamas
Barcelona
Beijing
Belgium, Holland & Luxembourg
Belize
Bermuda
Boston
Brazil
British Columbia & the Canadian
  Rockies
Brussels & Bruges
Budapest & the Best of Hungary
Buenos Aires
Calgary
California
Canada
Cancún, Cozumel & the Yucatán
Cape Cod, Nantucket & Martha's
  Vineyard
Caribbean
Caribbean Ports of Call
Carolinas & Georgia
Chicago
Chile & Easter Island
China
Colorado
Costa Rica
Croatia
Cuba
Denmark
Denver, Boulder & Colorado Springs
Eastern Europe
Ecuador & the Galapagos Islands
Edinburgh & Glasgow
England
Europe
Europe by Rail

Florence, Tuscany & Umbria
Florida
France
Germany
Greece
Greek Islands
Guatemala
Hawaii
Hong Kong
Honolulu, Waikiki & Oahu
India
Ireland
Israel
Italy
Jamaica
Japan
Kauai
Las Vegas
London
Los Angeles
Los Cabos & Baja
Madrid
Maine Coast
Maryland & Delaware
Maui
Mexico
Montana & Wyoming
Montréal & Québec City
Morocco
Moscow & St. Petersburg
Munich & the Bavarian Alps
Nashville & Memphis
New England
Newfoundland & Labrador
New Mexico
New Orleans
New York City
New York State
New Zealand
Northern Italy
Norway
Nova Scotia, New Brunswick &
  Prince Edward Island
Oregon
Paris
Peru

Philadelphia & the Amish Country
Portugal
Prague & the Best of the Czech
  Republic
Provence & the Riviera
Puerto Rico
Rome
San Antonio & Austin
San Diego
San Francisco
Santa Fe, Taos & Albuquerque
Scandinavia
Scotland
Seattle
Seville, Granada & the Best of
  Andalusia
Shanghai
Sicily
Singapore & Malaysia
South Africa
South America
South Florida
South Korea
South Pacific
Southeast Asia
Spain
Sweden
Switzerland
Tahiti & French Polynesia
Texas
Thailand
Tokyo
Toronto
Turkey
USA
Utah
Vancouver & Victoria
Vermont, New Hampshire & Maine
Vienna & the Danube Valley
Vietnam
Virgin Islands
Virginia
Walt Disney World® & Orlando
Washington, D.C.
Washington State

FROMMER'S® DAY BY DAY GUIDES

Amsterdam
Barcelona
Beijing
Boston
Cancun & the Yucatan
Chicago
Florence & Tuscany

Hong Kong
Honolulu & Oahu
London
Maui
Montréal
Napa & Sonoma
New York City

Paris
Provence & the Riviera
Rome
San Francisco
Venice
Washington D.C.

PAULINE FROMMER'S GUIDES: SEE MORE. SPEND LESS.

Alaska
Hawaii
Italy

Las Vegas
London
New York City

Paris
Walt Disney World®
Washington D.C.

FROMMER'S® PORTABLE GUIDES

Acapulco, Ixtapa & Zihuatanejo
Amsterdam
Aruba, Bonaire & Curacao
Australia's Great Barrier Reef
Bahamas
Big Island of Hawaii
Boston
California Wine Country
Cancún
Cayman Islands
Charleston
Chicago
Dominican Republic

Florence
Las Vegas
Las Vegas for Non-Gamblers
London
Maui
Nantucket & Martha's Vineyard
New Orleans
New York City
Paris
Portland
Puerto Rico
Puerto Vallarta, Manzanillo &
    Guadalajara

Rio de Janeiro
San Diego
San Francisco
Savannah
St. Martin, Sint Maarten, Anguilla &
    St. Bart's
Turks & Caicos
Vancouver
Venice
Virgin Islands
Washington, D.C.
Whistler

FROMMER'S® CRUISE GUIDES

Alaska Cruises & Ports of Call

Cruises & Ports of Call

European Cruises & Ports of Call

FROMMER'S® NATIONAL PARK GUIDES

Algonquin Provincial Park
Banff & Jasper
Grand Canyon

National Parks of the American West
Rocky Mountain
Yellowstone & Grand Teton

Yosemite and Sequoia & Kings
    Canyon
Zion & Bryce Canyon

FROMMER'S® WITH KIDS GUIDES

Chicago
Hawaii
Las Vegas
London

National Parks
New York City
San Francisco

Toronto
Walt Disney World® & Orlando
Washington, D.C.

FROMMER'S® PHRASEFINDER DICTIONARY GUIDES

Chinese
French

German
Italian

Japanese
Spanish

SUZY GERSHMAN'S BORN TO SHOP GUIDES

France
Hong Kong, Shanghai & Beijing
Italy

London
New York
Paris

San Francisco
Where to Buy the Best of Everything

FROMMER'S® BEST-LOVED DRIVING TOURS

Britain
California
France
Germany

Ireland
Italy
New England
Northern Italy

Scotland
Spain
Tuscany & Umbria

THE UNOFFICIAL GUIDES®

Adventure Travel in Alaska
Beyond Disney
California with Kids
Central Italy
Chicago
Cruises
Disneyland®
England
Hawaii

Ireland
Las Vegas
London
Maui
Mexico's Best Beach Resorts
Mini Mickey
New Orleans
New York City
Paris

San Francisco
South Florida including Miami &
    the Keys
Walt Disney World®
Walt Disney World® for
    Grown-ups
Walt Disney World® with Kids
Washington, D.C.

SPECIAL-INTEREST TITLES

Athens Past & Present
Best Places to Raise Your Family
Cities Ranked & Rated
500 Places to Take Your Kids Before They Grow Up
Frommer's Best Day Trips from London
Frommer's Best RV & Tent Campgrounds in the U.S.A.

Frommer's Exploring America by RV
Frommer's NYC Free & Dirt Cheap
Frommer's Road Atlas Europe
Frommer's Road Atlas Ireland
Retirement Places Rated

CLOSED
due to
accidental demolition

WEGEN BISSIGEN
EICHHÖRNCHEN GESCHLOSSEN

CERRADO
CABRAS

Κλειστό
Μετεωρίτες

POOL CLOSED
プール
も
ELECTRIC EELS
閉
鎖
中

Hotel
closed for
facelifting

FERMÉ POUR
RAISON
DE GRÈVE
DES BONNES

FECHADO!
POR CAUSA DE
ATAQUES DOS CROCODILOS

I don't speak sign language.

A hotel can close for all kinds of reasons.
Our Guarantee ensures that if your hotel's undergoing construction,
we'll let you know in advance. In fact, we cover your entire travel
experience. See www.travelocity.com/guarantee for details.

travelocity
You'll never roam alone.